100 GUIDE to the most Beautiful Beaches in the World

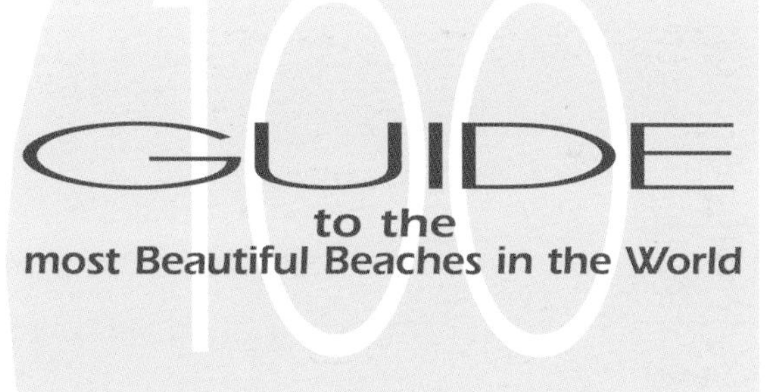
100
GUIDE
to the
most Beautiful Beaches in the World

www.grandsvoyageurs.com
e-mail : egv@grandsudpress.com

ISBN 2-915648-09-3

EDITORIAL

Once again this year, millions of us will choose holidays under the sign of the sea and the sun. Out of this inexhaustible enthusiasm for beaches was born the Guide to the 100 Best Beaches in the World.

This rather biased selection sets out to showcase outstanding destinations - be they world-renowned or secluded - scattered throughout the four corners of the world. Whether they are well-known beaches or paradisiacal islands, these enchanted getaways adhere to a common philosophy : they are within a preserved environment and offer a sophisticated tourism experience.

Each destination comes complete with useful tips to make your stay that much smoother : What airline to choose ? Do you need a visa or a vaccine ? Which are the best seasons ? What about nearby accommodation ? What spots to visit in the region ? What about the regional cuisine ? What kinds of souvenirs to bring back home ? What activities are available ?... The answers to these questions will allow you to get a clearer picture of each destination and to become aware of its particular attractions.

In short, these pages will allow us to become conscious of the incredible natural treasures found in our planet and our need to preserve them as such.

A breath of fresh air, a guide to look through as a prelude to your next vacation or simply a good read on a long winter's night...

Enjoy the reading and bon voyage !

Les Editions Grands Voyageurs

Africa

The Americas

Asia

- Cambodia
- India
- Indonesia
- Malaysia
- Maldives
- Myanmar
- Philippines
- Sri Lanka
- Thailand
- Vietnam

Europe

- Croatia
- Spain
- France
- Greece
- Italy
- Portugal

Oceania

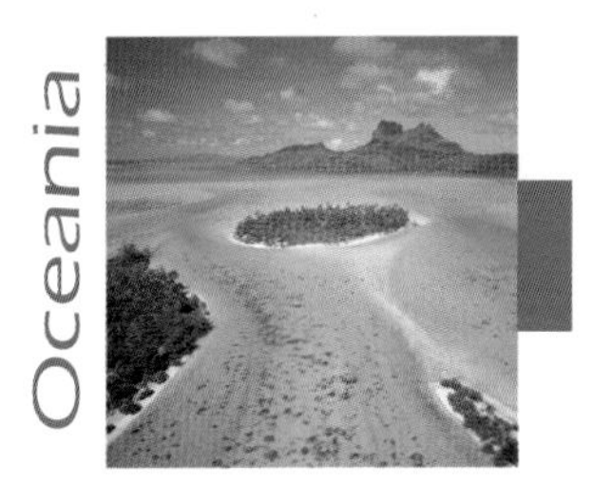

- Australia
- Fiji
- Hawaii
- Cook Islands
- New Caledonia
- New Zealand
- Palau
- French Polynesia
- Samoa

AFRICA

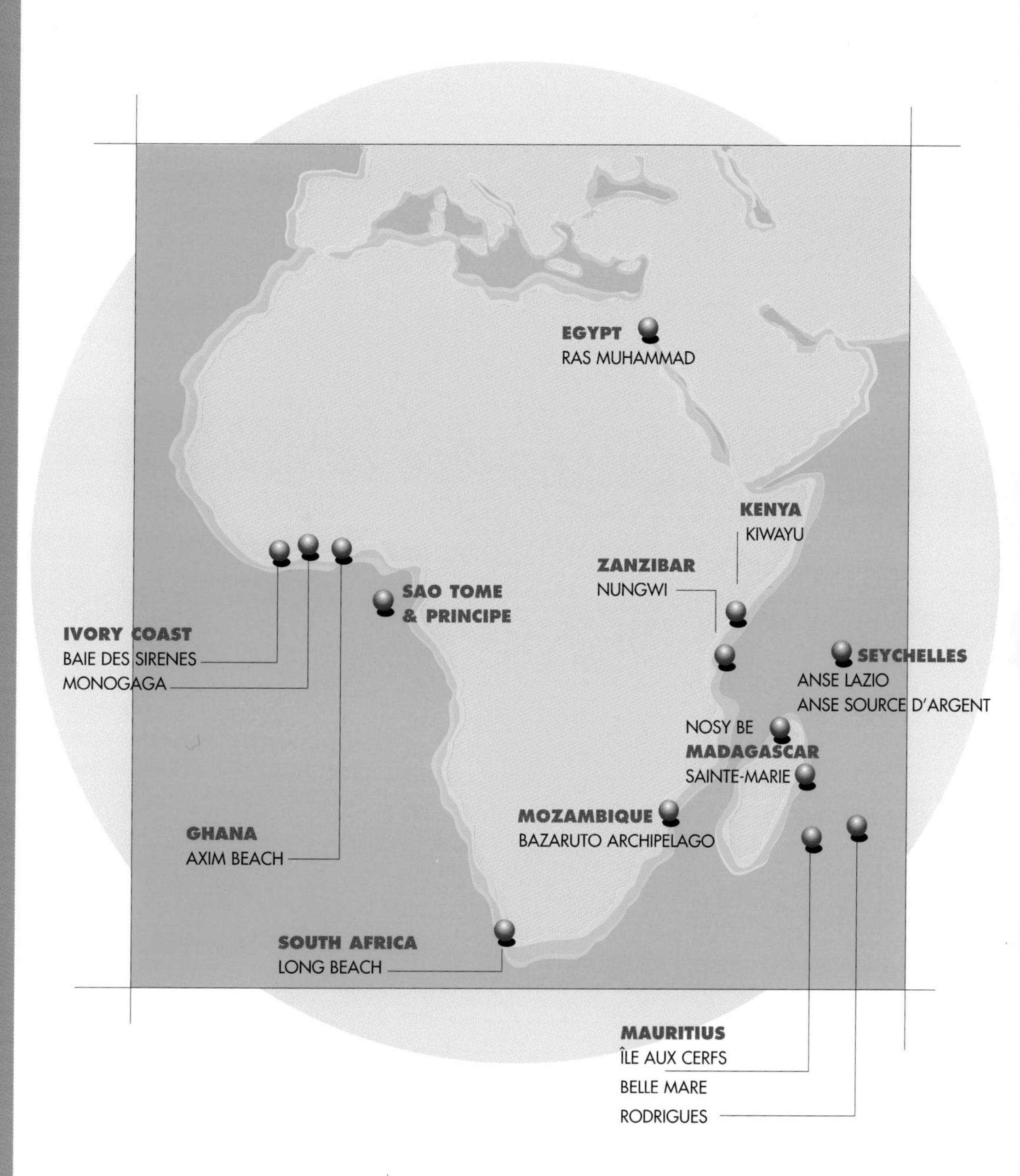

EGYPT
RAS MUHAMMAD
KENYA
KIWAYU
ZANZIBAR
NUNGWI
SAO TOME & PRINCIPE
IVORY COAST
BAIE DES SIRENES
MONOGAGA
SEYCHELLES
ANSE LAZIO
ANSE SOURCE D'ARGENT
NOSY BE
MADAGASCAR
SAINTE-MARIE
MOZAMBIQUE
BAZARUTO ARCHIPELAGO
GHANA
AXIM BEACH
SOUTH AFRICA
LONG BEACH
MAURITIUS
ÎLE AUX CERFS
BELLE MARE
RODRIGUES

SOUTH AFRICA • LONG BEACH

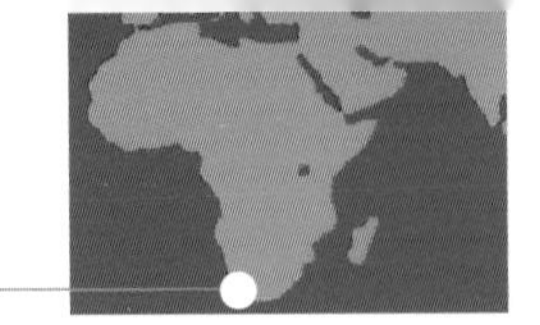

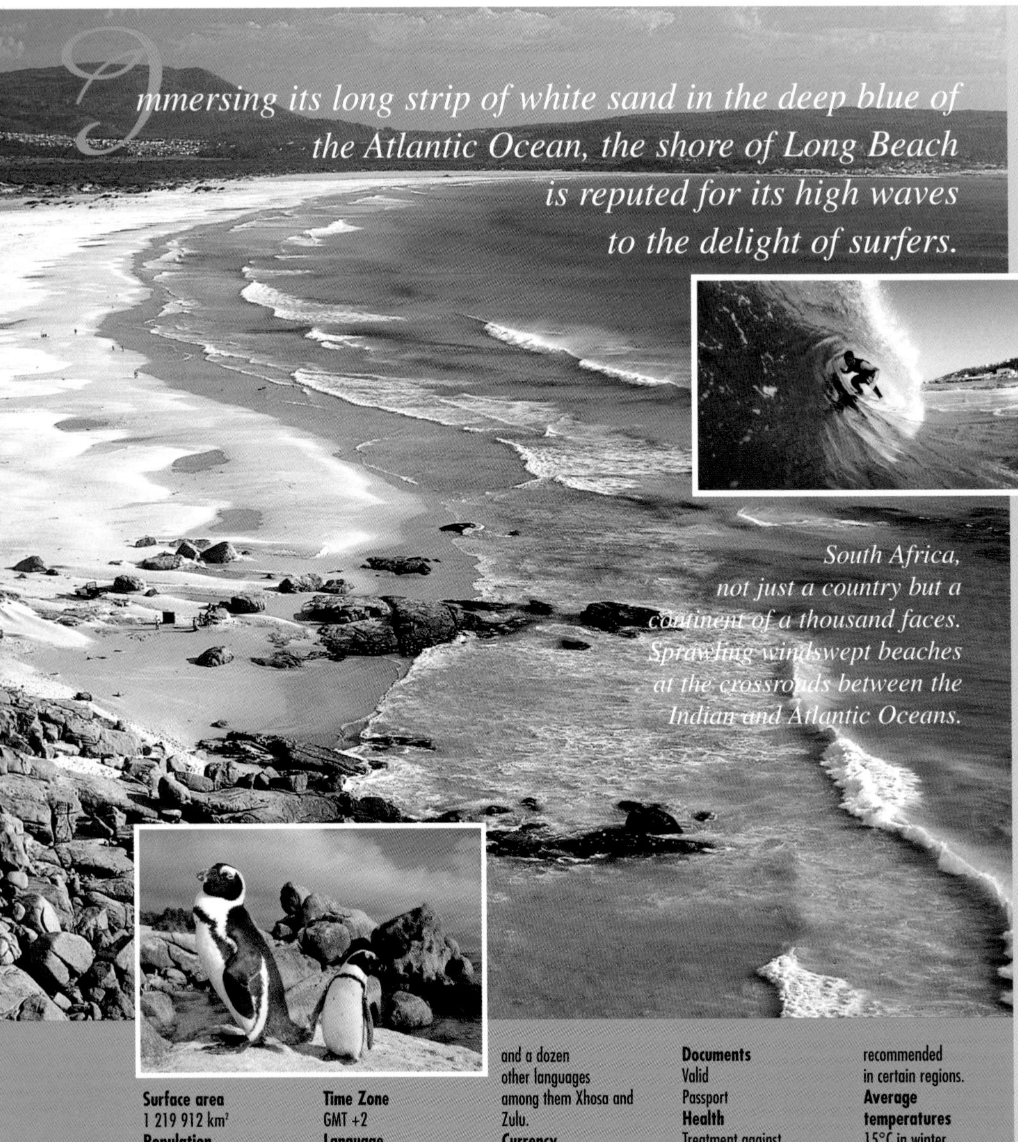

Immersing its long strip of white sand in the deep blue of the Atlantic Ocean, the shore of Long Beach is reputed for its high waves to the delight of surfers.

South Africa, not just a country but a continent of a thousand faces. Sprawling windswept beaches at the crossroads between the Indian and Atlantic Oceans.

Airline Companies
Air France, British Airways, South African Airways, Lufthansa.

How to get there
From Noordhoek, take the route heading south and travel for approximately ten kilometers.

Best seasons
The region of Long Beach has a warm and dry Mediterranean climate between September and April.

Accommodation
Hotels at Noordhoek or Cape Town and B&B at Kommetjie.

Local cuisine
This land saw the blending of several cultures and many dishes are the result of this mixture: bobotie (Malay curry), biltong (dried meat), mieliepap (goulash and corn purée).
Make sure to try the local wines from the Winelands, where vineyards are grown with a grape variety brought over by the French Huguenots in the 17th century.

Shopping
Wooden sculptures, traditional arts and crafts...

What to see
The Slangkoppunt lighthouse, the last standing steel lighthouse in the whole country; the Kakapo shipwreck, which sank in 1900 visible 45 minutes from Long Beach; Imhoff's Park, a Bird Park where one can admire the South African giant crane.

Activities
Sailing, surfing, horseback riding, lobster fishing...

Budget
Quite high

Contact
http://www.southafrican.net

Surface area
1 219 912 km²

Population
43.6 million

Time Zone
GMT +2

Language
Afrikaans, English and a dozen other languages among them Xhosa and Zulu.

Currency
Rand

Documents
Valid Passport

Health
Treatment against malaria recommended in certain regions.

Average temperatures
15°C in winter, 26°C in summer

+ *A pristine beach for lovers of wide spaces.*

- *Waves may reach 5 to 8 meters...*

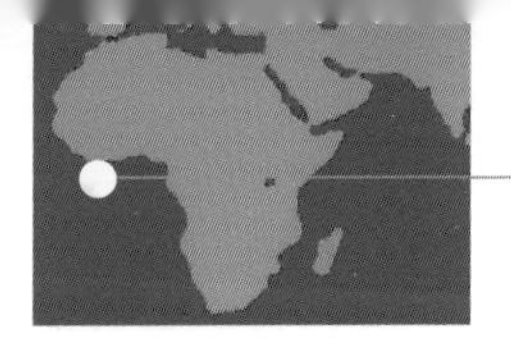

Airline Companies
Air France
How to get there
By bus: from Abidjan, take the bus at the Adjamé terminal (a four-hour ride).
By badjan (bush taxi) or by woro-woro (collective taxi).
Best seasons
The Ivory Coast has both an equatorial and tropical climate. The most pleasant period is between November and March in order to avoid the heat which at times can be overwhelming (from March to May) and the rainy season (from May to November with one interruption from July - August).
Accommodation
A nearby vacation resort and some small hotels at Grand Béréby.
Local cuisine
Ivory Coast cuisine features fried plantain (alloko), manioc and yam. Among the most popular dishes we find chicken kedjenou, braised fish and bush meat served with peanut or gombo sauce. For drinks, try the local beer (flag), an alcoholic drink made from sugar cane or palm wine (bangui).
Shopping
Traditional musical instruments (djembé...), good-luck-charm bracelets, kitchen linen and fabrics, basketware, statuettes and masks. Don´t hesitate to bargain !
What to see
The market at Grand Béréby; the sacred lake at Klana; the monkey forest; the savanna; the four forest rivers nearby (Nidja, Dodo, Néro and Gnagbagbo rivers)
Activities
Sport fishing and big game fishing (you can expect to catch marlins, barracudas, red carps, rays and carangues), excursion through the rivers on pirogue boat, atv...
Budget
Very affordable
Contact
http://www.abidjan.net

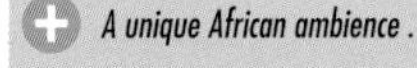
A unique African ambience .

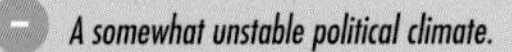
A somewhat unstable political climate.

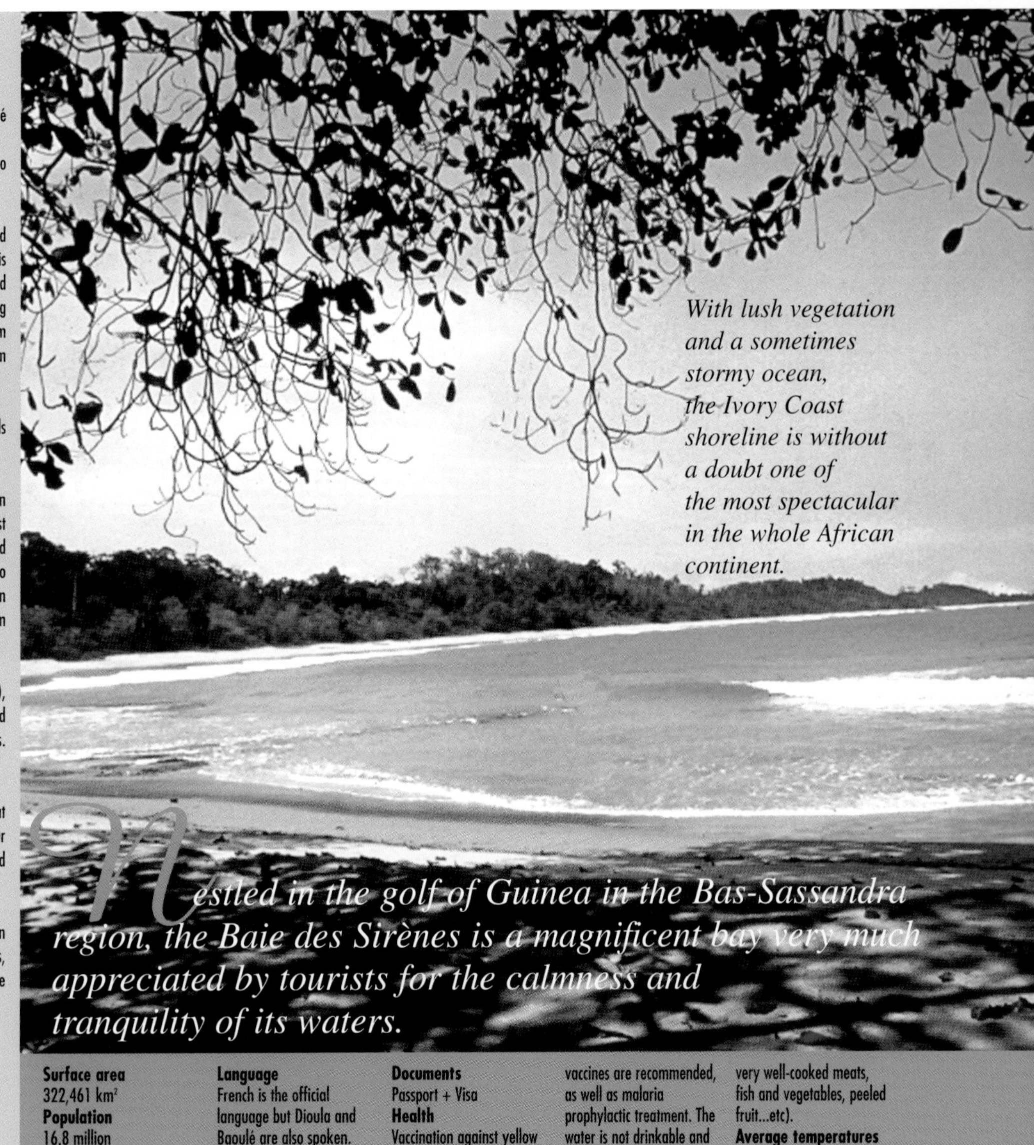

With lush vegetation and a sometimes stormy ocean, the Ivory Coast shoreline is without a doubt one of the most spectacular in the whole African continent.

Nestled in the golf of Guinea in the Bas-Sassandra region, the Baie des Sirènes is a magnificent bay very much appreciated by tourists for the calmness and tranquility of its waters.

Surface area
322,461 km²
Population
16.8 million
Time Zone
GMT
Language
French is the official language but Dioula and Baoulé are also spoken.
Currency
Franc CFA
Documents
Passport + Visa
Health
Vaccination against yellow fever is mandatory, typhoid and hepatitis A and B vaccines are recommended, as well as malaria prophylactic treatment. The water is not drinkable and care must be taken when preparing food (eat only very well-cooked meats, fish and vegetables, peeled fruit...etc).
Average temperatures
24°C in winter,
32°C in summer

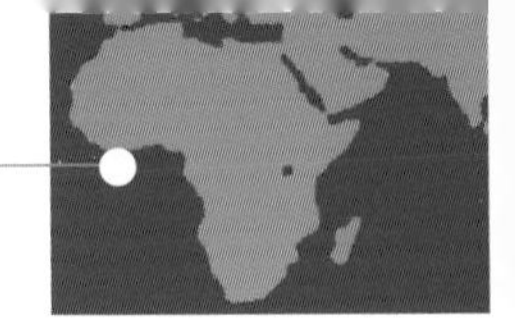

Not far from the small town of San Pedro and the border with Liberia, the small fishing village of Monogaga lies at the edge of a primary forest. The sparsely treed pristine beach is particularly appreciated by surfers because of the high waves that break on the sand.

Airline Companies
Air France.

How to get there
By bus: From Abidjan, take the bus at the Adjacent terminal (it takes a little more than four hours of traveling).
By badjan (bush taxi) or by woro-woro (collective taxi)

Best seasons
The Ivory Coast has both an equatorial and tropical climate. The most pleasant period is between November and March in order to avoid the heat which at times can be overwhelming (from March to May) and the rainy season (from May to November with one interruption from July - August).

Accommodation
Bungalows on the beach at very attractive prices.

Local cuisine
Ivory Coast cuisine features fried plantain (alloko), manioc and yam. Among the most popular dishes we find chicken kedjenou, braised fish and bush meat served with peanut or gombo sauce. For drinks, try the local beer (flag), an alcoholic drink made from sugar cane or palm wine (bangui).

Shopping
Traditional musical instruments (djembé...), good-luck-charm bracelets, kitchen linen and fabrics, basketware, statuettes and masks. Don't hesitate to bargain !

What to see
The classified forest of Monogaga; the San Pedro port, buffaloes that sometimes venture on the beach.

Activities
Big game fishing, pirogue boat rides, atv ...

Budget
Very affordable

Contact
http://www.abidjan.net

➕ *You will appreciate the beauty and the serenity of this place.*

➖ *Beware of waves and currents !*

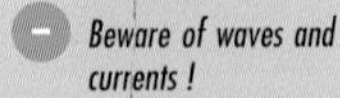

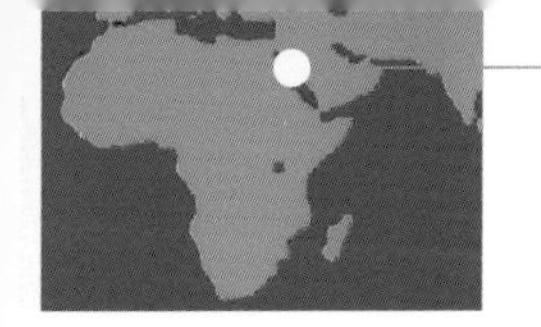

Airline Companies
Air France, Alitalia, Egyptair, British Airways, Lufthansa.
How to get there
By air : From Cairo, take a local flight to Sharm el Sheikh.
By bus : leaves from Sharm el Sheikh.
Best seasons
Between October and May
Accommodation
Hotels of all categories
Local cuisine
Tahina (sesame seed cream spread), homos (chickpea purée), babaghanouj (eggplant purée), pigeons, grape vine leaves, lima beans...
Shopping
Gold and silver jewelry, copper and brass objects, spices, papyrus, carpets, narguiles (water pipe), pottery...
What to see
The Sinai desert where you can go on cammel back rides.
Activities
Diving, sailing, snorkeling, desert safaris...
Budget
Average
Contact
http://www.egypttourisme.org

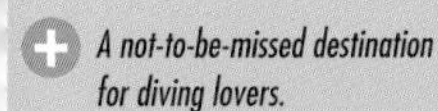

+ *A not-to-be-missed destination for diving lovers.*

– *Suffocating summer heat.*

At the southern tip of the Sinai peninsula, not far from Sharm el Sheikh, Ras Muhammad is a National Park created in 1963 sprinkled with extensive beaches of yellow sand and fragile coral reefs.

Egypt, an age-old civilization full of natural wonders that make it one of the most fascinating and most visited countries in the world.

Surface area
1,001,449 km²
Population
69 million
Time Zone
GMT +2
Language
Arabic, English
Currency
Egyptian pound

Documents
Passport + Visa
Health
Anti-diarrhea treatment, be up-to-date with vaccinations particularly for hepatitis A.
Average temperatures
26°C in winter,
37°C in summer (Red Sea)

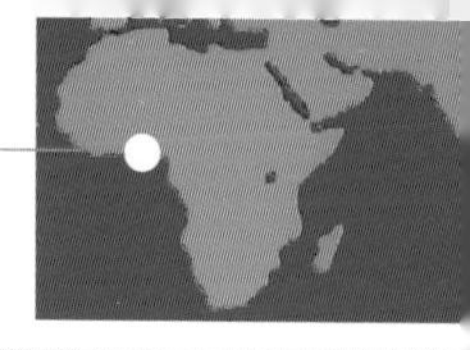

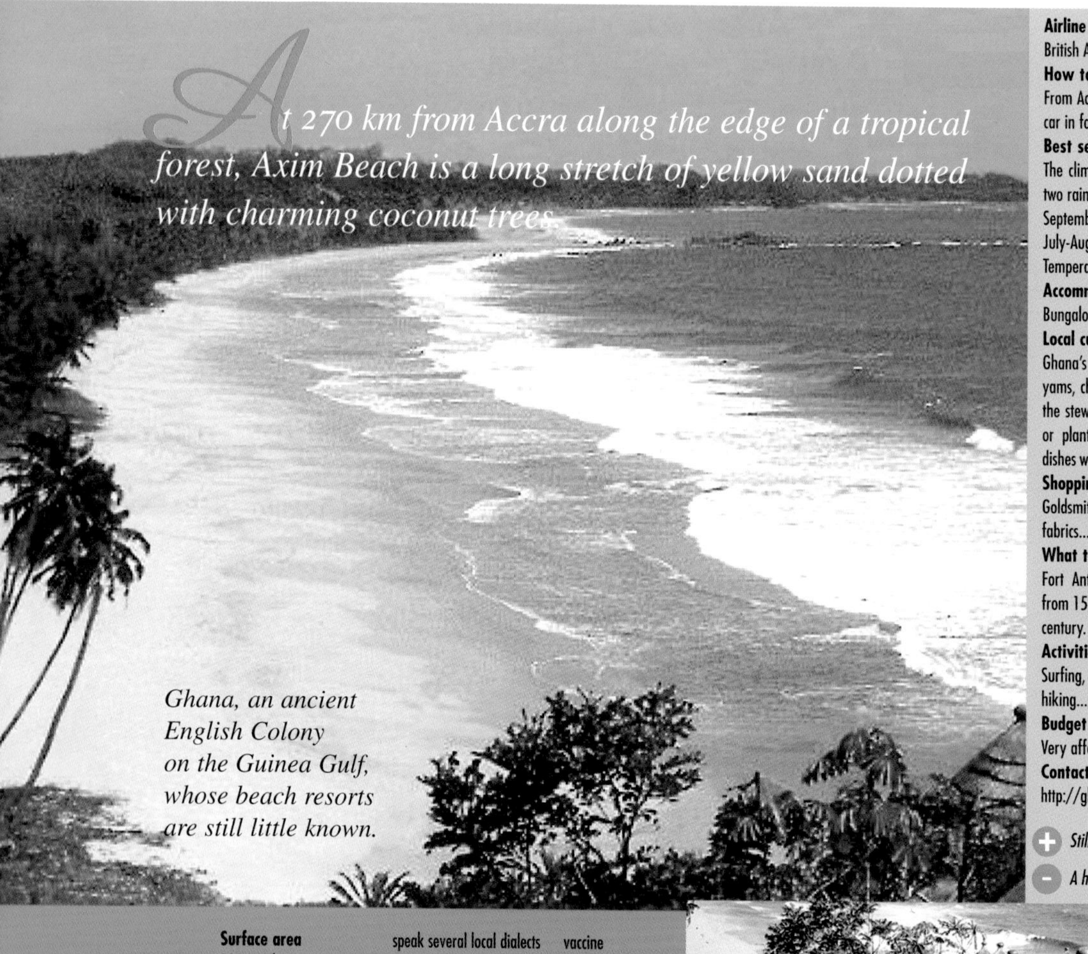

At 270 km from Accra along the edge of a tropical forest, Axim Beach is a long stretch of yellow sand dotted with charming coconut trees.

Ghana, an ancient English Colony on the Guinea Gulf, whose beach resorts are still little known.

Airline Companies
British Airways, KLM, Lufthansa.

How to get there
From Accra, Axim can be reached by bus or by car in four hours.

Best seasons
The climate in the south of Ghana is ruled by two rainy seasons, from April to June and from September to November. It is best to visit it in July-August or between December and March. Temperatures are pleasant all year round.

Accommodation
Bungalows on the beach.

Local cuisine
Ghana's cuisine is usually prepared using rice, yams, chicken and seafood. Don't forget to try the stews (kontomere, okro) and foufou (yam or plantain purée) and to accompany these dishes with local beers and palm alcoholic drink.

Shopping
Goldsmith, leather and wooden carved objects, fabrics...

What to see
Fort Antonio (Portuguese construction dating from 1515); Château d'Elmina built in the 15th century.

Activities
Surfing, sailing, snorkeling, canoeing, fishing, hiking...

Budget
Very affordable even for backpackers.

Contact
http://ghanatourism.gov.gh

+ *Still just a few tourists.*

– *A humid climate even during the dry season.*

Surface area
238,540 km²

Population
20 million

Time Zone
GMT

Language
English is the official language, although people speak several local dialects (Akan, Twi, Fante, Ga, Ewe...)

Currency
Cedi

Documents
Passport + Visa

Health
Mandatory yellow fever vaccine and preventative treatment against malaria is recommended.

Average temperatures
24°C in winter, 28°C in summer

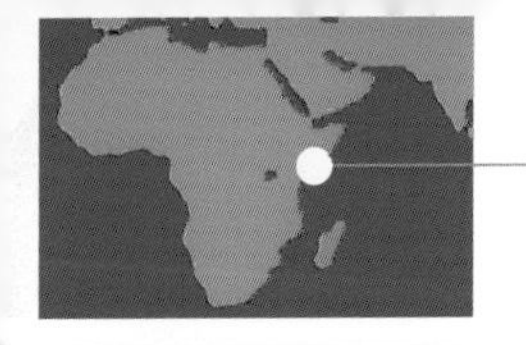

Lost in the heart of a small archipelago protected by a huge coral reef, the island of Kiwayu offers a captivating contrast of color and sensations.

As the most popular African tourist destination, Kenya is renowned for its many wildlife reserves which are now, for the most part, open to the public. In addition, the country boasts superb unusual beaches of surprising beauty.

Surface area
582,644 km²
Population
29 million
Time Zone
GMT +3
Language
Swahili, English
Currency
Kenyan Shilling
Documents
Passport + Visa
Health
Yellow fever vaccine and treatment against malaria are strongly recommended.
Average temperatures
Between 28°C and 32°C all year round on the coast

Airline Companies
KLM, British Airways.
How to get there
Air Kenya offers flights between Nairobi and Kiwayu by small propeller planes. The trip lasts around two hours and the plane then lands on a beaten-earth runway.
Best seasons
It is dry season from October to March when the winds on the coast blow with less strength.
Accommodation
A few bungalows right in the middle of nature offering adequate comfort and also a high-end resort.
Local cuisine
Barbecued meat «nyama choma» (lamb, goat, chicken and beef) served with lugali, a kind of corn porridge.
Shopping
Ebony sculptures (makonde), wooden animals, batiks, cotton goods, precious stones, tea and coffee, soapstone, kiondos (baggages)...
What to see
Paté, an ancient sultanate where the buildings are half-sunk in the sand; the Dodori Reserve, where you can take part in a safari; and for the lucky ones, the possibility to sight small groups of elephants bathing as a family, and also turtles and dolphins.
Activities
Safari, big game fishing, sailing, water skiing, diving (a must in the island due to the abundance of the coral reef)...
Budget
High
Contact
http://www.tourismkenya.com

+ *A pristine island with a delightful sea and the discovery of African reserves.*
- *This wilderness experience comes with a price...*

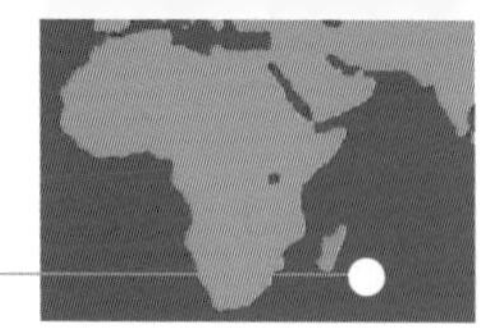

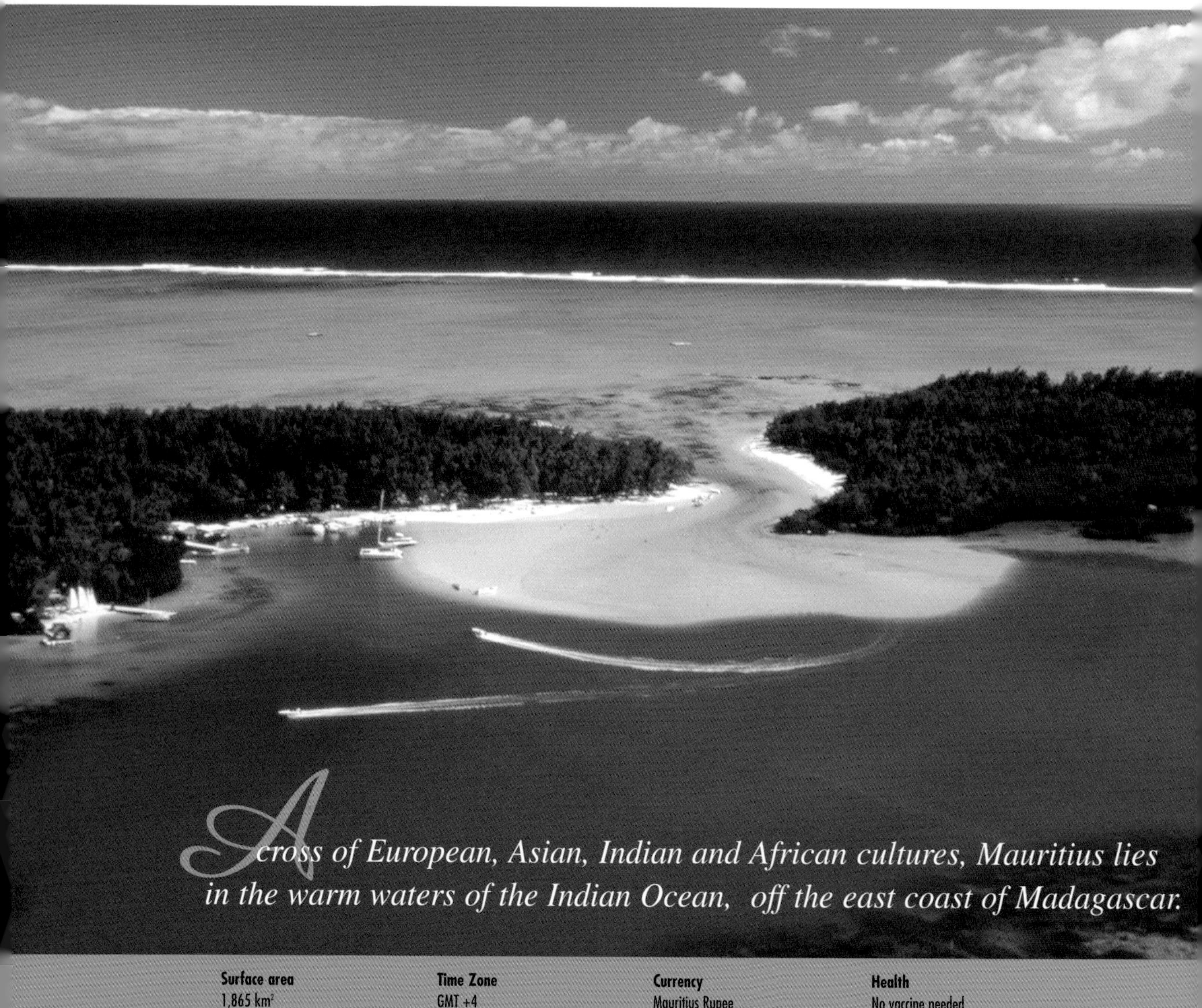

Across of European, Asian, Indian and African cultures, Mauritius lies in the warm waters of the Indian Ocean, off the east coast of Madagascar.

Surface area
1,865 km²

Population
1.1 million

Time Zone
GMT +4

Language
French, English, Creole

Currency
Mauritius Rupee

Documents
Valid Passport

Health
No vaccine needed

Average temperatures
22°C in winter, 27°C in summer

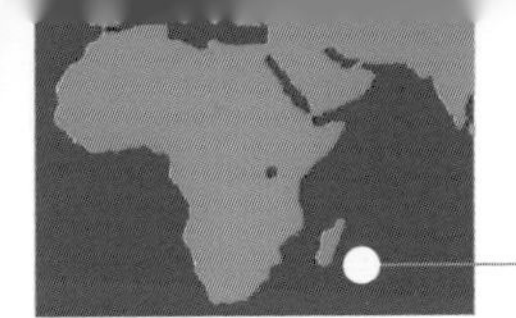

Airline Companies
Air France, Air Mauritius, British Airways.

How to get there
From Trou d'Eau Douce, it is possible to hire «taxi-boats»: it takes 20 minutes by fishing boat and 10 minutes by speed boat.

Best seasons
The climate is pleasant all year round. Winter is from June to September when temperatures vary between 17°C and 25°C. In summer, temperatures can surpass the 30°C mark, however it is the season that gets most rain.

Accommodation
There is no accommodation available on site however many hotels and guesthouses can be found on the other shore.

Local cuisine
A concoction of Creole, Indian, Asian and European, the local cuisine is well worth the detour: Vindaye (a dish of Indian origin consisting of fish marinated in mustard, spices, onions and vinegar), rougail (a Creole specialty with tomatoes, onions, garlic and spices), curry, biriani (Indian dish), samosas (philo dough with meat or vegetable filling), chutney, daubes (beef stew), fish barbecues and don't forget the ti-punch !

Shopping
Wooden sculptures, Indian fabrics, arts and crafts, precious stones, seashells, spices...

What to see
A fast boat tours the island and makes a stop near a waterfall accessible only from the sea, you can bathe in amazingly warm water and jump from the rocks.

Activities
Sailing, water skiing, diving...

Budget
High

Contact
http://www.mauritius.net

\+ *The incredible beauty of this lagoon is making news the world over !*

\- *Very busy on weekends.*

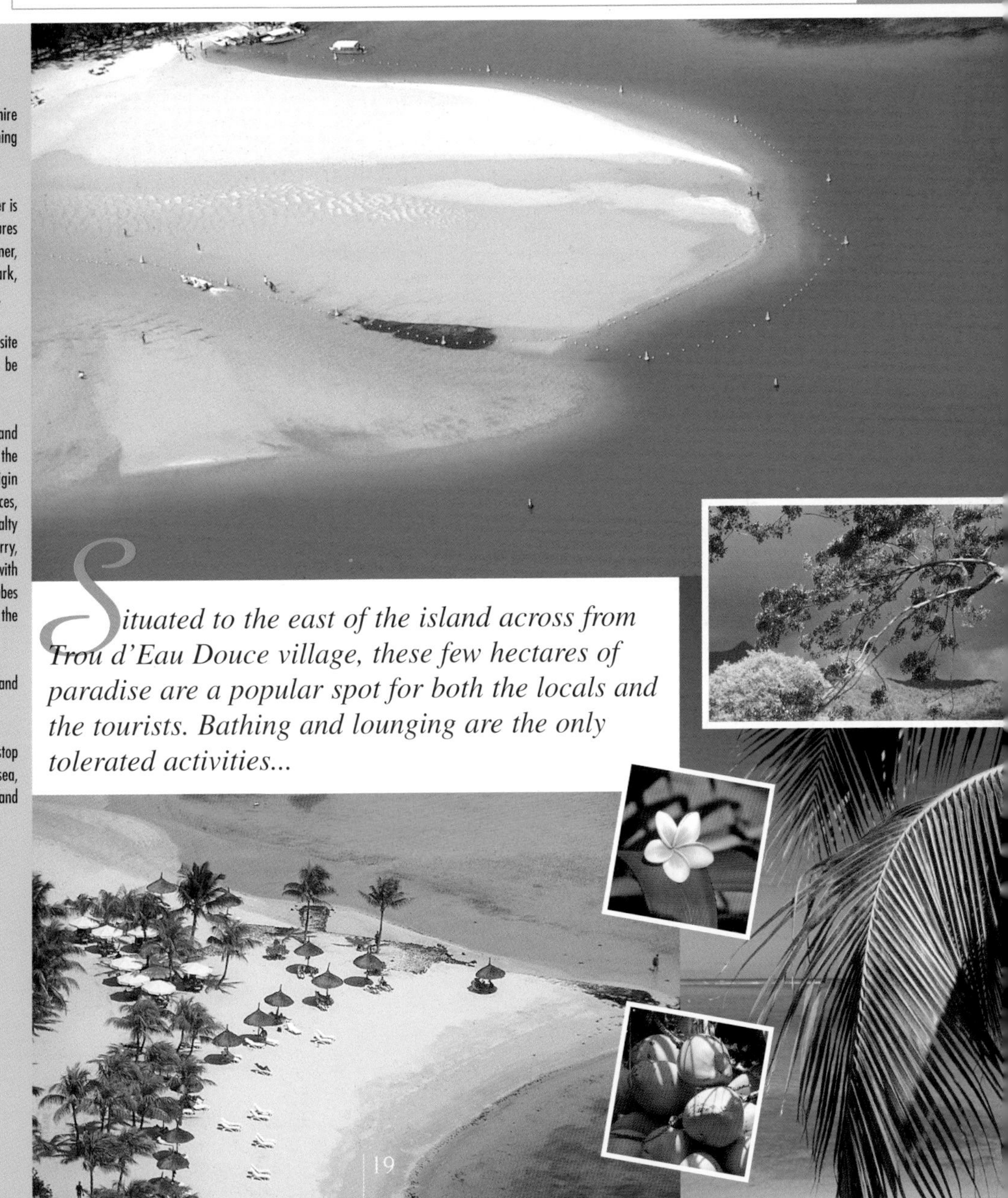

Situated to the east of the island across from Trou d'Eau Douce village, these few hectares of paradise are a popular spot for both the locals and the tourists. Bathing and lounging are the only tolerated activities...

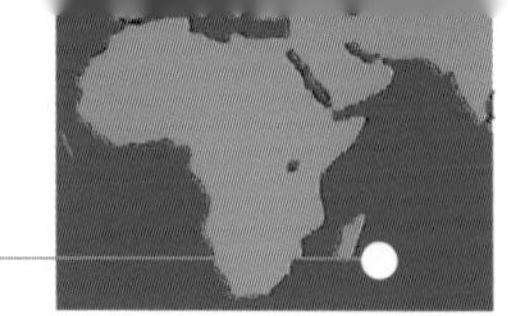

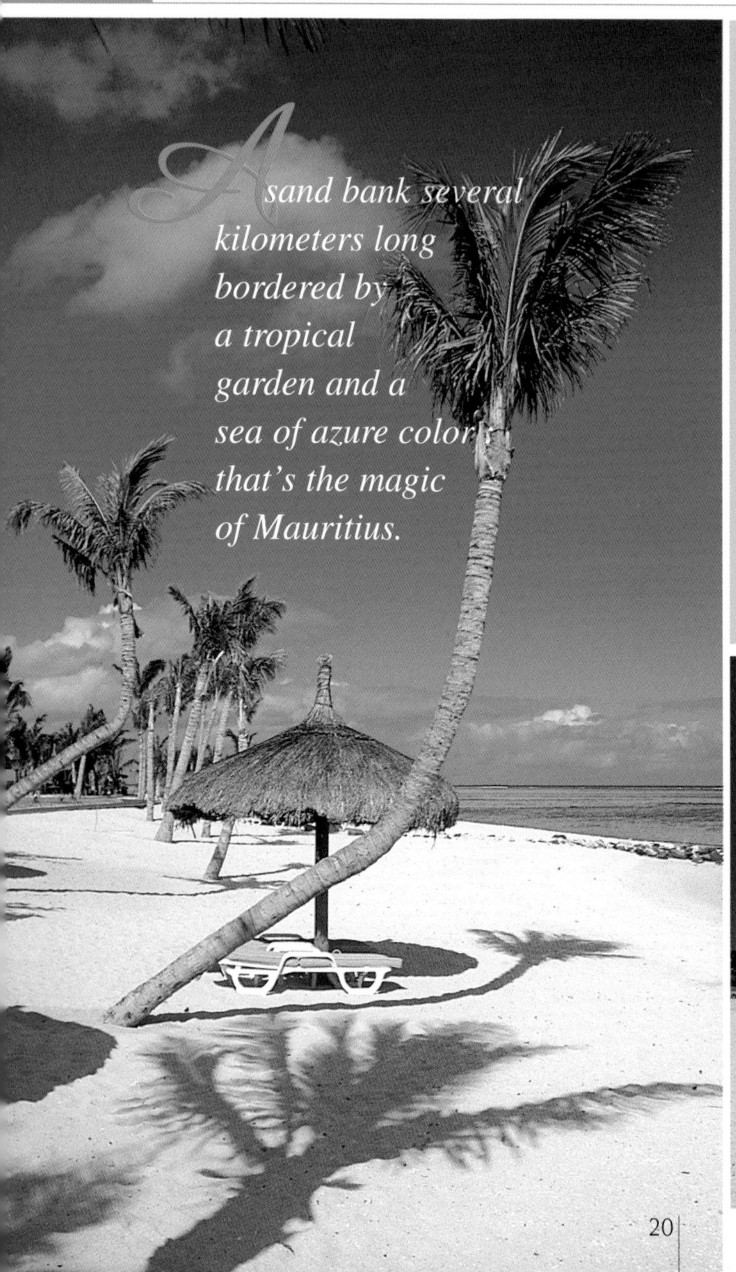

A sand bank several kilometers long bordered by a tropical garden and a sea of azure color that's the magic of Mauritius.

Airline Companies
Air France, Air Mauritius, British Airways.

How to get there
From the capital Port-Louis you travel the length of the island on the A7, then you take the coastal route B15.

Best seasons
The climate is pleasant all year round. Winter is from June to September when temperatures vary between 17°C and 25°C. In summer, temperatures can surpass the 30°C mark, although it is the season that gets most rain.

Accommodation
Several good hotels and many bungalows along the beach.

Local cuisine
A concoction of Creole, Indian, Asian and European, the local cuisine is well worth the detour: Vindaye (a dish of Indian origin consisting of fish marinated in mustard, spices, onions and vinegar), rougail (a Creole specialty with tomatoes, onions, garlic and spices), curry, biriani (Indian dish), samosas (philo dough with meat or vegetable filling), chutney, daubes (beef stew), fish barbecues and don't forget the ti-punch !

Shopping
Wooden sculptures, Indian fabrics, arts and crafts, precious stones, spices...

What to see
Heading a little to the south, you reach Trou d'eau douce, a small village from which it is possible to access Ile aux Cerfs.

Activities
Sailing, water skiing, golf, diving (Belle Mare pass)...

Budget
High

Contact
http://www.mauritius.net

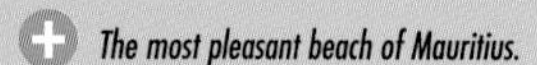
The most pleasant beach of Mauritius.

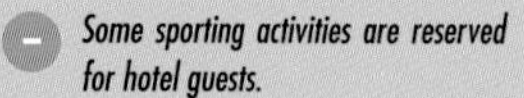
Some sporting activities are reserved for hotel guests.

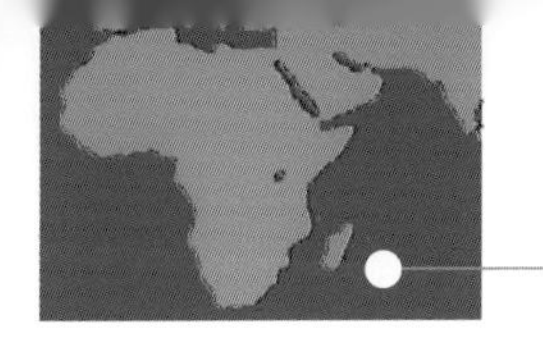

Nicknamed the « Cinderella of Mascareignes », this peaceful dependence of Mauritius hides a lot of treasures, especially an immense 200 km² lagoon and extensive deserted beaches of golden sand.

Airline Companies
Air Mauritius.

How to get there
By air: daily flights link Rodrigues with Mauritius (one-and-a-half hour flight time) and Reunion Island.
By boat: The Mauritius Pride sails two to three times per month between Reunion Island, Mauritius and Rodrigues (approximately 24 h crossing time).

Best seasons
The climate is drier and warmer than in Mauritius and allows pleasant visiting all year round. However, the times between April and June and September to November are best. Beware of the possibility of cyclones between December and March.

Accommodation
In Rodrigues, a handful of simple lodgings can be found at very affordable prices as well as more comfortable accommodations in a few hotels.

Local cuisine
Vindaye (a dish of Indian origin consisting of fish marinated in mustard, spices, onions and vinegar), rougail (a Creole specialty with tomatoes, onions, garlic and spices), curry, biriani (Indian dish), samosas (philo dough with meat or vegetable filling). For drinks, the local «Green Island» rum is very popular.

Shopping
Basketware, jewelry, boat models, spices, fabrics...

What to see
Ile aux Cocos (you can bathe and admire the birds); Mont Limon (highest point in the island at 390 m).

Activities
Big game fishing, canoeing, diving, hiking...

Budget
Average

Contact
http://www.mauritius.net

+ *Less touristy than Mauritius.*

- *The island is prone to cyclones.*

MADAGASCAR • SAINTE-MARIE

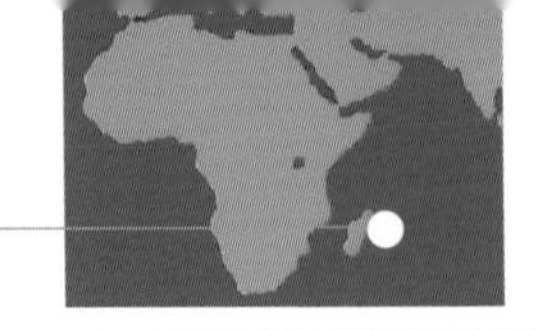

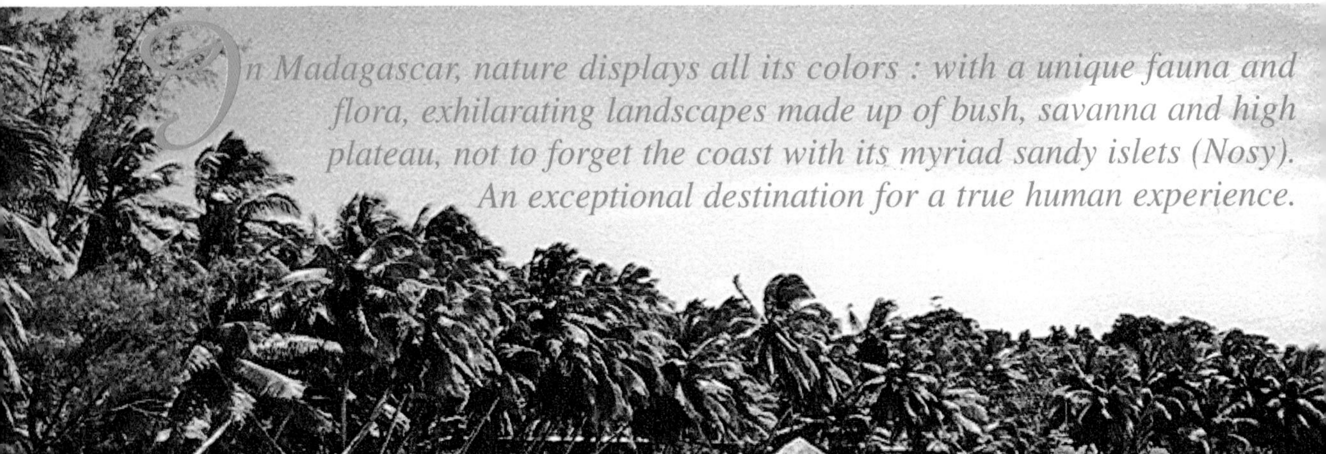

In Madagascar, nature displays all its colors : with a unique fauna and flora, exhilarating landscapes made up of bush, savanna and high plateau, not to forget the coast with its myriad sandy islets (Nosy). An exceptional destination for a true human experience.

Ancient pirate hideaway, the small island of Sainte-Marie (Nosy Boraha) is still to this day home to fishermen with age-old traditions. Located on the east coast of Madagascar its lush vegetation, granite rock, mangroves and marvelous beaches lure the tourists.

Surface area
592,000 km²

Population
15.5 million

Time Zone
GMT +3

Language
Malgache, French

Currency
Malgache Franc

Documents
Passport + Visa

Health
Hepatitis A, cholera, typhoid and yellow fever vaccines are recommended as well as anti-malaria treatment.

Average temperatures
20°C in winter,
29°C in summer on the coast

Airline Companies
Air France, Corsair, Air Madagascar

How to get there
By air: from Antananarivo to Tamatave with Air Madagascar.
By boat: from Tamatave

Best seasons
On the east coast the rain and cyclone season is from December to March. September, October and November are the driest months.

Accommodation
Several smaller hotels and bungalows right in the middle of the greenery or along the beaches.

Local cuisine
Malgache cuisine is prepared using rice which is often served with romazava (a beef stock and simmered pork stew with mashed manioc). Indulge in fish, crustaceans, and dishes prepared with vanilla and coconut milk.

Shopping
Inlaid work, objects made from precious woods, silver jewelry, embroideries, leather, spices, vanilla, cotton goods, raffia, carpets of mohair, semi-precious stones …

What to see
Ampanihy forest; Pirate cemetery; île aux Nattes.

Activities
Sailing, snorkeling, diving, 4x4, ATV, hiking, whale watching (between July and September)...

Budget
Average

Contact
http://www.madagascar-tourisme.com

\+ *Exotic far away surroundings.*

\- *Mosquitoes with a voracious sting...*

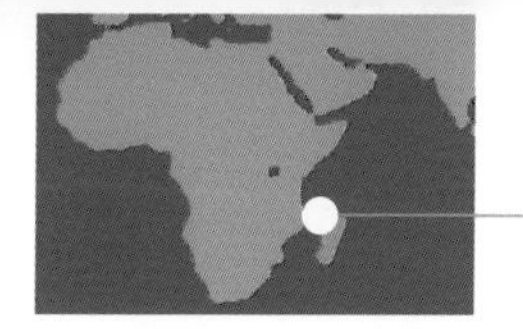

Airline Companies
Air France, Corsair, Air Madagascar
How to get there
By air: from Antananarivo with Air Madagascar
By boat: leaves from Antsahampano
Best seasons
Between May and October. Avoid the month of February when rains are torrential.
Accommodation
Hotels of all categories and comfortable resorts.
Local cuisine
Malgache cuisine is prepared using rice which is often served with romazava (a beef stock and simmered pork stew with mashed manioc). Indulge in fish, crustaceans, and dishes prepared with vanilla and coconut milk.
Shopping
Inlaid work, objects made from precious woods, silver jewelry, embroideries, leather, spices, vanilla, cotton goods, raffia, mohair carpets…
What to see
«L'arbre Sacré» (sacred tree), a gigantic ficus with branches and air roots that form a cathedral 50m in diameter; the cascade at Ampasindava; the Lokobe Natural Reserve, where crocodiles, pythons and lemurs can be seen; Mont Passos, highest point in the island (330 meters); the nearby islets (Nosy Tanikely, Nosy Iranja, Nosy Komba, Nosy Sakatia); the archipelagos of Mistio and Ramada.
Activities
Sailing, snorkeling, hiking, diving (dolphins, whales, sharks, manta rays, turtles and multicolored fish...)
Budget
Quite high
Contact
http://www.madagascar-tourisme.com

\+ *Tourism that is just awakening.*

\- *Prices are higher than anywhere else in the country.*

To the northwest of the Malgaches coast, on the Mozambique channel, Nosy Be - or Ile aux Parfums - welcomes its visitors with the aromas of ylang-ylang, coffee, clove, cocoa and vanilla. With its 200 km of virgin coast and its multitude of small paradisiacal islets (above Nosy Iranja), it is a not-to-be-missed beach experience for travelers seeking to relax after a long journey inland.

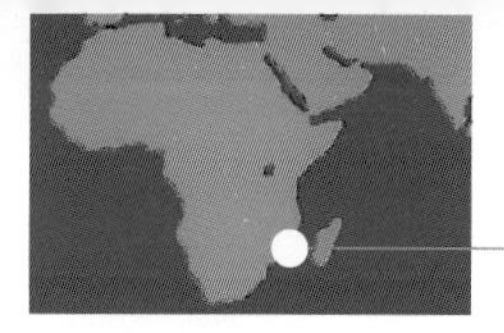

MOZAMBIQUE • BAZARUTO ARCHIPELAGO

Airline Companies
South African Airways
How to get there
By air: from Maputo or Beira.
By boat: from Vilanculos
Best seasons
Mozambique has a subtropical climate with warm temperatures and heavy precipitation. The dry season (from May to October) is the best time to visit. During the rest of the year the country is prone to floods and cyclones.
Accommodation
Small resorts and individual bungalows at Bazaruto and Benguerra.
Local cuisine
Mozambique cuisine resulted from the confluence of Portuguese and oriental culinary traditions. Specialties consist of piri-piri chicken, zambesi chicken, seafood, matapa (peanut or manioc sauce), all served with rice or corn.
Shopping
Wooden carvings, pottery, ceramics, paintings, percussion instruments (timbila)...
What to see
Boat excursions to the virgin island of Pansy.
Activities
Fishing, diving (the coral reefs are home to more than two thousand fish species, dolphins and whales, an aquatic fauna unique in the world !).
Budget
Low (Accommodation)
Contact
http://www.mozambique.mz

+ *Natural Marine Park of almost supernatural beauty.*

- *Little accommodation available.*

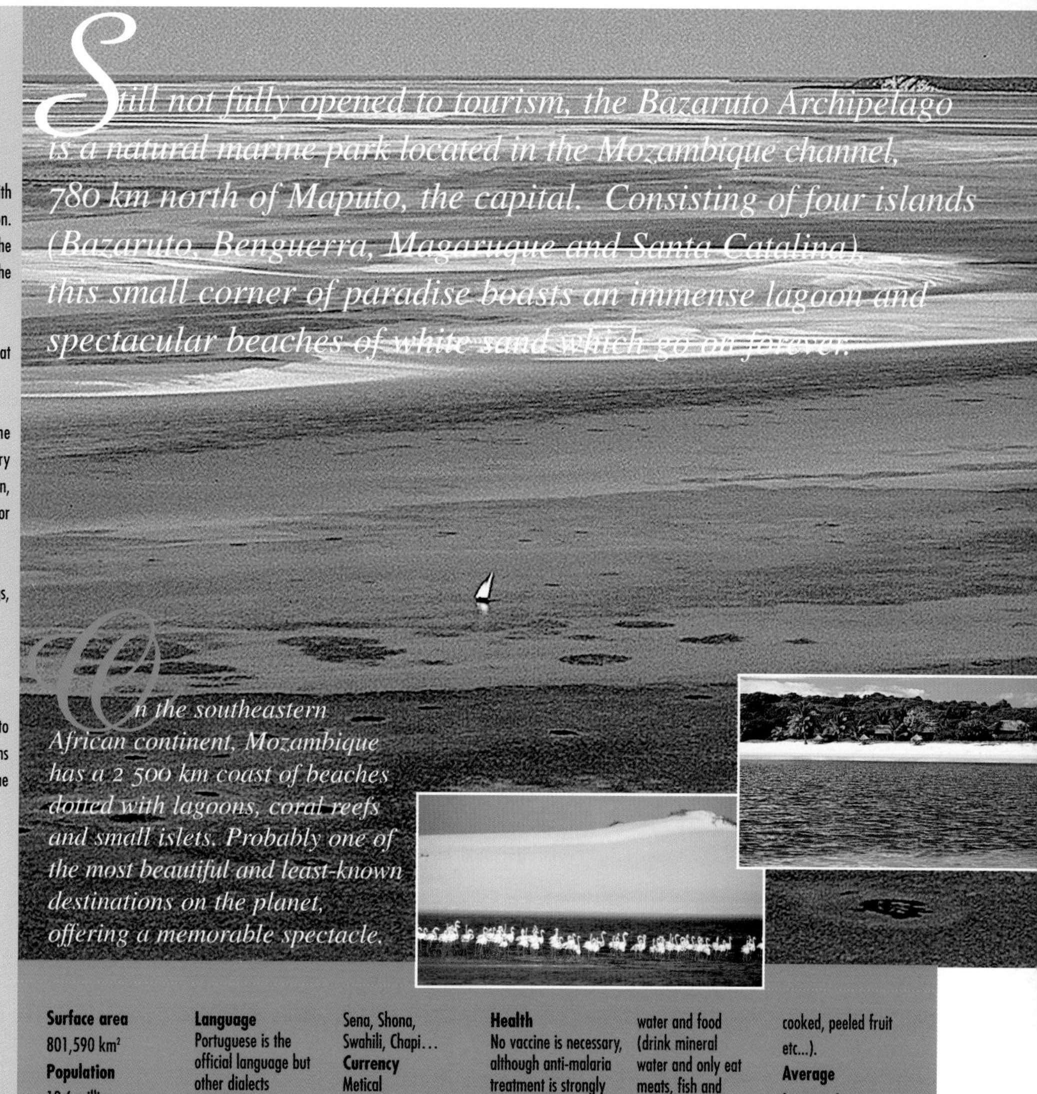

Still not fully opened to tourism, the Bazaruto Archipelago is a natural marine park located in the Mozambique channel, 780 km north of Maputo, the capital. Consisting of four islands (Bazaruto, Benguerra, Magaruque and Santa Catalina), this small corner of paradise boasts an immense lagoon and spectacular beaches of white sand which go on forever.

On the southeastern African continent, Mozambique has a 2 500 km coast of beaches dotted with lagoons, coral reefs and small islets. Probably one of the most beautiful and least-known destinations on the planet, offering a memorable spectacle.

Surface area
801,590 km²
Population
19.6 million
Time Zone
GMT +2
Language
Portuguese is the official language but other dialects arespoken by the population: Makua, Tsonga, Sena, Shona, Swahili, Chapi...
Currency
Metical
Documents
Passport + Visa
Health
No vaccine is necessary, although anti-malaria treatment is strongly recommended. Moreover, care must be taken with water and food (drink mineral water and only eat meats, fish and vegetables that have been previously well cooked, peeled fruit etc...).
Average temperatures
21°C in winter,
27 °C in summer

SAO TOME & PRINCIPE

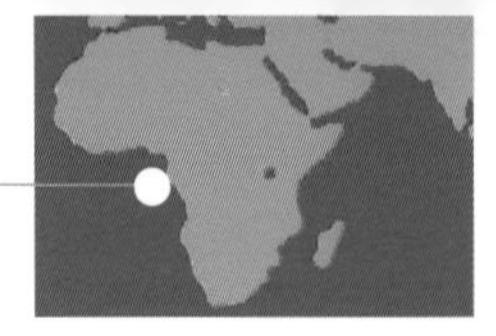

Surface area
Sao Tome : 850 km²
Principe : 130 km²
Population
140 000

Time Zone
GMT
Language
Portuguese is the official language although locals also speak Forro.
Currency
Dobra
Documents
Passport + Visa

Health
Mandatory yellow fever vaccine. Prophylactic malaria treatment is also recommended.

Average temperatures
Between 24°C and 27°C all year long

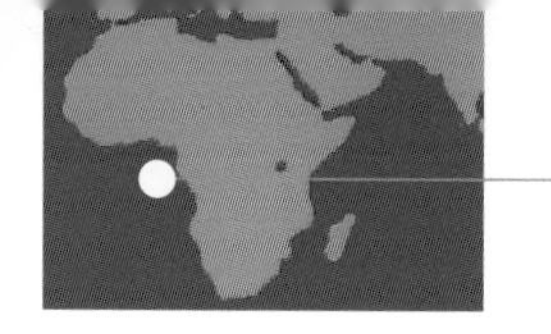

SAO TOME & PRINCIPE

Here, black and ocher-colored sand mix and beaches retain their original beauty. Some of them are today the object of special environmental protection since they are the breeding grounds of turtles.

Airline Companies
TAP.

How to get there
Air Sao Tome provides several flights per week between Sao Tome and Principe.

Best seasons
Located in an equatorial zone the archipelago enjoys a warm and humid climate all year round with heavy precipitation from September to March.

Accommodation
Lodgings, hotels and bungalows in all ranges on both islands.

Local cuisine
Calulu (an African dish of fish or meat and vegetables), cachupa (a sort of meat stew with corn and beans), and a variety of fish served with breadfruit or plantain bananas.

Shopping
Local arts and crafts, wood carvings, inlaid work, coffee, chocolate...

What to see
Obo Natural Park southwest of Sao Tome; Obo de Principe Park; cocoa plantations; the colonial buildings of the city of Sao Tome; Cao Grande (famous mountain of Sao Tome at 2024 m above sea level); the small island of Das Rolas (situated right on the Ecuator); «Boca do Inferno» (hell's mouth) near the beach at Sete Ondas.

Activities
Hiking through the jungle and mountains, big game fishing, diving. In November you can witness the turtles lay their eggs.

Budget
Affordable

Contact
http://www.saotome.st

+ *An unspoilt destination with very welcoming people.*

- *Very little tourism infrastructure.*

SEYCHELLES • ANSE LAZIO

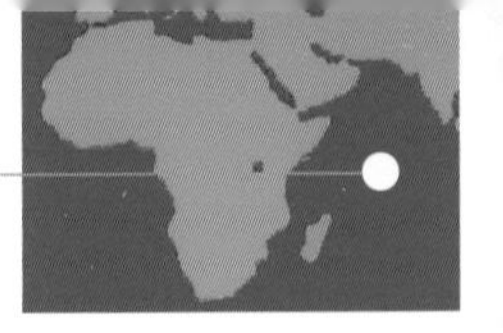

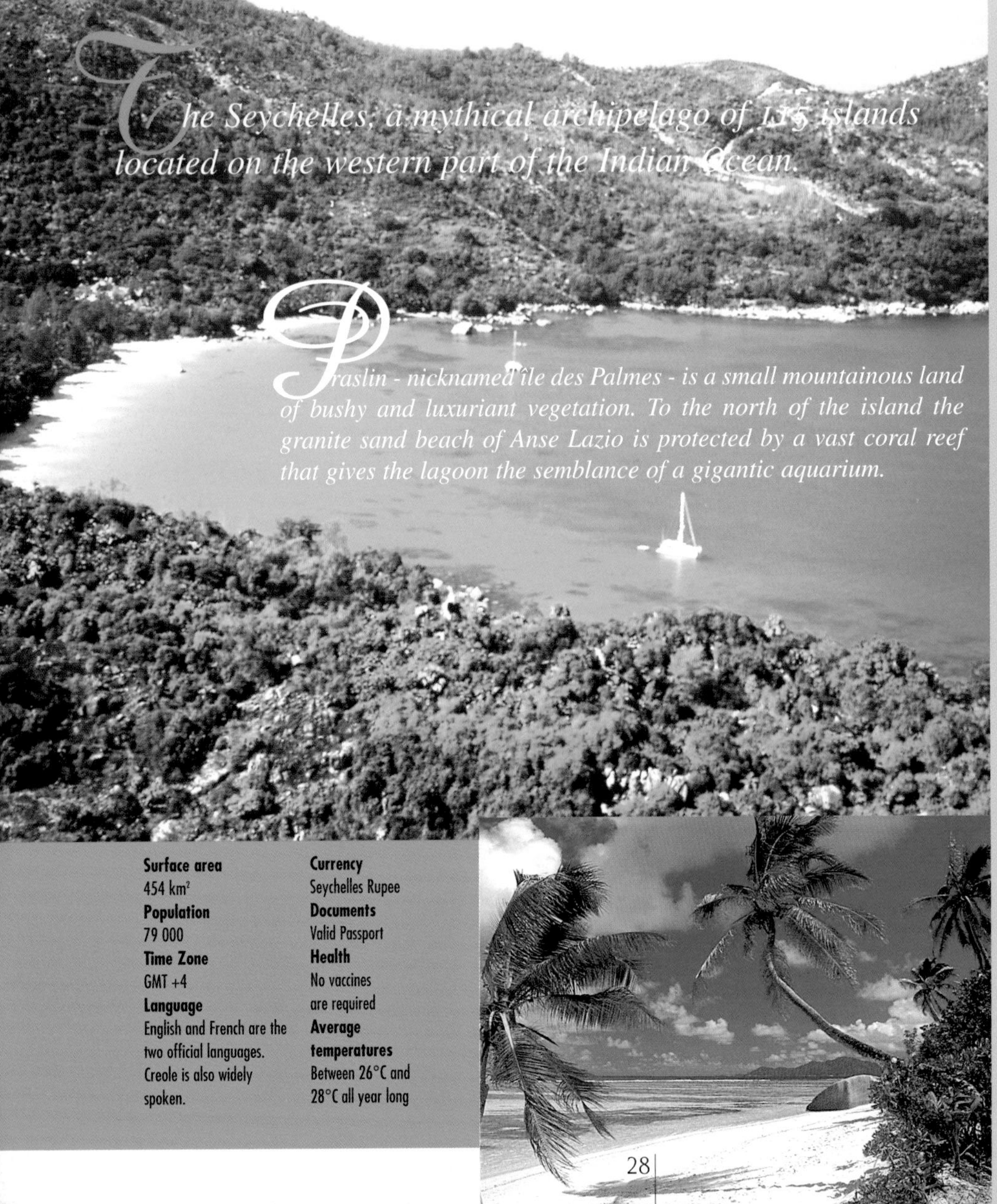

The Seychelles, a mythical archipelago of 115 islands located on the western part of the Indian Ocean.

Praslin - nicknamed île des Palmes - is a small mountainous land of bushy and luxuriant vegetation. To the north of the island the granite sand beach of Anse Lazio is protected by a vast coral reef that gives the lagoon the semblance of a gigantic aquarium.

Surface area
454 km²
Population
79 000
Time Zone
GMT +4
Language
English and French are the two official languages. Creole is also widely spoken.

Currency
Seychelles Rupee
Documents
Valid Passport
Health
No vaccines are required
Average temperatures
Between 26°C and 28°C all year long

Airline Companies
Air France, British Airways, Air Seychelles.
How to get there
By air: Air Seychelles has regular flights between islands.
By ferry: A ferry makes frequent trips from Mahé to Praslin and La Digue.
Best seasons
The months of May-June and September-November are the most pleasant. From December to February and in July-August the archipelago suffers from monsoons and trade winds.
Accommodation
Few amenities near Anse Lazio since the site falls under strict regulation of Natural Parks. Most hotels are located in Grande Anse and on Côte D'Or.
Local cuisine
Abundant fish (shark, barracuda, swordfish, octopus, cobbler tuna...), local palm-heart salad, Creole dishes : daube, rougail (fish or sausages with a tomato sauce), carii coco (meat curry or fish curry cooked with coconut milk), exotic fruits (papayas, tamarind, pineapple, mangos, pomegranate, guava, litchis, jeanmalac) and an interesting local specialty: bat. Glasses filled with local beer and the ubiquitous punch.
Shopping
Hats and baskets made from coconut leaves, wooden Creole furniture, coral jewelry, batiks and sarongs...
What to see
Vallée de Mai is a National Park classified as World Heritage Site known for its exotic forest of Coco-de-Mer giant palms found only in the Seychelles; Baie de Sainte-Anne, where cargo boats from other islands dock.
Activities
Scuba diving, surfing, big game fishing, mountain climbing, hiking, atv...
Budget
For those with a comfortable budget
Contact
http://www.seychelles.com

+ *A lagoon ? No, it's an aquarium !*

− *Cost of living is very high.*

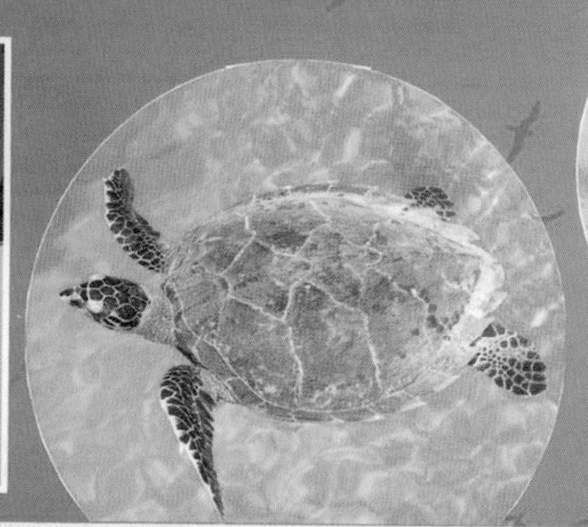

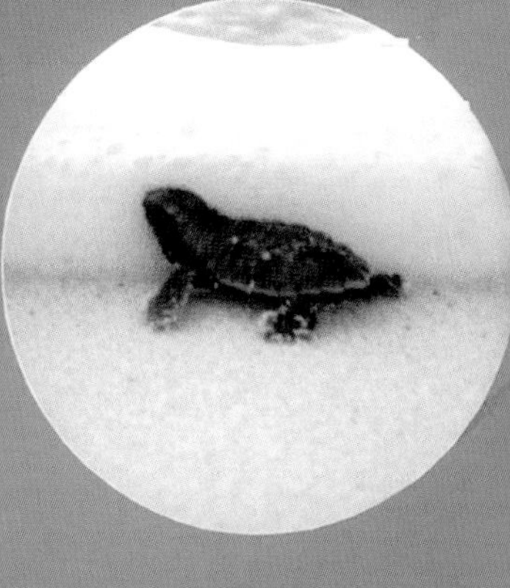

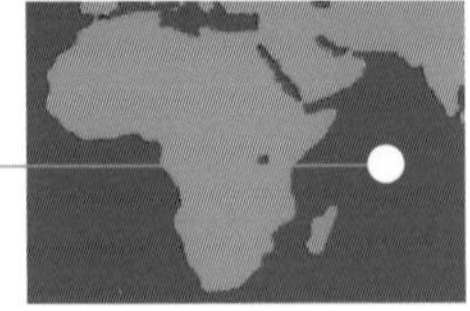

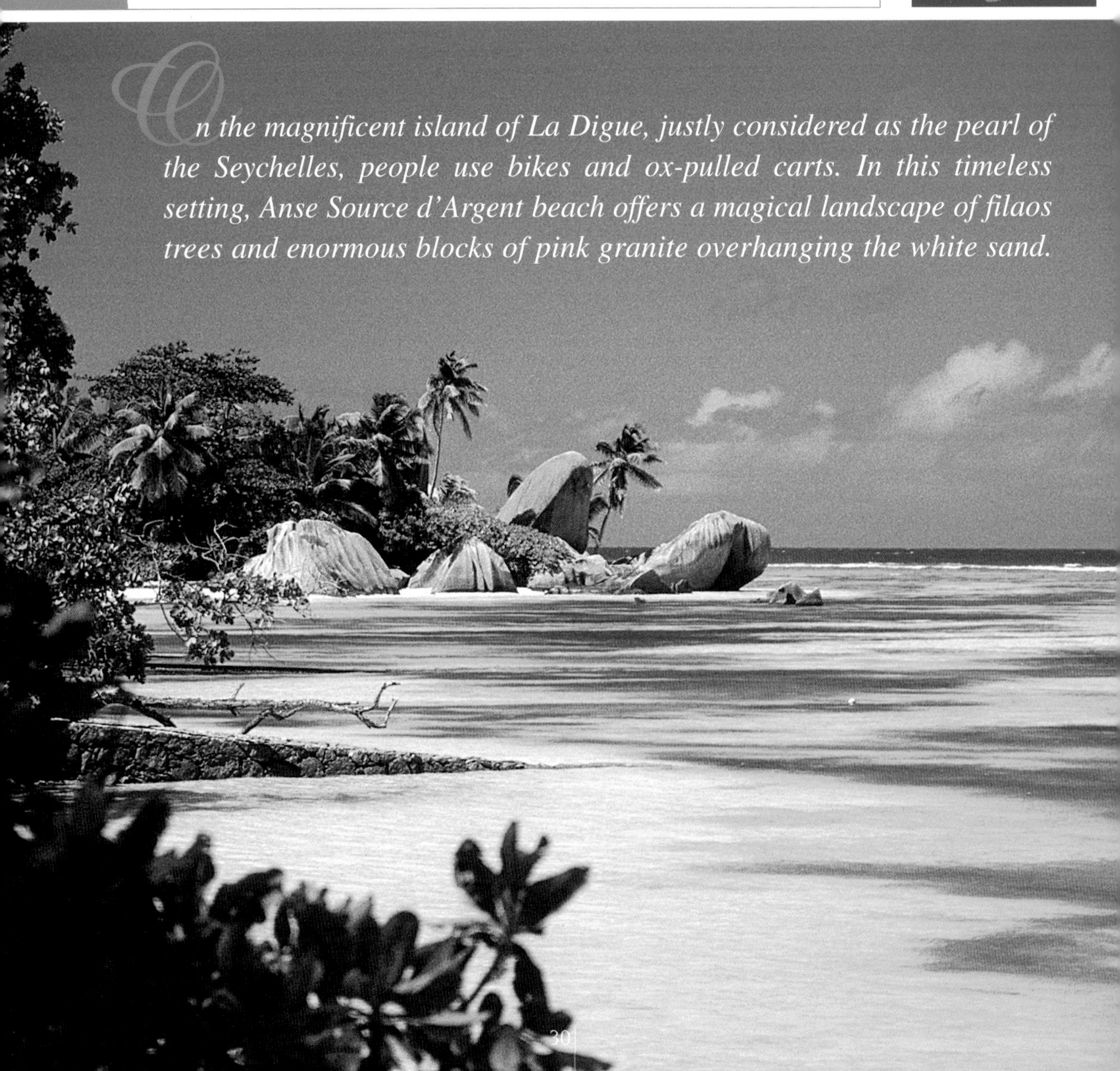

On the magnificent island of La Digue, justly considered as the pearl of the Seychelles, people use bikes and ox-pulled carts. In this timeless setting, Anse Source d'Argent beach offers a magical landscape of filaos trees and enormous blocks of pink granite overhanging the white sand.

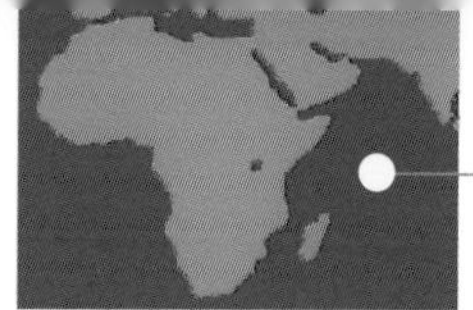

Airline Companies
Air France, British Airways, Air Seychelles.

How to get there
The island of La Digue can be accessed by boat or helicopter from Mahé.
By ferry: A ferry makes frequent trips from Mahé to Praslin and La Digue.

Best seasons
The months of May-June and September-November are the most pleasant. From December to February and in July-August the archipelago suffers from monsoons and trade winds.

Accommodation
Most of the hotels are concentrated on the west coast, between La Passe, Union and Anse Réunion.

Local cuisine
Abundant fish (shark, barracuda, swordfish, octopus, cobbler tuna…), local palm-heart salad, Creole dishes: daube (stew), rougail (fish or sausages with a tomato sauce), carii coco (meat curry or fish curry cooked with coconut milk), exotic fruits (papayas, tamarind, pineapple, mangos, pomegranate, guava, litchis, jeanmalac) and an interesting local specialty: bat. Glasses filled with local beer and the ubiquitous punch.

Shopping
Hats and baskets made from coconut leaves, wooden Creole furniture, coral jewelry, batiks and sarongs, spices grown on the island such as vanilla and cinnamon...

What to see
The old Creole-style houses such as Château Saint-Cloud; visit the «La Digue Veuve Réserve» where you can observe the last specimen of a rare protected bird species: Veuve des Seychelles; the presidential residence and its park complete with giant turtles.

Activities
Big game fishing, hiking, atv, scuba diving (very controlled in order to avoid harpoon fishing).

Budget
For those with a comfortable budget

Contact
http://www.seychelles.com

\+ *Welcome to paradise...*

\- *Very few activities apart from beach-related ones.*

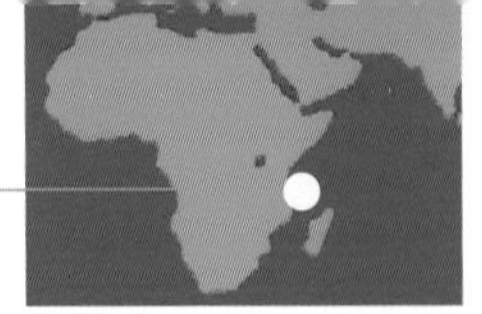

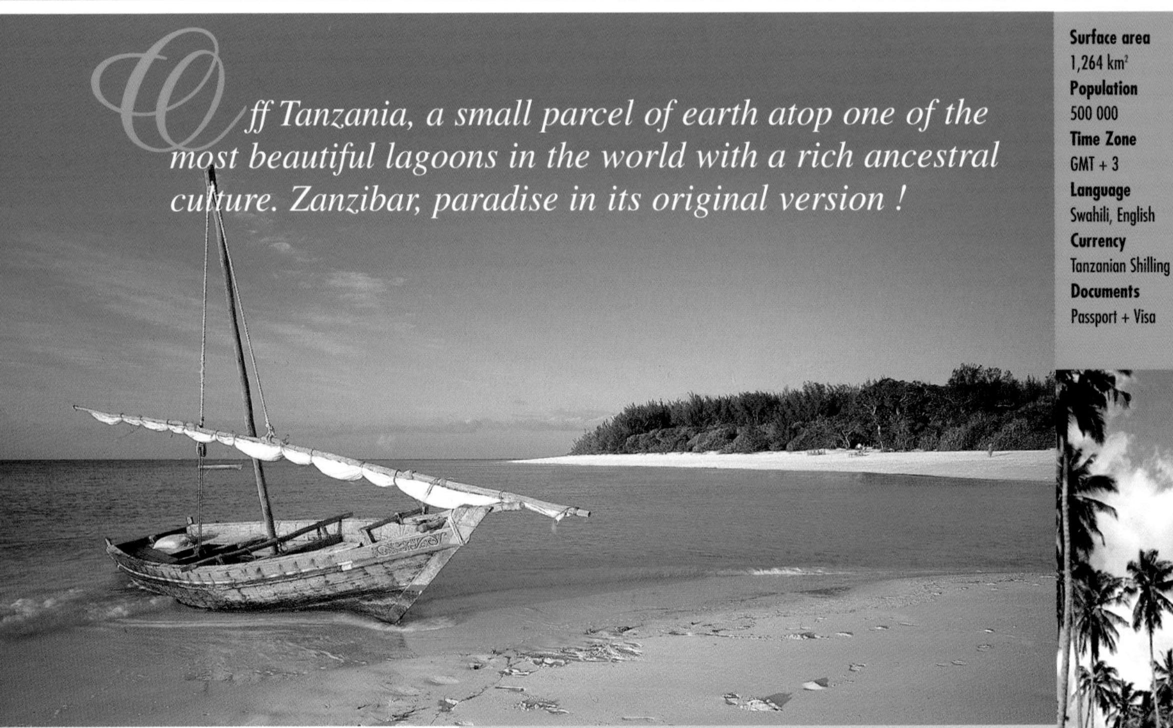

Off Tanzania, a small parcel of earth atop one of the most beautiful lagoons in the world with a rich ancestral culture. Zanzibar, paradise in its original version !

Surface area
1,264 km²
Population
500 000
Time Zone
GMT + 3
Language
Swahili, English
Currency
Tanzanian Shilling
Documents
Passport + Visa
Health
Hepatitis A and yellow fever vaccines are strongly recommended as well as anti-malaria treatment.
Average temperatures
22°C in winter, 32°C in summer

In the north of the island, Nungwi beach is a postcard landscape : white sand, turquoise water and leaning palm trees which provide a protective shadow... It is one of the rare beaches that have no coral barrier which allows for easy bathing at low tide.

Airline Companies
By air: British Airways, KLM up to Dar-el-Salam then take a local flight.
By ferry: depart from Dar el Salam.

How to get there
Take the route heading north until Nungwi.

Best seasons
Zanzibar has an equatorial climate. Rainy season is from March to the end of May, it would be better to take advantage of the dry season (between June and October) when it is warmer and relatively dry.

Accommodation
Wide range of accommodation. The less expensive rooms offer basic comfort, although hygienic conditions prevail in most places. A more comfortable hotel is found in Nungwi offering a wide range of sporting activities.

Local cuisine
If you are sensitive to spiced up food beware the local cuisine ! Hotels serve a fare better suited to the taste and stomach of tourists. In addition, you may find a large variety of fish prepared different ways: grilled, curried, in masala (a mix of spices), served with a dish of rice pilaf or ugali (boiled manioc).

Shopping
Carved wooden objects, mirrors, baskets, spices, aromatics, essential oils...

What to see
Les Jardins d'Epices (spice tour), where one can smell and learn how to recognize the grains right from the original trees; shipbuilding shops where typical flat-bottomed boutres are built.

Activities
Sailing, canoeing, diving (Zanzibar is home to a marine life reputed to be one of the most beautiful of the Indian Ocean).

Budget
Not too high

Contact
http://www.zanzibar.net

\+ *Double your pleasure - the beach and the culture.*

\- *Be careful of sanitary conditions in food preparation !*

THE AMERICAS

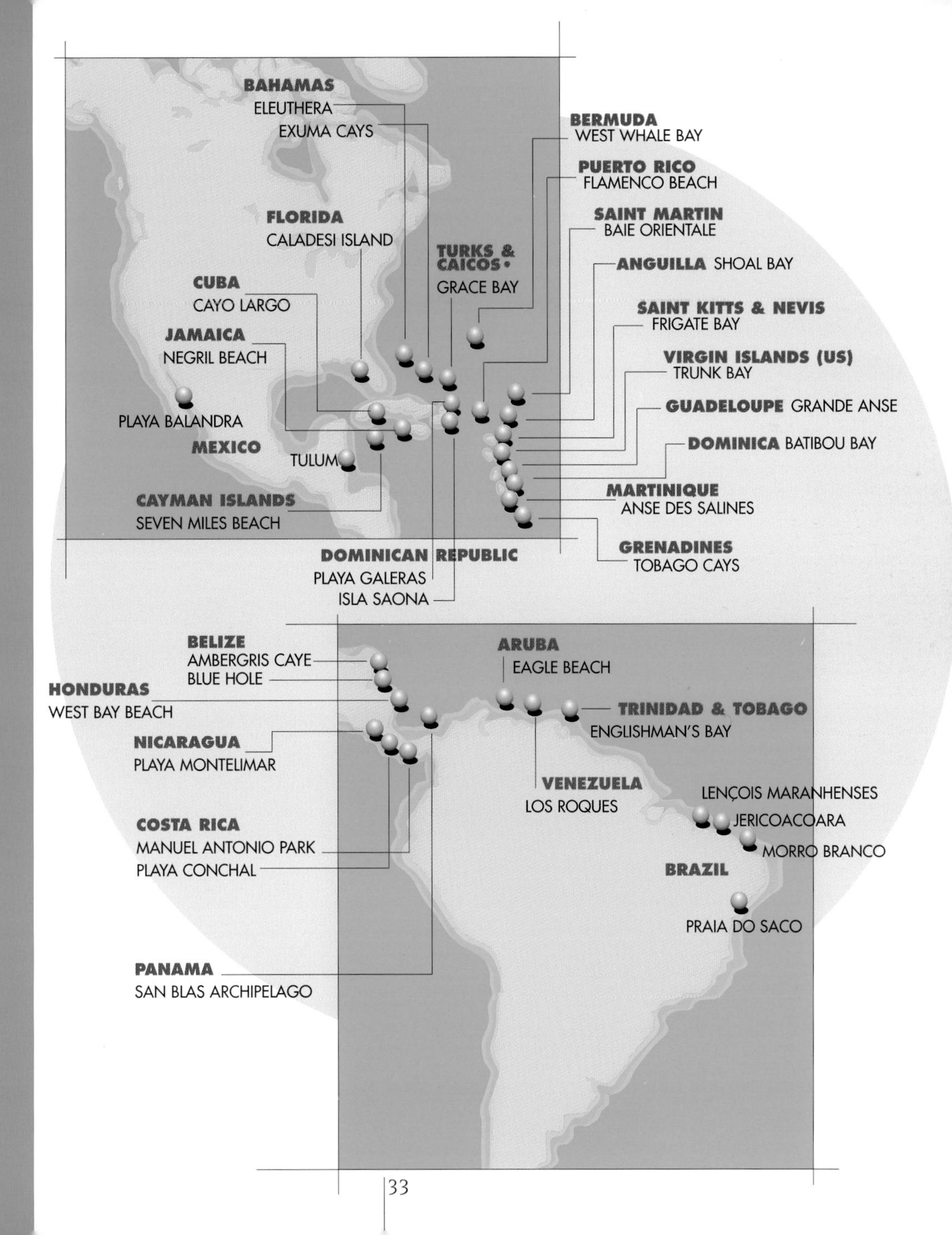

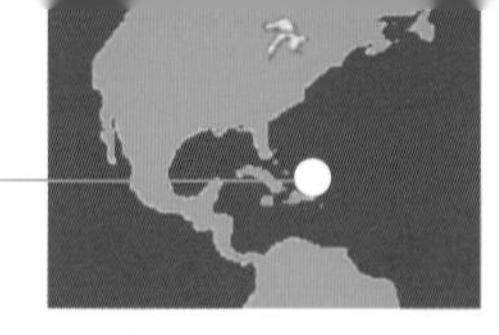

Stretched like an eel, the small island of Anguilla is truly worth the detour thanks to its incredible turquoise waters and its depths teeming with lobster.

Nestled in the southern corner of the island, Shoal Bay beach is often referred to as one of the most seductive in the Caribbean.

Surface area
91 km^2
Population
12 000
Time Zone
GMT -4
Language
English
Currency
Caribbean Dollar

Documents
Valid Passport
Health
No vaccine required
Average temperatures
26°C in winter, 29°C in summer

Airline Companies
By air: Air France (via Saint Martin), Air Caraïbes, Windward Islands Airways.
By ferry: from Saint-Martin.

How to get there
A single route crosses the length of the entire island. From the capital The Valley, head for Stoney Groud and turn left toward Shoal Bay.

Best seasons
Between December and April.

Accommodation
Some good resorts and villas to rent.

Local cuisine
Lobster (the island's specialty), clawless lobster, fish and seafood, tropical fruits...

Shopping
Souvenirs with the face of Anguilla's bear, rum, cigars, perfumes, pottery...

What to see
Sandy Island is a small islet of white sand and coconut trees that can be toured in ten minutes and is perfect for diving; the submarine caves of Prickly Pear Cays.

Activities
Sailing, water skiing, diving (some ships have been sunk on purpose to create new submarine environments)...

Budget
Quite high

Contact
http://net.ai

+ *A destination little known to European tourists.*

- *Little recreational activity except for the «beach ones».*

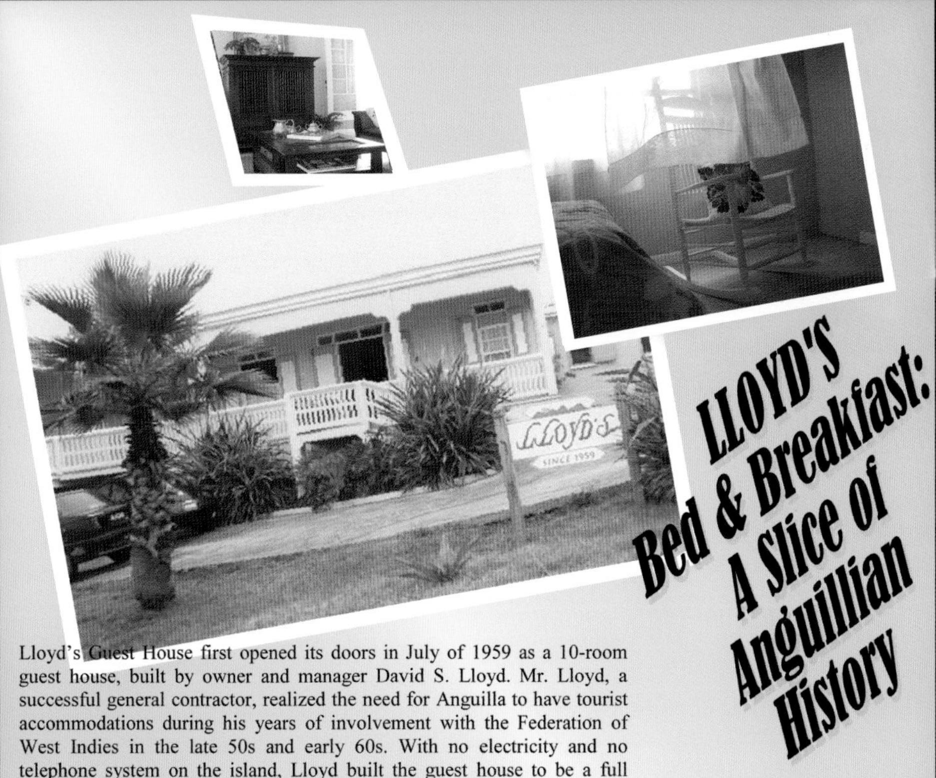

LLOYD'S Bed & Breakfast: A Slice of Anguillian History

Lloyd's Guest House first opened its doors in July of 1959 as a 10-room guest house, built by owner and manager David S. Lloyd. Mr. Lloyd, a successful general contractor, realized the need for Anguilla to have tourist accommodations during his years of involvement with the Federation of West Indies in the late 50s and early 60s. With no electricity and no telephone system on the island, Lloyd built the guest house to be a full service establishment that would provide three home-cooked meals a day to guests, as there were no restaurants on island. All for the price of US $8.00 per day!

As the only place in town that offered rooms and meals to visitors, Lloyd's hosted many dignitaries and VIPs during the early years. And even after other hotels and restaurants opened on island in later years, Lloyd's was the caterer of choice to provide sandwiches for the reception held in honour of Prince Charles' visit in 1973.

In response to heavy demand, the small inn grew to 12 rooms in 1960 and 14 rooms by the mid 70s. But despite the bigger facilities, Lloyd's has remained true to its roots over the past 40 years. Mr. Lloyd's wife, Vida, took over as the manager of the property when David passed away in 1989, and along with their children David and Christine, Mrs. Lloyd has kept the same family atmosphere at the inn, which continues to charm guests.

Today, meals at Lloyd's are only offered as part of an optional meal plan, rates have increased to US$70 per day, and there are plans for further expansion and renovation. But despite these changes, Lloyd's stays refreshingly the same as it was when it opened in 1959.

Lloyd's Guest House is a slice of Anguillian history and culture. The original architecture is intact and is a reflection of tradition and simplicity. A spacious living room/lounge segues into a smaller dining room where people from all backgrounds and cultures meld, a feat made easy by old-fashioned, family-style dining.

The guest house sits atop Crocus Hill and is a stone's throw from the capital, Crocus Bay and Little Bay (two of the many beaches). The long, breezy corridor that abuts the living room opens up to a panoramic view of The Valley and sea at the eastern end of the island. The vantage positioning of Lloyd's also offers glimpses into surrounding villages, and keeps one attuned to the sounds and rhythms of island life.

ARUBA • EAGLE BEACH

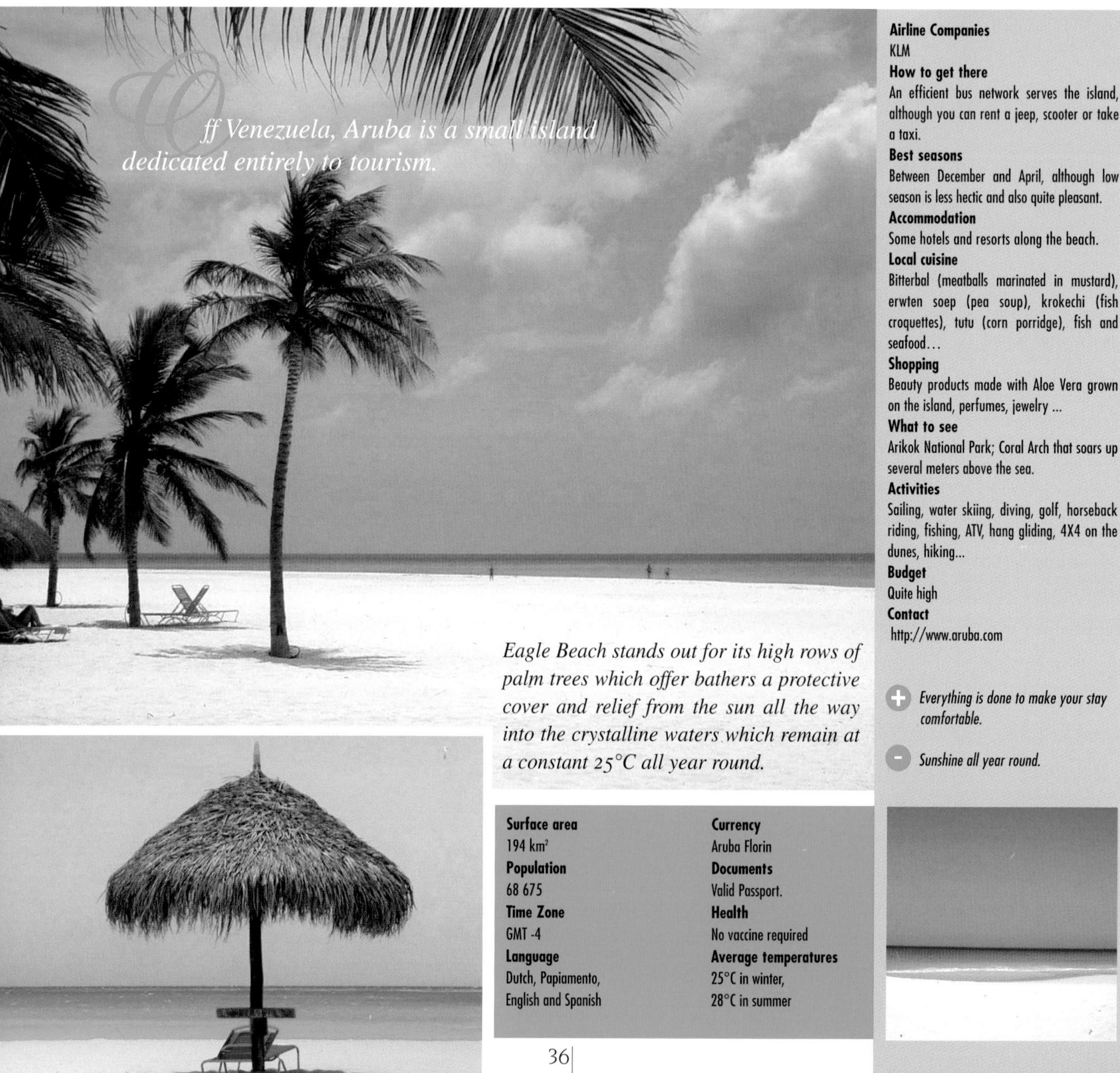

Off Venezuela, Aruba is a small island dedicated entirely to tourism.

Eagle Beach stands out for its high rows of palm trees which offer bathers a protective cover and relief from the sun all the way into the crystalline waters which remain at a constant 25°C all year round.

Surface area	**Currency**
194 km²	Aruba Florin
Population	**Documents**
68 675	Valid Passport.
Time Zone	**Health**
GMT -4	No vaccine required
Language	**Average temperatures**
Dutch, Papiamento, English and Spanish	25°C in winter, 28°C in summer

Airline Companies
KLM

How to get there
An efficient bus network serves the island, although you can rent a jeep, scooter or take a taxi.

Best seasons
Between December and April, although low season is less hectic and also quite pleasant.

Accommodation
Some hotels and resorts along the beach.

Local cuisine
Bitterbal (meatballs marinated in mustard), erwten soep (pea soup), krokechi (fish croquettes), tutu (corn porridge), fish and seafood…

Shopping
Beauty products made with Aloe Vera grown on the island, perfumes, jewelry ...

What to see
Arikok National Park; Coral Arch that soars up several meters above the sea.

Activities
Sailing, water skiing, diving, golf, horseback riding, fishing, ATV, hang gliding, 4X4 on the dunes, hiking...

Budget
Quite high

Contact
http://www.aruba.com

+ *Everything is done to make your stay comfortable.*

- *Sunshine all year round.*

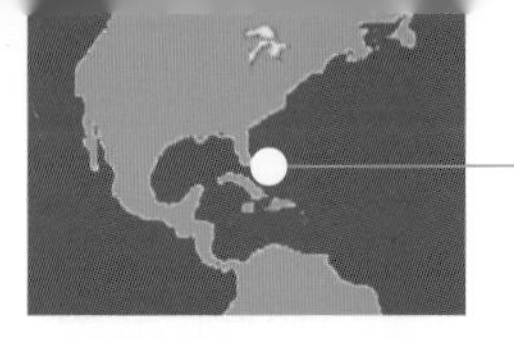

The 700 islands of the Bahamas are dispersed in the Atlantic Ocean, 140 km south of the Florida coast. The archipelago extends over 1200 km all the way to Cuba.

Eleuthera island is shaped like an arch and looks to the Atlantic Ocean on one side and to the Caribbean Sea on the other. A stunning spectacle !

Surface area
14 000 km²
Population
300 000
Time Zone
GMT - 5
Language
English

Currency
American or Bahamian Dollar
Documents
Valid Passport
Health
No vaccine required
Average temperatures
25°C in winter,
32°C in summer

Airline Companies
British Airways, Continental Airlines, American Airlines
How to get there
By air: Some international flights land in Eleuthera and the carrier Bahamas Air has local links departing from Nassau.
By high-speed catamaran: departing from Nassau.
Best seasons
A mild spring-like climate prevails all year round in the archipelago.

Accommodation
Many top-notch hotels, at Governor's Harbour or Harbour Island (small islet situated 1.5 km northeast of the island).
Local cuisine
Fish and seafood, chicken, peas 'n' rice and don't miss out on Eleuthera's specialty: pineapple.
Shopping
Local arts and crafts, seashells, hand-braided hats from Spanish Wells...

What to see
Dunmore Town dates back to the 18th century; pineapple plantations; Devil's Backbone reef where you can see a variety of species lured by the shipwrecks that are found here.
Activities
Sailing, water skiing, bonefish fishing and fly fishing, diving (a marine environment replete with jacks, barracudas and tiger sharks)...

Budget
High
Contact
http://www.bahamas.com

+ *The ultimate beach destination !*

- *Avoid American school vacation time.*

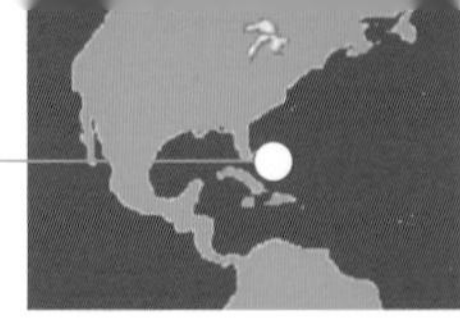

The Exuma Cays archipelago is made up of more than 300 lush islands of which the two main ones, Great Exuma and Little Exuma, are connected by a small bridge. A string of fine sand beaches which sprawl under the tropical sun with azure waters completing this paradisiacal image. This spot is so picture-perfect that it was used as a backdrop location in two James Bond movies (Thunderball and Never Say Never Again).

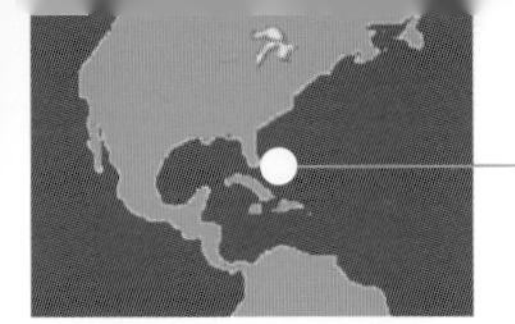

Airline Companies
British Airways, Continental Airlines, American Airlines

How to get there
By air: from Nassau, with Bahamas Air which provides local flights.
By «mail-boat»: In charge of delivering the mail to the different islands of the archipelago, these boats accept travelers on board. An original mode of transportation if you are not in a hurry...

Best seasons
Spring-like conditions all year round.

Accommodation
Most hotels are found at George Town on the island of Great Exuma.

Local cuisine
Lobster, conch, grouper, «peas ' n' rice»...

Shopping
Local arts and crafts, basketware, paintings, sculptures...

What to see
Exuma Cays Land & Sea Park, a 3000 m^2 natural reserve where you can walk amidst the iguanas and discover the underwater world in these magnificent coral gardens.

Activities
Water skiing, diving, big game and bonefish fishing, canoeing-kayaking, biking, sailing (in April you can take in the Family Islands regatta).

Budget
High

Contact
http://www.bahamas.com

+ *Photos speak for themselves...*

- *Cost of living.*

BELIZE • AMBERGRIS CAYE

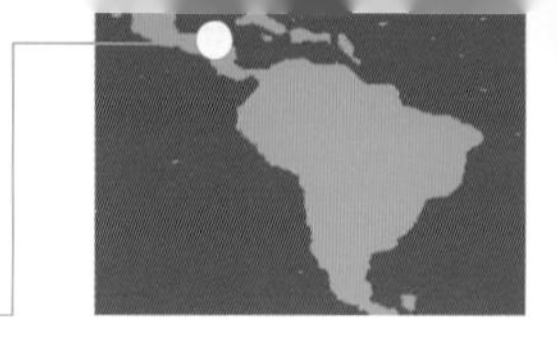

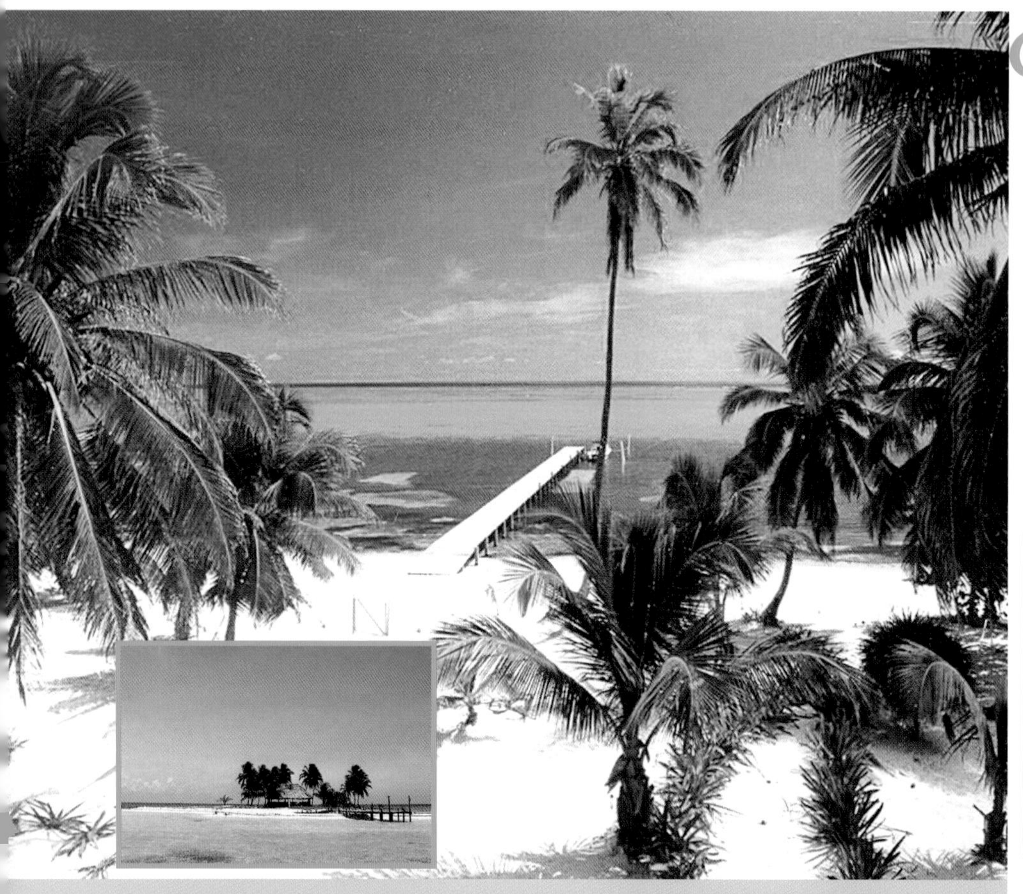

Belize is a small Central American country tucked between Mexico, Guatemala and the Caribbean Sea. Jungle, Inca ruins, coral reef islands and exceptional diving spots are the main points of attraction of this destination which is at the first stages of tourism development. An exotic experience is guaranteed.

Surface area
23,300 km²
Population
250 000
Time Zone
GMT -6
Language
Spanish, English, Mayan dialects
Currency
Belize Dollar
Documents
Valid Passport
Health
Hepatitis A and typhoid vaccines are recommended as well as anti-mosquito treatment against malaria and dengue
Average temperatures
23°C in winter, 27°C in summer

Airline Companies
Iberia, American Airlines via Mexico or the USA, British Airways.
How to get there
Ferries provide regular service to Ambergris Cayre departing from Belize City.
Best seasons
Between November and May
Accommodation
Some rooms in the local charming wood houses and small bungalows right in the water.
Local cuisine
Seafood products and Mexican specialties…
Shopping
Mayan art reproductions, ceramics, paintings, musical instruments...
What to see
On the continent, the ruins of Mayan villages and temples (Altun ha, Caracol, Xunantunich…), the Belize zoo and the many Natural Parks.
Activities
Sailing, canoeing, hiking, diving (on one of the most beautiful coral barriers of the world)
Budget
Average
Contact
http://www.travelbelize.org

+ *A destination off the beaten path.*

- *Road conditions are very poor.*

This small island of only 2000 inhabitants is located along the longest coral barrier on the American continent. The local motto ? «Shirtless, barefoot and no problems!». What an agenda !

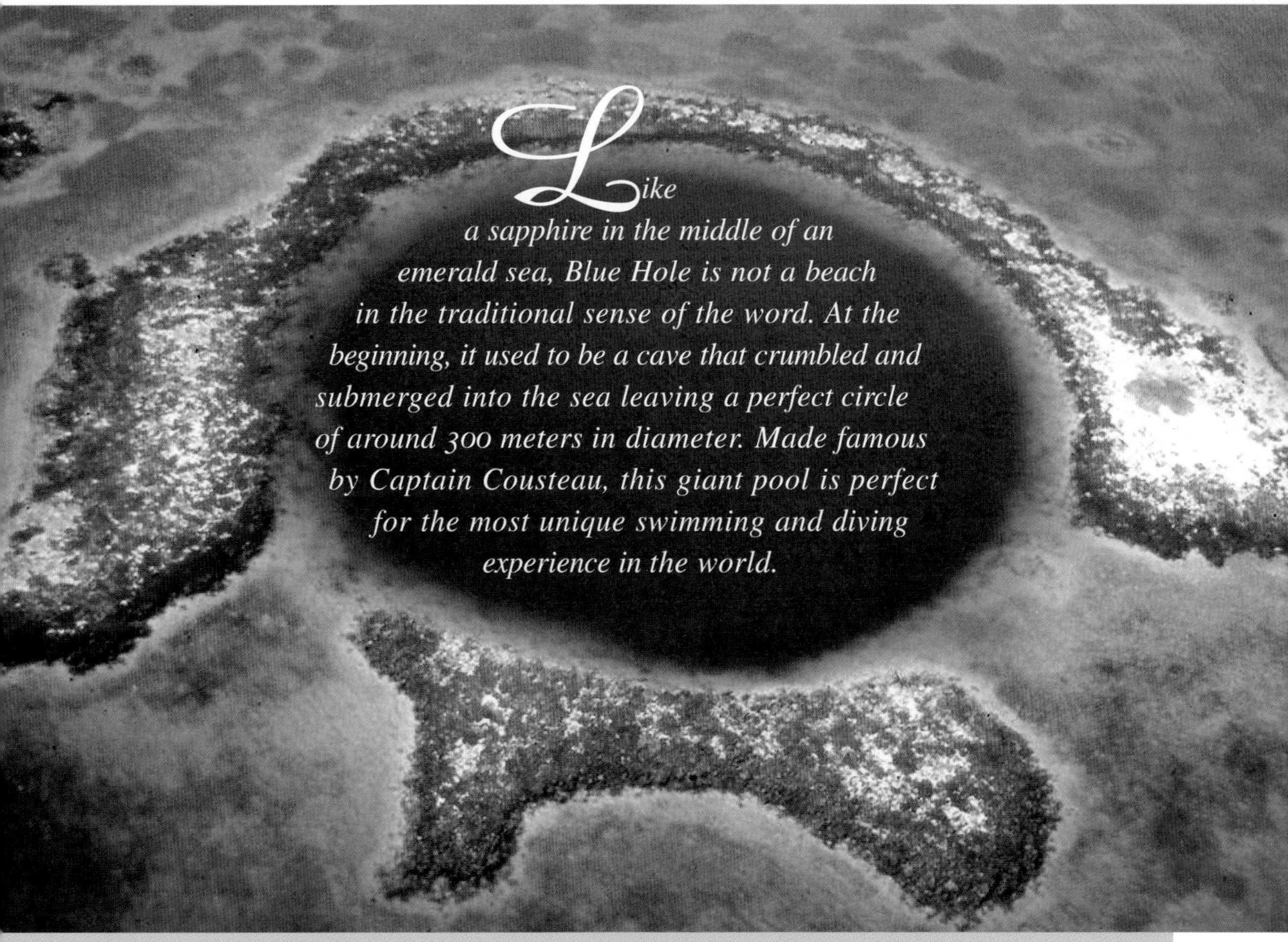

Like a sapphire in the middle of an emerald sea, Blue Hole is not a beach in the traditional sense of the word. At the beginning, it used to be a cave that crumbled and submerged into the sea leaving a perfect circle of around 300 meters in diameter. Made famous by Captain Cousteau, this giant pool is perfect for the most unique swimming and diving experience in the world.

Airline Companies
Iberia, American Airlines via Mexico or the USA, British Airways.

How to get there
Most agencies in the country offer excursions. Finding a boat to get here should be no problem.

Best seasons
Between November and May

Accommodation
No accommodation available here but you can easily stay on a neighboring island or on a boat.

Local cuisine
Seafood products and Mexican specialties…

Shopping
Mayan art reproductions, ceramics, paintings, musical instruments...

What to see
The Marine Reserve at Glovers Reef, the islands of Turnefee and Half Moon Caye. On the continent, the ruins of Mayan villages and temples (Altun ha, Caracol, Xunantunich…), the Belize zoo and the many Natural Parks.

Activities
Snorkeling, diving...

Budget
Average

Contact
http://www.travelbelize.org

\+ *The most beautiful seawater pool in the whole planet.*

\- *Hard to avoid organized excursions.*

BERMUDA • WEST WHALE BAY

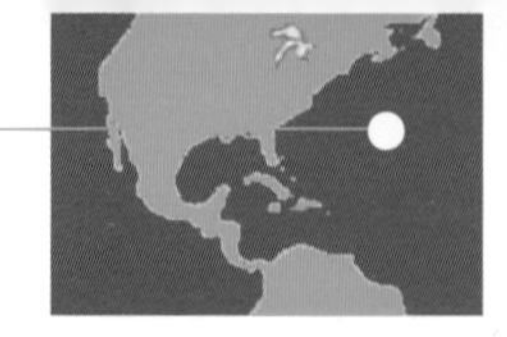

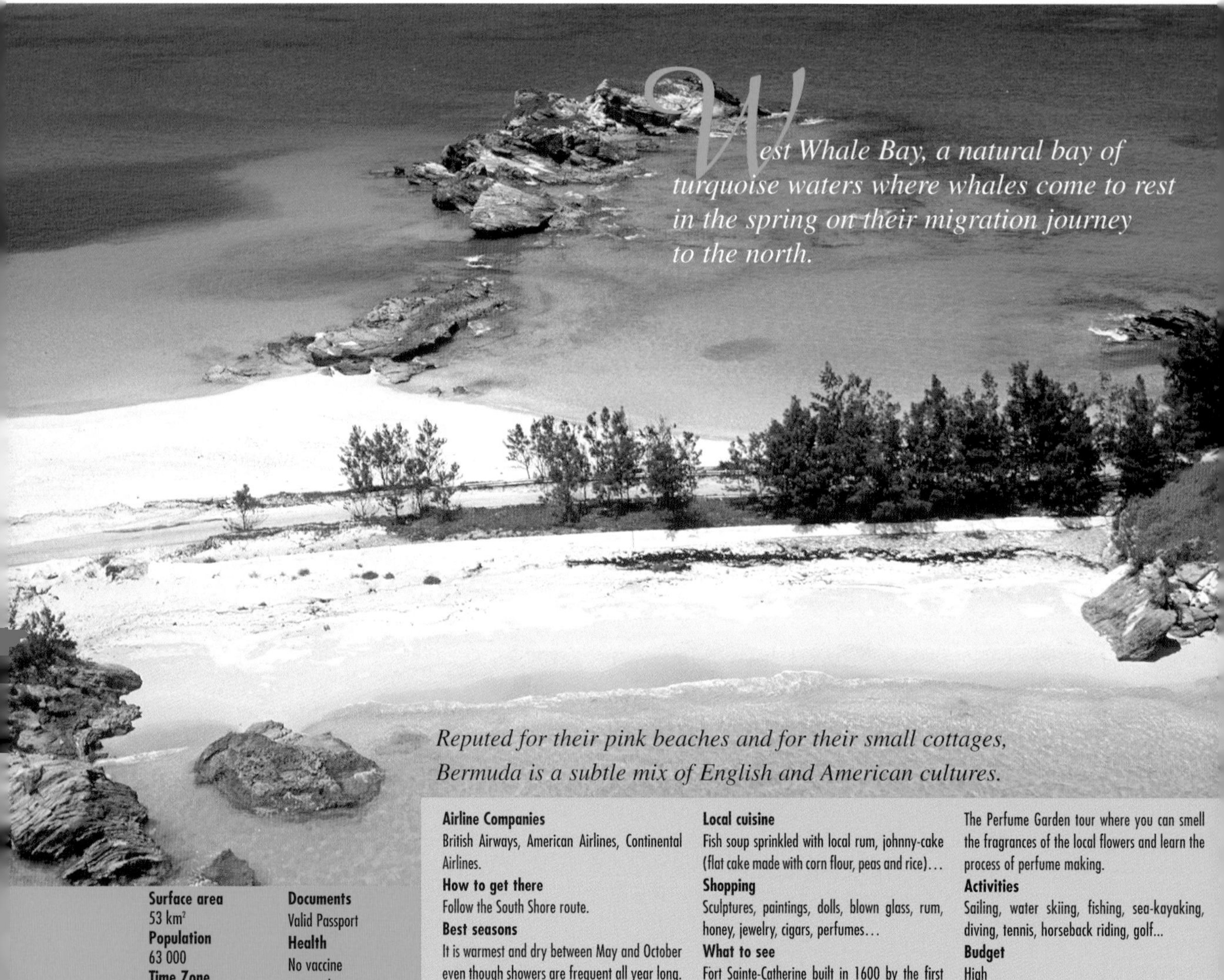

West Whale Bay, a natural bay of turquoise waters where whales come to rest in the spring on their migration journey to the north.

Reputed for their pink beaches and for their small cottages, Bermuda is a subtle mix of English and American cultures.

Surface area
53 km²
Population
63 000
Time Zone
GMT -4
Language
English
Currency
Bermuda Dollar

Documents
Valid Passport
Health
No vaccine required
Average temperatures
17°C in winter, 27°C in summer

Airline Companies
British Airways, American Airlines, Continental Airlines.
How to get there
Follow the South Shore route.
Best seasons
It is warmest and dry between May and October even though showers are frequent all year long.
Accommodation
Renowned hotels to luxury resorts, not to mention cottages, B&B and apartments for rent.

Local cuisine
Fish soup sprinkled with local rum, johnny-cake (flat cake made with corn flour, peas and rice)…
Shopping
Sculptures, paintings, dolls, blown glass, rum, honey, jewelry, cigars, perfumes…
What to see
Fort Sainte-Catherine built in 1600 by the first residents of the island; the Maritime Museum; Crystal Cave, where caves go to a depth of 240 meters and also its underground lake; The Perfume Garden tour where you can smell the fragrances of the local flowers and learn the process of perfume making.
Activities
Sailing, water skiing, fishing, sea-kayaking, diving, tennis, horseback riding, golf...
Budget
High
Contact
http://www.bermudatourism.com

+ *Beaches of pink sand*

- *A very visited location especially by their American neighbors*

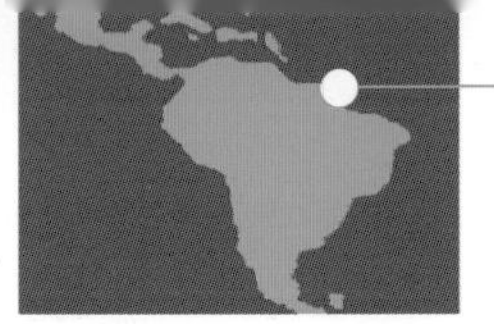

BRAZIL • JERICOACOARA

Surface area
8,511,965 km²
Population
166 million
Time Zone
4 time zones
(GMT –2 to –5)
Language
Portuguese
Currency
Real

Documents
Valid Passport
Health
Out of the cities, an anti-mosquito treatment against dengue and malaria is recommended. Drink mineral water.
Average temperatures
21°C in winter,
26°C in summer

Airline Companies
To Fortaleza: Varig, TAP
How to get there
From Fortaleza's airport situated at 300 km from Jericoacoara, you can go by car (5-hour ride) or by plane. To get to the beach it is best to do so by 4X4
Best seasons
Spring and autumn are ideal seasons if you want to escape the overwhelming heat.
Accommodation
All new hotel construction is no longer allowed on this site, but you can easily find accommodation in lodges or pension houses as long as you reserve a little in advance.
Local cuisine
Churrasco (grilled beef), buchada de carneiro (stuffed mutton tripe), carne de sol (salted beef meat), feijoada (black beans simmered with salt pork and smoked beef). For drinks, the unavoidable caipirinha.
Shopping
Local arts and crafts, hammocks, leathers, embroidery, precious stones (don't be swindled)...
What to see
All the area is protected. You will have a total natural experience.
Activities
Sailing, hiking, horseback riding, dune buggy...
Budget
Average
Contact
http://braziltourism.org

➕ *A genuine and protected location.*

➖ *Basic comfort.*

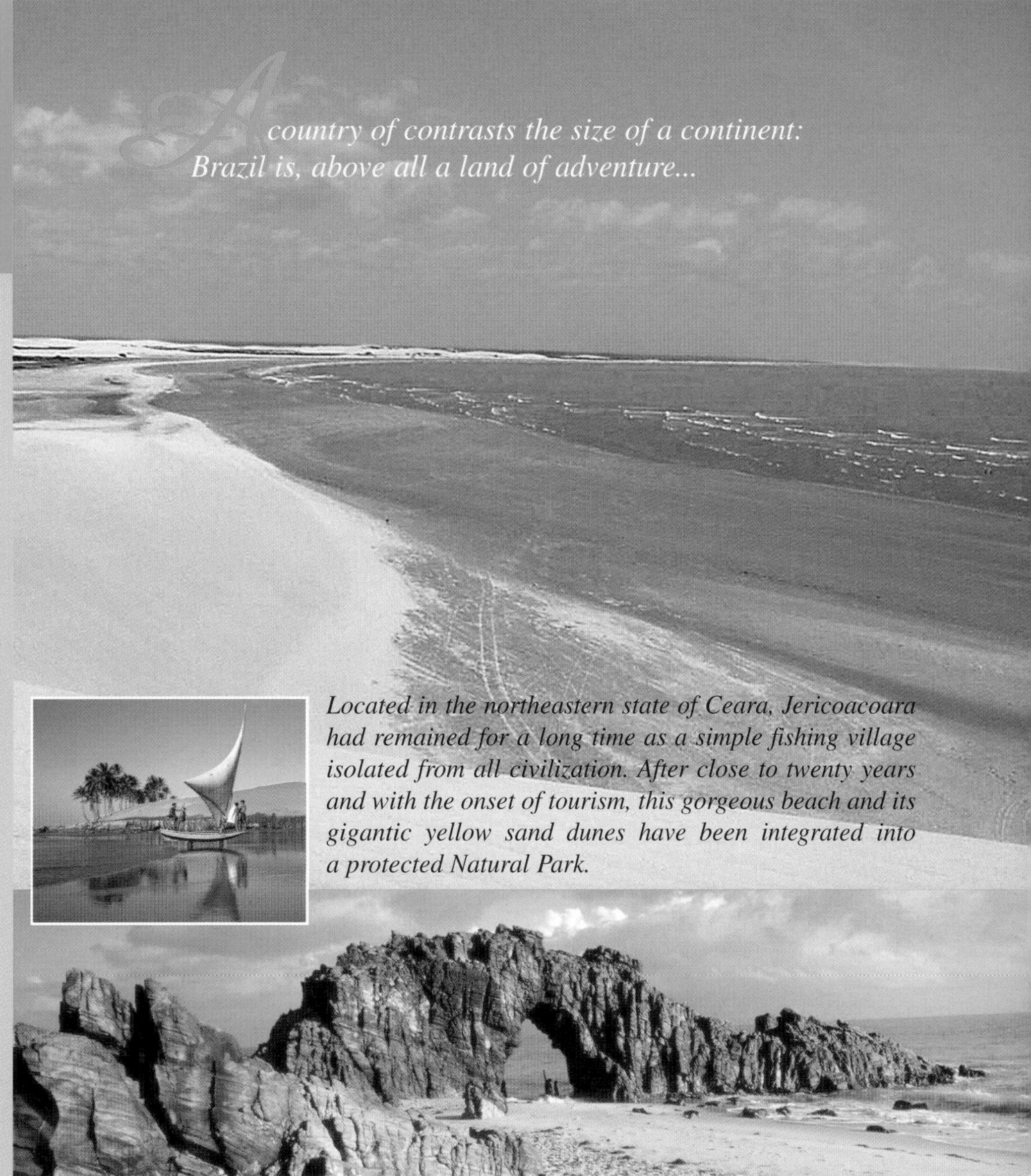

A country of contrasts the size of a continent: Brazil is, above all a land of adventure...

Located in the northeastern state of Ceara, Jericoacoara had remained for a long time as a simple fishing village isolated from all civilization. After close to twenty years and with the onset of tourism, this gorgeous beach and its gigantic yellow sand dunes have been integrated into a protected Natural Park.

Not far from the village of Salvador de Bahia, already popular for its superb coastline, Praia do Saco beach is located in the heart of a vast ecologically protected zone : Costas das Dunas. At its farthest corner, a sand as fine as flour sinks in the deep blue of the Atlantic Ocean.

Airline Companies
To Salvador de Bahia: Air France, Varig, TAP

How to get there
From the town of Estancia, to the north of Salvador de Bahia, take the SE 100 for about forty kilometers. An all-terrain vehicle might be necessary to travel the dunes alongside the coast.

Best seasons
Spring and autumn are ideal seasons if you want to escape the overwhelming heat.

Accommodation
Some hotels, pausadas and camping grounds nearby.

Local cuisine
Churrasco (grilled beef), buchada de carneiro (stuffed mutton tripe), carne de sol (salted beef meat), feijoada (black beans simmered with salt pork and smoked beef). For drinks, the unavoidable caipirinha.

Shopping
Local arts and crafts, hammocks, leathers, embroidery, precious stones (don't be swindled)...

What to see
The outlying beaches are just as magnificent; the towns of Estancia and Salvador de Bahia.

Activities
Water sports, hiking, 4X4 on the dunes...

Budget
Average

Contact
http://braziltourism.org

+ *An almost pristine island at the edge of the ocean.*

- *Little accommodation available on site.*

Airline Companies
Air France, Varig, TAP

How to get there
From the town of Barreirinhas, which has an airport, the Park is only a few kilometers away.

Best seasons
Spring and autumn are ideal seasons if you want to escape the overwhelming heat.

Accommodation
Comfortable hotels and rooms in the local homes at Barreirinhas.

Local cuisine
Churrasco (grilled beef), buchada de carneiro (stuffed mutton tripe), carne de sol (salted beef meat), feijoada (black beans simmered with salt pork and smoked beef). For drinks, the unavoidable caipirinha.

Shopping
Local arts and crafts, hammocks, leathers, embroidery, precious stones (don't be swindled)...

What to see
The Natural Park and its treasures; the Parnaiba Delta and its lagoons that go on forever; the Sao Domingo village on the shore of the Preguiças River.

Activities
Hiking, 4X4 on the dunes...

Budget
Average

Contact
http://braziltourism.org

+ *An unforgettable spectacle.*

- *Some dunes can be as high as several tens of meters !*

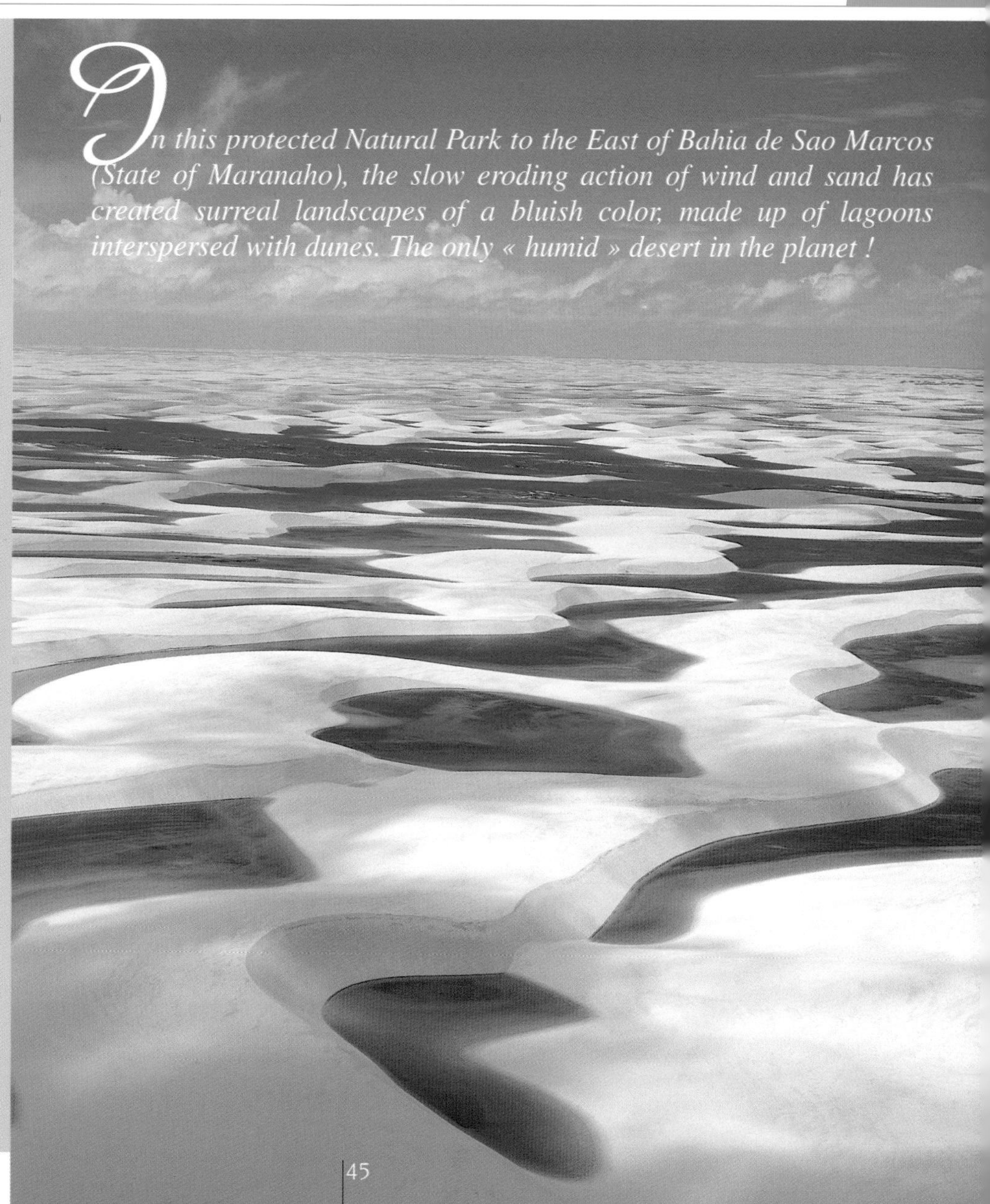

In this protected Natural Park to the East of Bahia de Sao Marcos (State of Maranaho), the slow eroding action of wind and sand has created surreal landscapes of a bluish color, made up of lagoons interspersed with dunes. The only « humid » desert in the planet !

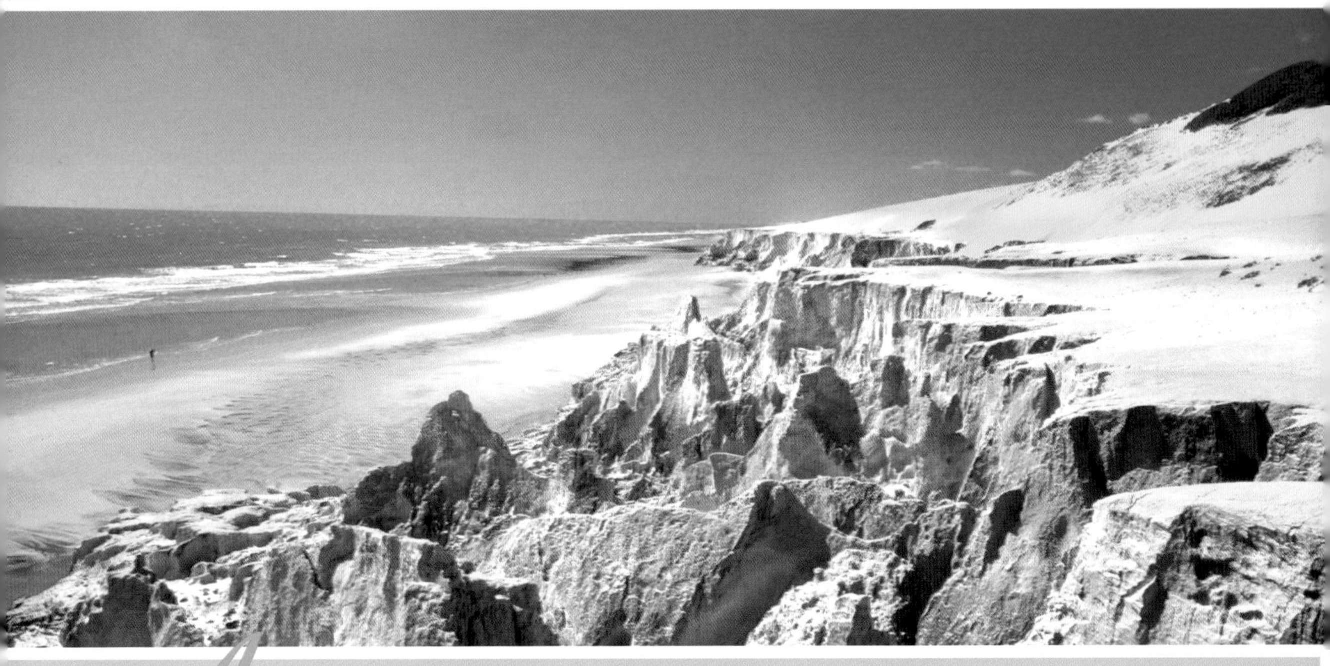

At 80 kilometers to the East of Fortaleza town, Morro Branco is a special beach. You won't find here white sand or coconut trees, but rather red cliffs that plunge down to the azure sea below. A decor that regularly inspires studios of both cinema and television. Astounding and beautiful !

Airline Companies
Air France, Varig, TAP

How to get there
From Fortaleza, take the scenic route «Sol Nascente» until Caponga.

Best seasons
Spring and autumn are ideal seasons if you want to escape the overwhelming heat.

Accommodation
Some beautiful hotels and some comfortable «pausadas».

Local cuisine
The Morro Branco village specializes in lobster fishing. Churrasco (grilled beef), buchada de carneiro (stuffed mutton tripe), carne de sol (salted beef meat), feijoada (black beans simmered with salt pork and smoked beef). As for drinks, the unavoidable caipirinha.

Shopping
Local arts and crafts, weaved baskets...

What to see
The town of Fortaleza.

Activities
Sailing, hiking, show off your photographic ability...

Budget
Average

Contact
http://braziltourism.org

+ *A beautiful setting.*

- *Difficult to access.*

Belize, Central America

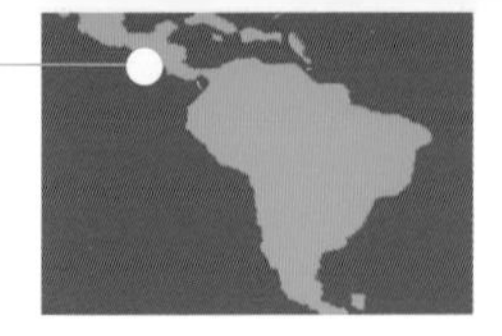

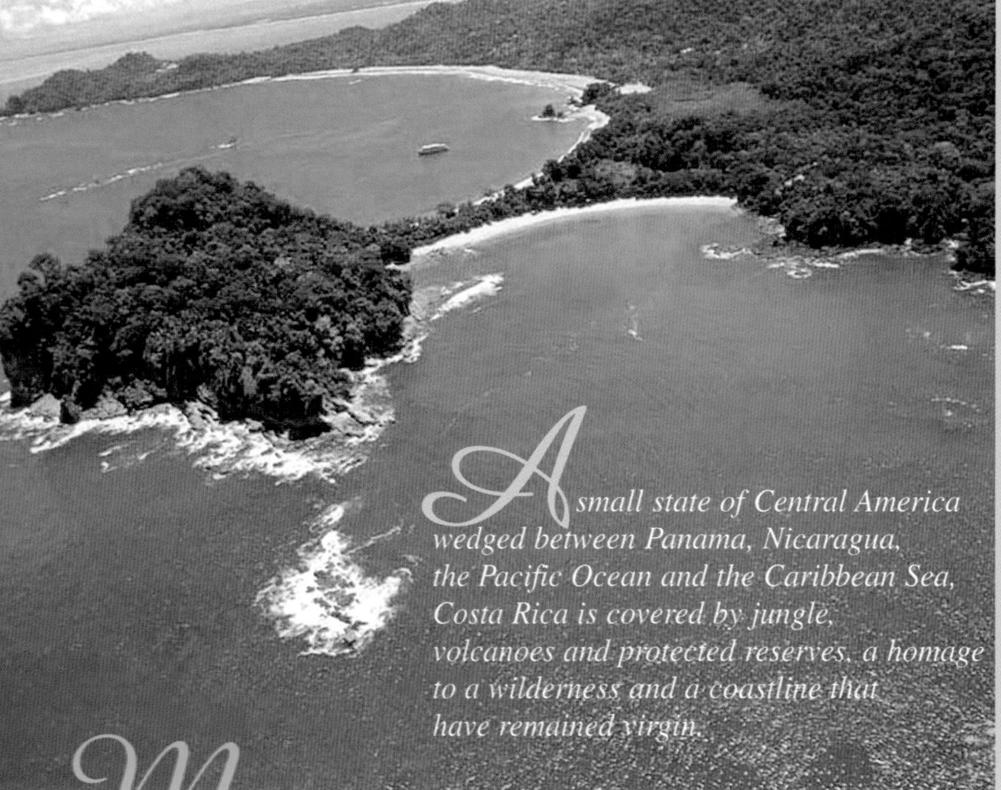

A small state of Central America wedged between Panama, Nicaragua, the Pacific Ocean and the Caribbean Sea, Costa Rica is covered by jungle, volcanoes and protected reserves, a homage to a wilderness and a coastline that have remained virgin.

Manuel Antonio Park is one of the most popular for the richness of both its fauna and flora. Its long beach of white sand draws a wide arch on the horizon-blue sea.

Surface area
51,000 km²
Population
3.5 million
Time Zone
GMT -6
Language
Spanish
Currency
Colon
Documents
Valid Passport
Health
Vaccines against diphtheria and hepatitis are recommended for long stays.
Average temperatures
19° C in winter, 22° C in summer

Airline Companies
Iberia, Continental Airlines, American Airlines, British Airways.

How to get there
Manuel Antonio Park is 3-hours drive away from San José on the Panamerican Highway. You can also go by plane thanks to the two local carriers Sansa and Travel Air.

Best seasons
On the Pacific side, the dry season (from December to May) is the most agreeable.

Accommodation
Several high-end hotels and some villas for rent.

Local cuisine
The national dish is gallo pinto (rice, red bean, onions) and is often had with tortillas or wheat flat cakes. A must-have: strong aroma coffee...

Shopping
Hammocks, pre-Columbian art imitations, coffee, cigars, paper made from banana or coffee leaves...

What to see
In San José, the capital, the National Museum, the Jade Museum and the central market; in the northwestern part of the country, the still active Arenal volcano.

Activities
Sailing, surfing, fishing, kayaking, rafting, hiking, diving (the island of Coco serves as a refuge for thousands of species of fish and is a World Heritage Site).

Budget
Quite high

Contact
http://www.tourism-costarica.com

+ *Nature at its purest.*

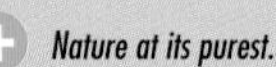

− *Poor road conditions.*

Airline Companies
Iberia, Continental Airlines, American Airlines, British Airways.

How to get there
From the airport at Tamarindo, it is a fifteen-minute ride.

Best seasons
On the Pacific side, the dry season (from December to May) is the most pleasant.

Accommodation
Some guesthouses nearby and a good hotel.

Local cuisine
The national dish is gallo pinto (rice, red bean, onions) and is often had with tortillas or wheat flat cakes. A must-have: strong aroma coffee...

Shopping
Hammocks, pre-Columbian art imitations, coffee, cigars, paper made from banana or coffee leaves...

What to see
Various nearby National Parks (Santa Rosa, Palo Verde...); Las Tortugas, a haven for turtles; Manlagres, a wildlife reserve where you can admire crocodiles and exotic birds.

Activities
Sailing, hiking, surfing, diving, fishing, kayaking, rafting...

Budget
Quite high

Contact
http://www.tourism-costarica.com

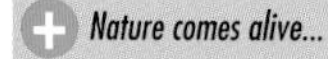

Nature comes alive...

A much appreciated destination by American tourists.

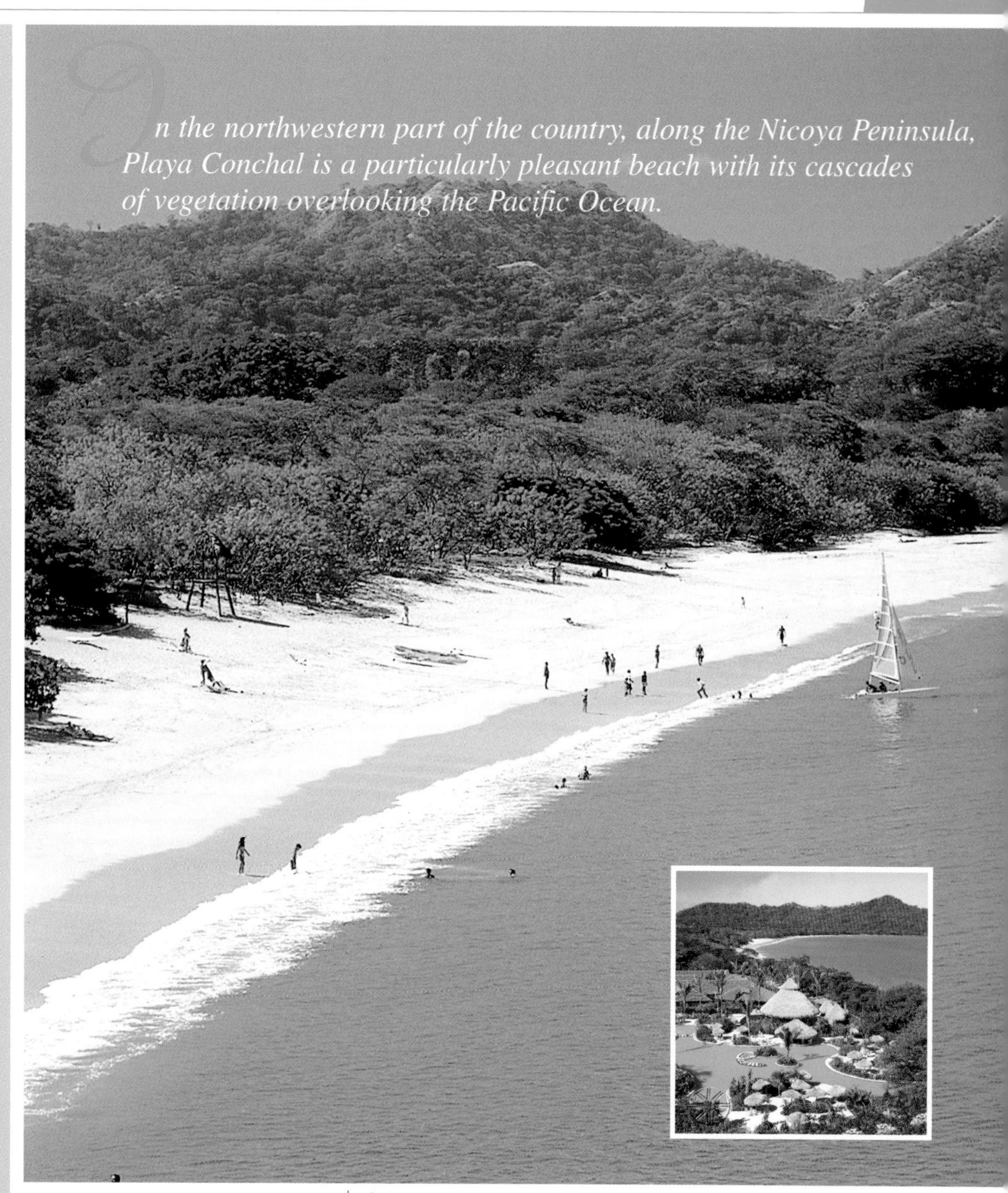

In the northwestern part of the country, along the Nicoya Peninsula, Playa Conchal is a particularly pleasant beach with its cascades of vegetation overlooking the Pacific Ocean.

CUBA • CAYO LARGO

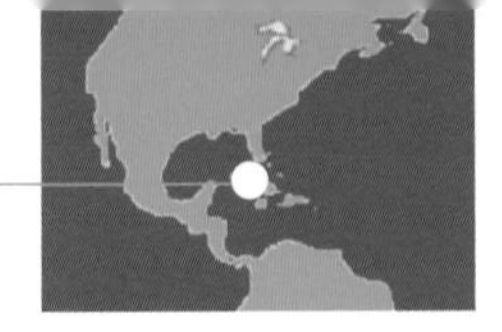

Cuba, a relaxed way of life and a population that has been traditionally welcoming, making it one of the most popular tourist destinations in the Caribbean. Its beaches are known the world over...

Cayo Largo lies on the Caribbean Sea, to the east of the archipelago of Canarreos, not far from the Island of Youth. The south side of the island has impressive white sand beaches which stretch for more than 24 km and the water temperature never goes below 24°C.

Airline Companies
Air France, Ibéria, Cubana de Aviacion, British Airways.

How to get there
The island has an airport. Regular links are assured between Havana and other Cuban cities such as Trinidad, Santiago de Cuba, Cienfuegos and Varadero.

Best seasons
From October to April so as to avoid the extreme heat and the rainy season.

Accommodation
A handful of comfortable hotels mainly found around Playa Lindamar.

Local cuisine
Rice and black beans, chicken and roasted piglets, lobster, fried bananas...

Shopping
Rum, cigars, «son» CDs (traditional Cuban music)...

What to see
Excursions to the surrounding small islands (Cayo Cantiles, Cayo Iguana); pink flamingo watching.

Activities
Sailing, water skiing, diving, horseback riding...

Budget
Quite expensive since everything is in dollars

Contact
http://www.cubatravel.cu

Surface area
110,861 km^2

Population
11.5 million

Time Zone
GMT –5

Language
Spanish

Currency
The Cuban peso, however the American dollar is used in transactions with tourists.

Documents
Passport + Cuban Tourist Card provided by the tourism agencies

Health
No vaccine required

Average temperatures
25 °C in winter,
30°C in summer

\+ *This island is everything you expect from a small tropical paradise.*

\- *You don't get to see many Cubans...*

Sol Cayo Largo

Sol Pelícano

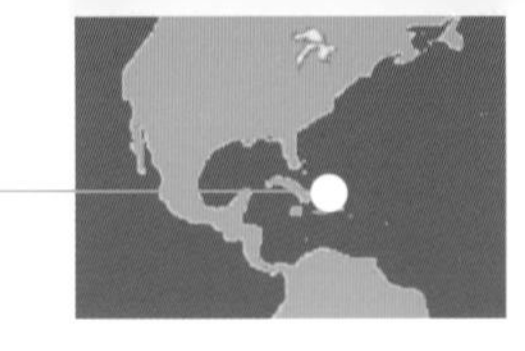

Dominica is a distinct small island in the volcanic string that makes up the Petites Antilles. Its varied terrain and lush vegetation are pure natural elements that attract thrill-seekers.

Batibou Bay, a ravishing beach of black sand tucked in the midd of vegetation.

Airline Companies
American Airlines, British Airways, Lufthansa, Alitalia.

How to get there
From Marigot, the beach is accessible by jeep from the route that leads to Calibishie.

Best seasons
Between December and May

Accommodation
Nearby bungalows and hotels of all categories scattered throughout the island.

Surface area
751 km²

Population
71 000

Time Zone
GMT -4

Language
English and Creole

Currency
East Caribbean Dollar

Documents
Valid Passport

Health
No vaccine required

Average temperatures
23°C in winter,
29°C in summer

Local cuisine
Mountain chicken (actually frog legs !), crab cake, rum and exotic fruits...

Shopping
Jewelry, fabrics, pottery...

What to see
Roseau, the capital; Cabrits National Park where an English fort dating from the 18th century still towers over; the Layour River lined with bamboo.

Activities
Hiking, diving, and watching of whales and dolphins that swim near the coasts...

Budget
Average

Contact
http://www.dominica.dm

+ *A small peaceful haven.*

- *Hurricane advisory in autumn.*

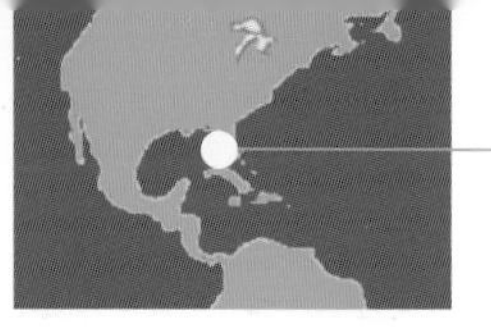

Florida is blessed with a mild climate and is sunny all year round, an advantage that makes it the number 1 tourist destination in the United States.

Surface area	**Currency**
9.3 million km²	Dollar
Population	**Documents**
272 million	Valid Passport
Time Zone	**Health**
GMT – 6	No vaccine required.
Language	**Average temperatures**
English	19°C in winter, 28°C in summer

Not far from Tampa, the small island of Caladesi lies in the warm waters of the Mexican Gulf. At 3 km from the small town of Dunedin, its magnificent white sand dunes and emerald-colored waters are a protected Natural Park.

Airline Companies
Air France, American Airlines, Continental Airlines

How to get there
During many years, the island of Caladesi could only be accessed by boat, but since Hurricane Elena en 1985, the passage of Dunedin has been covered with sand. It is now possible to reach the island on foot from the beach at Clearwater. You can also take a ferry which leaves from Honeymoon Island.

Best seasons
It is best to avoid hurricane season between June and November.

Accommodation
Camping is prohibited on the island. You can stay overnight on board a boat in the marina although it is more practical to stay at one of the motels in Dunedin or along Clearwater Beach.

Local cuisine
Hamburgers, grilled food, milk-shakes and some local specialties such as alligator, or «key lime pie», a lime pie.

Shopping
Great photos and seashells collected on the seashore will be your treasured holiday trophies !

What to see
Honeymoon Island; Keys (the southern tip of Florida); Orlando's amusement parks for children.

Activities
Stroll along the coastal road, fishing, sailing, canoeing, biking, bird watching, diving (some excursions on the sea to sight sea turtles and dolphins).

Budget
Quite high

Contact
http://www.flausa.com

+ *A preserved environment perfect for those who engage in ecotourism.*

- *Blood-thirsty mosquitoes !*

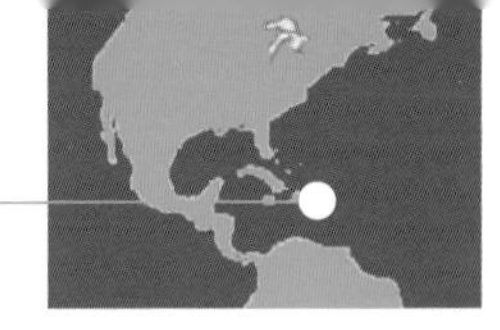

Between Saint Lucia and Martinique, Grenadines [illegible] a group of charming small paradisiacal islands - Grenade, Union, Canouan, Palm, Moustique, Bequia, Mayreau, Carriacou, Saint Vincent et les Tobago Cays - where the living is good all year round.

Surface area
388 km²
Population
120 000
Time Zone
GMT -4
Language
English
Currency
Caribbean Dollar

Documents
Valid Passport
Health
Hepatitis A vaccine recommended
Average temperatures
Between 24°C and 27°C all year long

These four uninhabited islands make the Grenadines very popular and are a true natural border between the Atlantic Ocean and the Caribbean Sea. You can hop from one island to the other in less time than it takes you to say it !

Airline Companies
Air France (via Fort de France), British Airways (via Londres) then LIAT.

How to get there
The only international airport is at Saint-Vincent, the principal island of the Grenadines. You can then continue traveling by boat or small plane.

Best seasons
The months of March and April are particularly pleasant since the trade winds cool down temperatures which can sometimes be unbearable.

Accommodation
A few high-end resorts, guesthouses and bungalows on the surrounding small islands.

Local cuisine
Fish, lobster, chicken with peppers served with Caribbean cabbage, sweet potato and taro root, exotic fruit (guava, coconut, mangos)...

Shopping
Rum, basketware, wooden sculptures, Creole dolls, spices, jewelry and clothing....

What to see
The best option is to access the Grenadines by sea and navigate around the islands.

Activities
Sailing, water skiing, diving (the marine environment is what the Grenadines are famous for).

Budget
Very high

Contact
http://www.grenadines.net

+ *Absolute tranquility.*

- *Things of interest are found in the water rather than on land.*

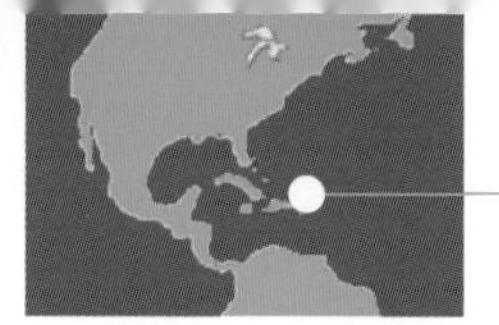

Surface area
1,438 km²
Population
422 000
Time Zone
GMT -4
Language
French and Creole
Currency
Euro

Documents
Identification Card
Health
No vaccine required
Average Temperatures
24°C in winter, 28°C in summer

Airline Companies
Air France, Corsair.

How to get there
From Pointe à Pitre, head for Deshaies sur Basse Terre. The beach is found at the entrance to the village.

Best seasons
Between December and April rather than autumn when it is more humid and the risk of a cyclone is greater.

Accommodation
Beachside camping, star-rated hotels as well as «relais créoles» (very affordable) and excursions all over the island.

Local cuisine
Creole cuisine : cod accras, fricassée de chatrou (octopus), ray colombo, lambi lasagna, Creole puddings and of course the local ti-punch…

Shopping
Rum (white or aged), punch, spices, traditional hats made from coconut leaves, madras cloth, embroidery, Creole jewelry...

What to see
Several excursions in the region of Basse-Terre ; Batterie lookout point offering a breathtaking view of the Bay; the Botanical Garden of Deshaies; Exotica Park; the Garden of Scents and Spices; the coffee plantations (at Sainte-Marie and Vanibel); the small villages and the old Creole houses.

Activities
Sailing, snorkeling, hiking.

Budget
Average

Contact
http://www.lesilesdeguadeloupe.com

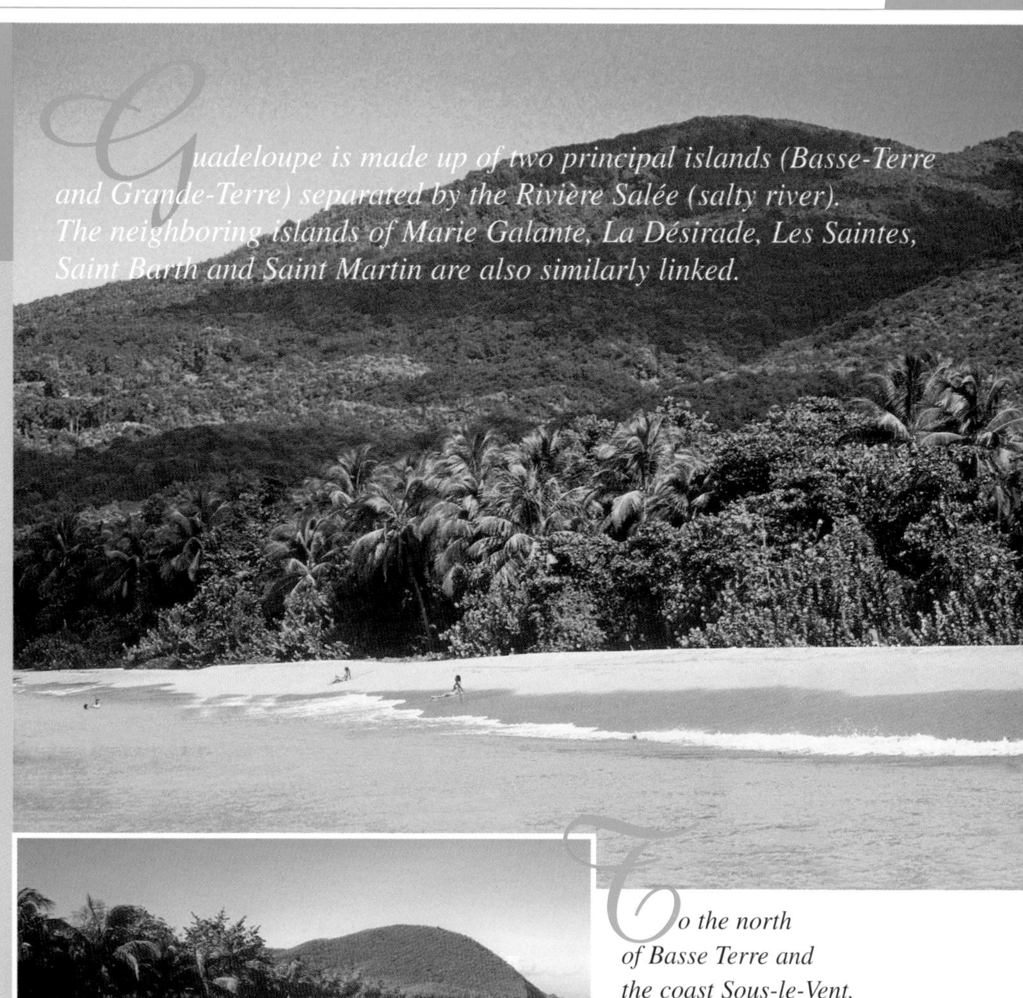

Guadeloupe is made up of two principal islands (Basse-Terre and Grande-Terre) separated by the Rivière Salée (salty river). The neighboring islands of Marie Galante, La Désirade, Les Saintes, Saint Barth and Saint Martin are also similarly linked.

+ The beach is vast and of unspoilt beauty

− Beware of currents an sharks !

To the north of Basse Terre and the coast Sous-le-Vent, the beach at Grande Anse offers a unique yellow ocher sand and a natural pool of seawater that makes safe swimming possible.

HONDURAS • WEST WHALE BAY

Wedged between Nicaragua, Guatemala and El Salvador, Honduras is a small Central American country boasting a mountainous and maritime geography. Even though it has little tourism development, it holds dazzling landscapes that are pristine and exotic.

Surface area
112,492 km²
Population
6 million
Time Zone
GMT -6
Language
Spanish is the official language, however the locals speak Creole as well as other Indian languages (Lenca, Paya, Sumo, Miskito).
Currency
Lempira
Documents
Valid Passport
Health
Anti-malaria treatment and hepatitis A vaccine are recommended.
Average temperatures
23°C in winter, 28°C in summer

Airline Companies
Iberia, American Airlines.
How to get there
By air: from Tegucigalpa, the capital, the carriers Sol Air and Taca Airlines provide regular flights to Roatan.
By ferry: from the town of La Ceiba.
Best seasons
Hot all year long and not much rain. A little fresher between October and January, though.
Accommodation
Some comfortable hotels and bungalows on piles.
Local cuisine
Rice, tortillas, red beans, fried bananas...
Shopping
Wooden sculptures, basketware, woven goods, embroidery,ceramics...
What to see
The Carembola Botanical Garden with its iguanas; the Butterfly Garden, where you can admire more than 200 species; some archeological sites dating from the Mayan times.
Activities
Sailing, snorkeling, high-sea fishing, hiking, horseback riding, diving (you can especially admire the sumptuous marine turtles)
Budget
Quite high
Contact
http://www.letsgohonduras.com

+ *A very lively island.*

– *American tour operators offer most of the programs in the island.*

Reputed for its underwater marine life and waters a constant 29°C all year long, Roatan Island is located in the Caribbean Sea, north of Honduras' coast. Bordering the jungle, the stunning West Bay beach stands out due to the rust-colored hues of the sand especially at dusk.

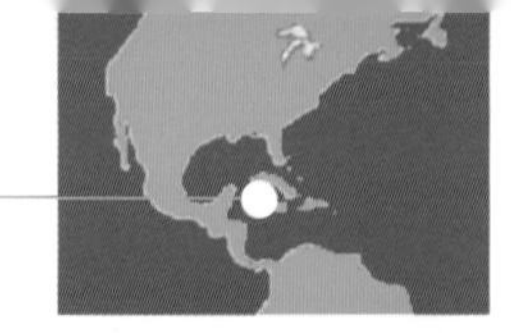

Surface area
260 km²

Population
39 000

Time Zone
GMT -5

Language
English

Currency
Cayman Dollar

Documents
Valid Passport

Health
No vaccine required

Average temperatures
21°C in winter,
30° in summer

Airline Companies
British Airways

How to get there
Seven Miles Beach is very easily accessible by car, bus or taxi from George Town.

Best seasons
Between December and April

Accommodation
Many high-end hotels make their presence here due to the business clientele. For those on a tighter budget, some B&B, guest-houses and a large choice of weekend houses and apartments for rent.

Local cuisine
Smoked and spiced meat, peppered sauteed fish, shellfish. Turtle dishes, which were once all the rave, are no longer that popular nowadays.

Shopping
Local arts and crafts, shell jewelry, Cayman island bird stores, rum...

What to see
The turtle farm, where you can see more than 16 000 sea turtles; Queen Elizabeth II Botanical Garden; the National Museum.

Activities
Sailing, water skiing, golf, underwater excursions, fishing, diving (water so clear that visibility can be several tens of meters).

Budget
High

Contact
http://www.caymanislands.ky

+ *More than 200 diving spots !*

- *Since it caters mainly to a business clientele prices are quite steep.*

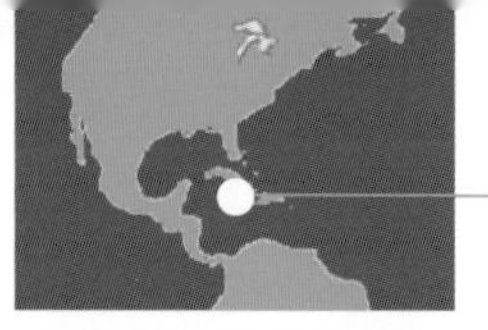

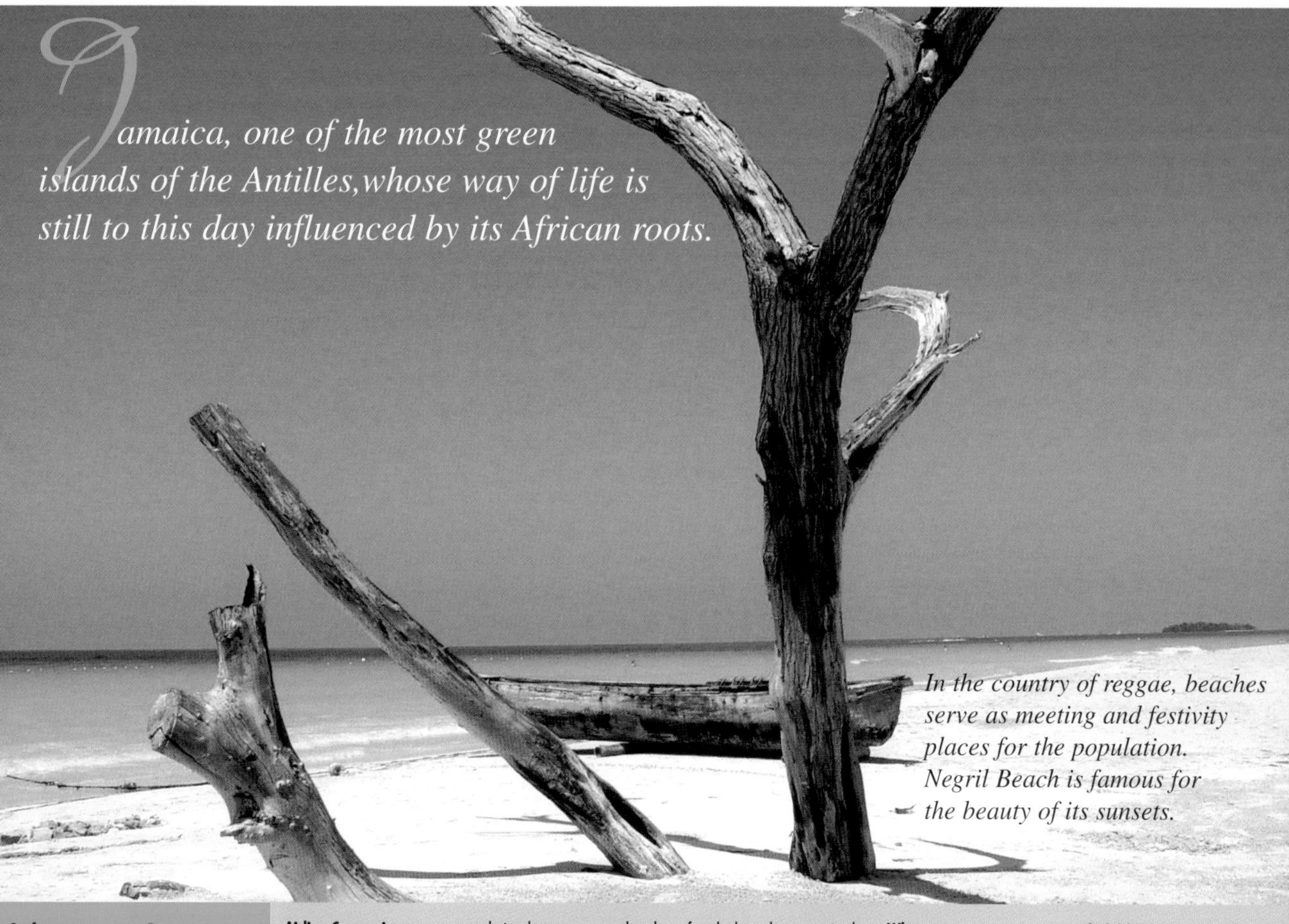

Jamaica, one of the most green islands of the Antilles, whose way of life is still to this day influenced by its African roots.

In the country of reggae, beaches serve as meeting and festivity places for the population. Negril Beach is famous for the beauty of its sunsets.

Surface area
10,991 km²
Population
2.5 million
Time Zone
GMT -6
Language
English
Currency
Jay

Documents
Valid passport
Health
No vaccine required
Average temperatures
20°C in winter, 29°C in summer

Airline Companies
British Airways, American Airlines, Air Jamaica.
How to get there
Located at the western tip of the island, Negril Beach is easy to access.
Best seasons
Between December and April during dry season, even though the rainy season is less troublesome in Jamaica than in the rest of the Antilles.
Accommodation
Bungalows, full range of hotels and cottages for rent.
Local cuisine
The national dish, jerk, is made from barbecued meat previously marinated in spices. Seafood is marinated then fried with peppers and onions. Everything is gulped down with rum or coconut milk.
Shopping
Reggae CDs, cigars, coral jewelry, rum…
What to see
Kingston's Reggae Museum ; Bob Marley's Mausoleum ; the colonial towns (Spanish Town, Port Royal); Long Bay Beach with its crescent shape; Cockpit Country, a remote limestone plateau, a bird-watcher's paradise.
Activities
Sailing, water skiing, snorkeling, horseback riding, diving (Negril is a wonderful marine park).
Budget
Not too high
Contact
http://www.jamaicatravel.com

+ *Full of excitement from dusk to dawn.*

− *Those who prefer quieter surroundings would do well to stay at a more isolated beach.*

Martinique, a passionate and endearing island.

Surface area
1,100 km²
Population
388 000
Time Zone
GMT -4
Language
French and Creole
Currency
Euro
Documents
Identification Card
Health
No vaccine required
Average temperatures
24°C in winter,
27°C in summer

Airline Companies
Air France, Corsair.
How to get there
From Sainte-Anne, take D9 to Pointe des Salines.
Best seasons
Between December and April rather than autumn when it is more humid and the risk of a cyclone is greater.
Accommodation
A camping ground, bungalows and some smaller hotels next to the beach and also in Saint-Anne.
Local cuisine
Cod accras, colombo, blaff, «z'habitants» (delicious crawfish), stuffed crab, Creole pudding and don't forget to try the local ti-punch.
Shopping
Madras garments, seashell jewelry, bakoua hats, dolls, watercolors, bamboo crafts...
What to see
Fort-de-France, the capital, and its parks, market and library; the tropical forest at the north side of the island; the sugar cane plantations; Pelée mountain.
Activities
Sailing, water skiing, hiking, horseback riding, ATV, canoeing, diving (some excursions to the shipwrecks that resulted from the eruption of Pelee Mountain at the beginning of the century).
Budget
Average
Contact
http://www.martiniquetourism.com

+ *A dramatic landscape.*

- *The east side of the island is prone to currents.*

With the majestic Rocher du Diamant as a backdrop, the beach at Salines is a charming place popular with tourists and Martinique people alike.

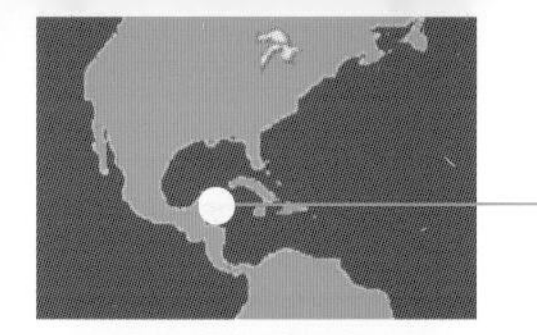

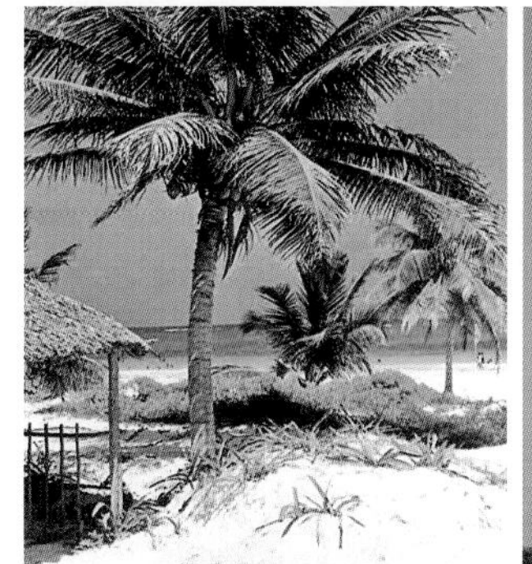

Mexico, a vast country with a dramatic history and majestic landscapes, with the most beautiful beaches in Central America.

Surface area
1,967,183 km²
Population
99 million
Time Zone
GMT -6
Language
Spanish
Currency
Mexican Peso
Documents
Valid Passport

Health
Hepatitis A and typhoid fever vaccines are strongly recommended as well as anti-malaria treatment in certain regions.
Average temperatures
25°C in winter, 30°C in summer (Yucatan)

Airline Companies
Air France, American Airlines, Aeromexico, British Airways.

How to get there
From Cancun, it is a 3-hour ride by bus or car.

Best seasons
During dry season (from October to April) temperatures are agreeable.

Accommodation
Some small huts with very basic comfort scattered along the beach as well as more comfortable resorts.

Local cuisine
Chicken pibil (Yucatan specialty), tacos, enchiladas, tortillas, cactus salad (nopal), frijoles (red or black beans), chilies (hot peppers), guacamole, quesadillas...

Shopping
Carpets, sombreros, wooden carvings, hammocks, basketware, Aztec-motif ceramics (it is forbidden, of course, to take antiques away from the country).

What to see
The magnificent Tulum archeological site overlooking the bay; the Ecological Reserve of the Maya Riviera; the archeological site at Coba, where the Nohoc Mul pyramid stands 42 meters tall; Sian Ka'an, the biosphere reserve located 11 km from Tulum declared World Heritage Site by UNESCO; Xcaret, an Eco-archeological Park where the Maya conducted many ceremonies.

Activities
Sailing, water skiing, snorkeling, horseback riding, diving...

Budget
Average

Contact
http://www.visitmexico.com

+ *A spellbinding beach and a unique archeological site.*

− *Make sure to bring enough sunscreen lotion !*

To the south of the Yucatan, Tulum is an ancient fortified city built by the Maya between 1200 and 1500 A.D. facing the Caribbean Sea. At the foot of the ruins, the beach lies next to turquoise waters that change in hue with the intensity of the light and impart an unreal and timeless quality to the setting.

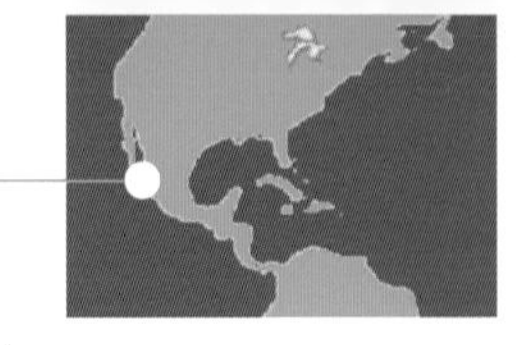

The south of the Baja California Peninsula, at about twenty kilometers from La Paz, Playa Balandra is a magnificent pristine bay framed by a strange rock formation.

Airline Companies
Air France, American Airlines, Aeromexico, Aerocalifornia, British Airways.

How to get there
Balandra Bay is located around twenty kilometers to the north of La Paz. You can get there by bus or by car.

Best seasons
In spring, when temperatures are not so high.

Accommodation
Camping grounds, B&B and hotels of all categories in La Paz.

Local cuisine
Tacos, enchiladas, sopas (soups), tortillas, cactus salad (nopal), frijoles (red or black beans), chilies (hot peppers), guacamole, quesadillas…

Shopping
Carpets, sombreros, wooden carvings, hammocks, basketware, Aztec-motif ceramics...

What to see
The dunes and the underlying hills offer a stupendous lookout point of the bay. The region is also reputed for its breathtaking canyons.

Activities
Snorkeling, hiking, ATV, diving (programmed excursions to watch the gray whales and seals)...

Budget
Average

Contact
http://www.visitmexico.com

+ *A stunning destination little known by Europeans.*
- *No accommodations available on site.*

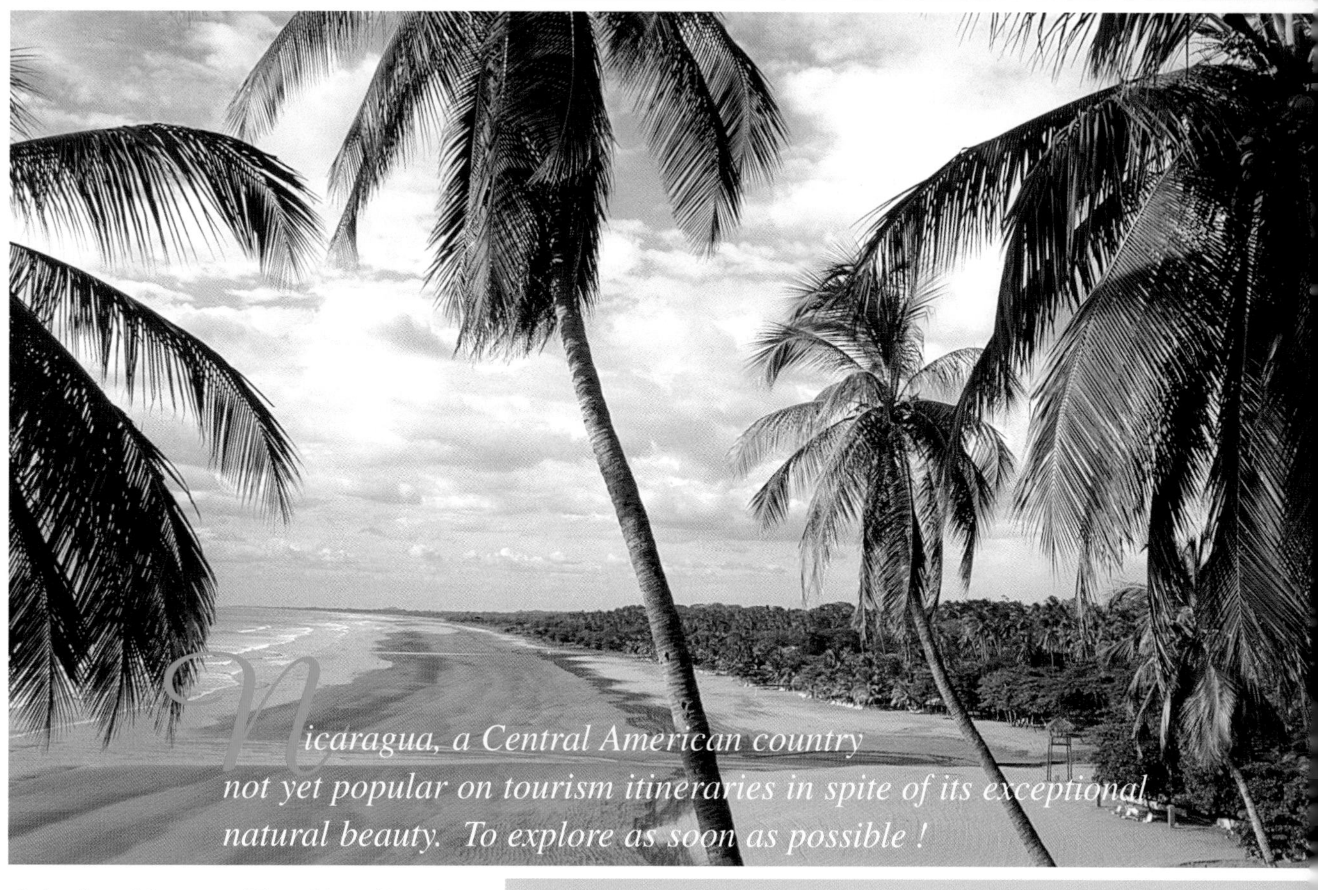

Nicaragua, a Central American country not yet popular on tourism itineraries in spite of its exceptional natural beauty. To explore as soon as possible !

60 km from Managua, Playa Montelimar is an endless stretch of light brown sand lined by a lush jungle.

Surface area
129,494 km²
Population
5.2 million
Time Zone
GMT -6
Language
Spanish, English, Creole, Miskito
Currency
Gold Cordoba
Documents
Passport + tourism card granted upon arrival.
Health
Be up to date with vaccines (hepatitis, rabies, tetanus, typhoid, cholera) and anti-mosquito treatment against dengue and malaria.
Average temperatures
25°C in winter, 28°C in summer

Airline Companies
American Airlines, British Airways.
How to get there
By car or taxi: from Managua, head for Masachapa and continue to Playa Montelimar.
Best seasons
Between December and January, the heat is more bearable...
Accommodation
Bungalows, rooms in the local homes and a high-end resort.
Local cuisine
Gallo pinto (white rice and red beans) ; tiste (a typical drink made from cocoa and cereals).
Shopping
Hammocks, textiles...
What to see
Managua, the capital, holds some interesting monuments.
Activities
Sailing, hiking, horseback riding, diving...
Budget
Average
Contact
http://www.intur.gob.ni

+ *A unique destination for the discerning nature lover.*
- *Getting around is sometimes difficult.*

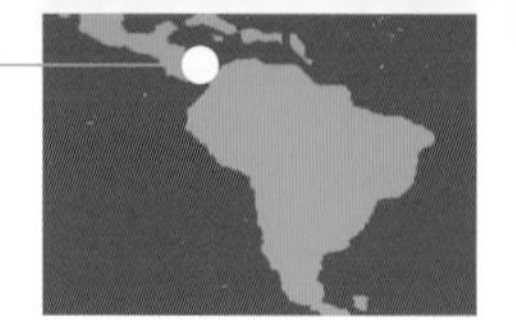

Famous for its canal rather than for its tourist attractions, Panama has the potential to become an important beach resort, especially due to a constellation of small paradisiacal islands scattered throughout the Caribbean Sea and the Pacific Ocean.

At one hundred kilometers to the northeast of the Panama coast, the 378 islets of the San Blas Archipelago constitute an autonomous province managed by the Kunas Indians. An exceptional voyage reminiscent of Robinson Crusoe.

Surface area
75,517 km²
Population
2.8 million
Time Zone
GMT -5
Language
Spanish, English and Native American languages
Currency
Balboa
Documents
Valid passport and tourism card granted at the airport.
Health
Certain vaccines are recommended (hepatitis A and B, yellow fever, typhoid). A preventative treatment against malaria is mandatory in San Blas.
Average temperatures
25°C in winter, 30°C in summer

Airline Companies
American airlines, British Airways.
How to get there
By air: from the capital Panama City
By boat: board the boats of Kunas merchants that take passengers from Colon.
Best seasons
The dry season, most pleasant from mid-December to mid-April.
Accommodation
Around forty inhabited islands, although there is little tourism infrastructure. However, some small hotels can be found in El Porvenir (capital), Wichubwala, Taboga, Nargana, Nalunega, Kuanidup, Carti-Sugtupu and Aligandi.
Local cuisine
The local specialty is sancocho, a kind of spicy chicken soup. You can also have gallo pinto (white rice and red beans), sopa vieja (local soup) and also lobster and giant crab served with coconut milk.
Shopping
Molas (textiles made by the Kunas Indians), ceramics, masks, wooden sculptures...
What to see
The mountains of San Blas, to the east of the Panama Canal, flanked with an immense tropical forest accessed by traditional pirogue.
Activities
Sailing, trolling (fishing), diving (the archipelago is a natural reserve protected by a vast coral barrier...).
Budget
High
Contact
http://www.visitpanama.com

+ *A paradise on earth with still very little tourism.*

- *Very basic comfort available.*

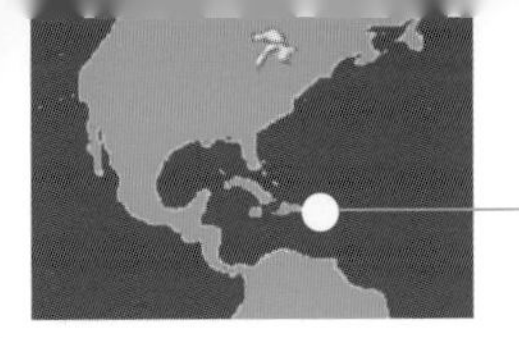

PUERTO RICO • FLAMENCO BEACH

Airline Companies
American Airlines, Continental Airlines, British Airways.

How to get there
By air: from the San Juan Airport (Puerto Rico) with the carrier Vieques Air-Link.
By ferry: two crossings daily from the port at Fajardo.

Best seasons
From December to April.

Accommodation
Camping, bungalows, comfortable hotels and rooms in local houses.

Local cuisine
Puerto Rican cuisine is a blend of Spanish and Creole. Some specialties: sancocho (thick meat soup), asopao (chicken fricassée), and don't forget to try the most famous local cocktail renowned the world over, pina colada.

Shopping
Small carved wooden figurines (santos), handmade lace (mundillo), carnival masks made from coconut or paper mache...

What to see
El Yunque National Park on the main island of Puerto Rico; the caves of Rio Camuys (where the longest underground river can be found), the islets of Culebrita and Mona.

Activities
Sailing, water skiing, snorkeling, fishing, ATV, diving (exceptionally abundant marine life)

Budget
Average

Contact
http://www.gotopuertorico.com

+ *A relaxed atmosphere typical of the Caribbean.*
- *Crowded during peak season.*

The smallest island of the Grandes Antilles, Puerto Rico was discovered in 1493 by Christopher Colombus who proclaimed : « All these islands are magnificent, but this one surpasses them all ». You can only agree with him...

Known for its turquoise beaches, marine underwater environment and bird sanctuary, the small island of Culebra is also reputed for its infamous history with its black chapter on pirates. Flamenco beach forms a horseshoe along the north coast.

Surface area
8,876 km²

Population
3 million

Time zone
GMT -4

Language
Spanish and English

Currency
American Dollar

Documents
Valid Passport

Health
No vaccine required

Average temperatures
23°C in winter, 27°C in summer

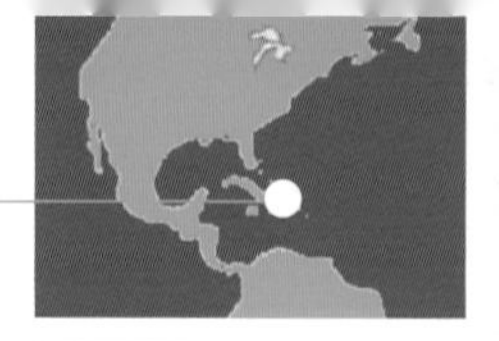

DOMINICAN REPUBLIC • PLAYA GALERAS

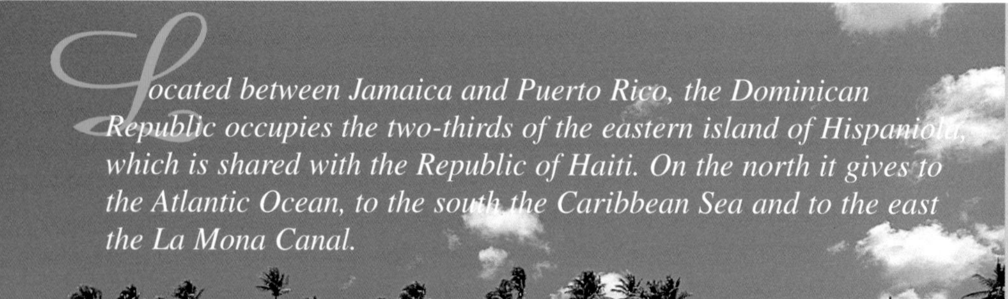

Located between Jamaica and Puerto Rico, the Dominican Republic occupies the two-thirds of the eastern island of Hispaniola, which is shared with the Republic of Haiti. On the north it gives to the Atlantic Ocean, to the south the Caribbean Sea and to the east the La Mona Canal.

On Samana, considered almost an island and located north of the country, Las Galeras beach stretches for thirty kilometers along the Atlantic Ocean protected by a coral reef. Between January and March, the perfect time to spot humpback whales that come to beach in this protected refuge.

Surface area
48,442 km²
Population
8.7 million
Time Zone
GMT –4
Language
Spanish
Currency
Dominican Peso

Documents
Valid Passport and tourism card granted upon arrival or beforehand at a consulate.
Health
Vaccines against polio and hepatitis A are recommended, also preventative malaria treatment.
Average Temperatures
24°C in winter, 27°C in summer

Airline Companies
Air France, Iberia, British Airways.
How to get there
By air: regular flights from Saint-Domingue with the carrier Air Santo Domingo.
By bus: Several daily links from Saint Domingue and Puerto Plata to Sanchez (15 km from Galeras), then take a «Guagua» (local collective transport) or a taxi.
By car or tax : from Saint Domingue's airport it is a 4h30 drive.
From Puerto Plata it is a 2h30 drive.
Best seasons
Between December and April
Accommodation
Bungalows, hotels of all categories and houses for rent.
Local cuisine
The Dominican cuisine is not so spicy and is the result of Creole, Spanish and French influences. Sancocho is the most popular dish (beef stew), mondongo (beef tripe with a zest of lime), asopao (thick soup made from rice, vegetables and meat)... For drinks, rum and more rum ! (amber, white, dark or aged).
Shopping
Cigars, amber and larimar (semi-precious light blue stone) jewelry, black coral, coffee, rum, Haitian arts and crafts, merengue CDs...
What to see
Haitian National Park; the cascade at El limón; the humpback whales at «Banco de la Plata».
Activities
Sailing, water skiing, snorkeling, diving, fishing, hiking, horseback riding, cock fighting (a local institution !), jeep safaris...
Budget
Not too high
Contact
http://wwwwebdominicana.com

+ *Almost and island and not found on the usual tourist itinerary.*

- *Road conditions are poor...*

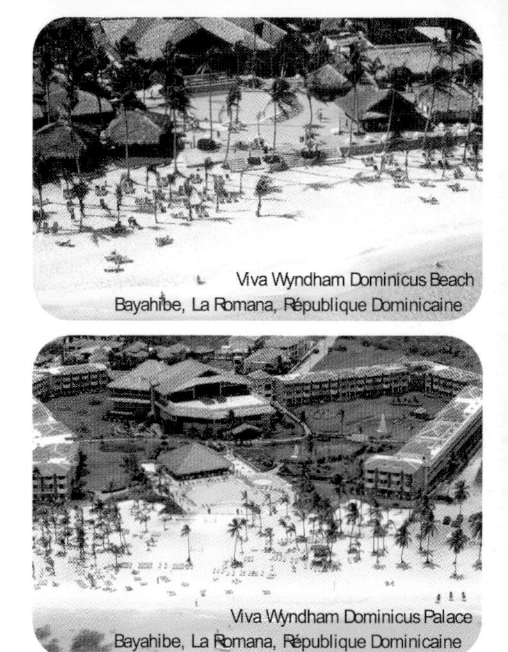

Viva Wyndham Dominicus Beach
Bayahibe, La Romana, République Dominicaine

Viva Wyndham Dominicus Palace
Bayahibe, La Romana, République Dominicaine

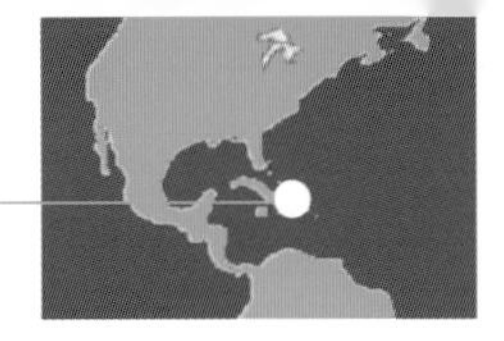

Airline Companies
Air France, Iberia, British Airways.

How to get there
From Santo Domingo, take the coast road to La Romana, then a boat to Isla Saona. The crossing takes about one hour.

Best seasons
The best time to visit, but also the busiest, is between December to April.

Accommodation
As this island is a National Park, there are no hotels where you can stay. So generally it is visited as a day trip.

Local cuisine
Dominican cooking, lightly spiced, is a mixture of Creole, Spanish and French influences. Favourite dishes include sancocho (a stew based on beef), mondongo (beef tripe with lime zest), asopao (a thick soup of rice and vegetables with meat) ... And for drinks, rum and more rum! (amber, white, dark or aged).

Shopping
Cigars, amber and larimar (a light-blue semi-precious stone) jewelry, black coral, coffee, rum, Haitian crafts, merengue music CDs etc.

What to see
The immense palm groves covering most of the island; the ruins of the Tainos culture, the Indians who lived in the area before the discovery of the New World.

Activities
Sailing, snorkeling, diving (the colonies of giant star fish to be seen in the lagoon must not be missed) ...

Budget
Not high

Contact
http://www.webdominicana.com

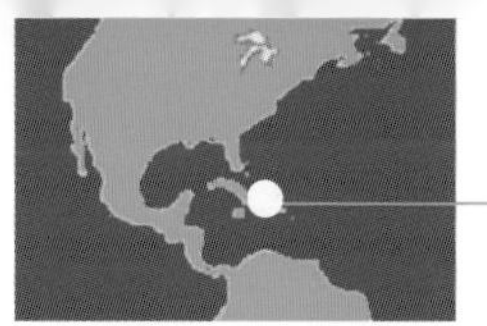

Isla Saona, beaches that are empty and secluded, and 26°C crystal clear water year-round: so when are you going?

- ⊕ *One of the most beautiful gems in the Caribbean!*
- ⊖ *No accommodation there.*

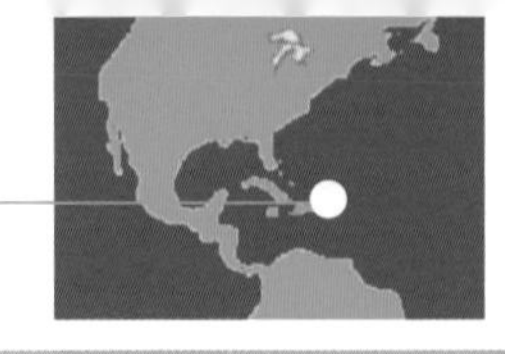

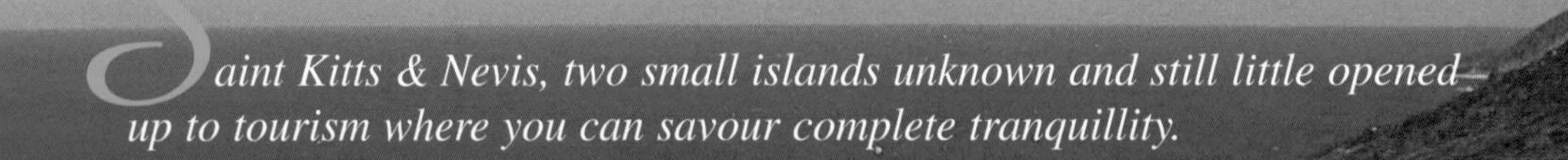

Saint Kitts & Nevis, two small islands unknown and still little opened up to tourism where you can savour complete tranquillity.

This superb beach of orange sand is found on the East coast of the islan of Saint Kitts, along a narrow band of land where the Caribbean Sea and the Atlantic Ocean almost touch.

Surface area
269 km²
Population
40 700
Time zone
GMT -4
Language
English

Currency
East Caribbean Dollar
Documents
Currently valid passport
Health
No vaccination is required
Average temperatures
25°C winter,
29°C summer

Airline Companies
Air France (via St Martin), British Airways.
How to get there
From Saint Kitts airport, drive south to Frigate Bay.
Best seasons
Between December and April but the climate is good year-round.
Accommodation
Guest houses, all grades of hotels, B&B and some villas to rent.

Local cuisine
Lobsters, crawfish, fish, chicken marinated in spices, exotic fruit...
Shopping
Clothes, jewelry, sculptures, objects made from coconut and shells...
What to see
Basseterre and its cathedral; Old Road Town, which follows the coast of Saint Kitts for almost its whole length and goes round the island; Brimstone Hill Fortress National Park, where you can admire the XVIIIth century Citadel.
Activities
Sailing, fishing, hiking, VTT, diving (some wrecks can be visited)...
Budget
Medium
Contact
http://www.stkitts-tourism.com

+ *A captivating destination which is still free from mass tourism.*

- *We quickly toured the island and its activities.*

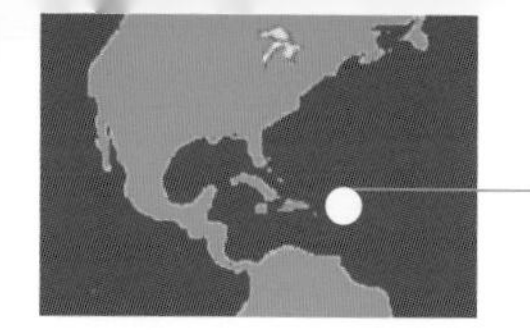

SAINT MARTIN • ORIENT BAY

Surface area
95 km²
Population
64 000
Time zone
GMT -4
Language
French, Dutch, Creole
Currency
Euro, Antilles florin, dollar
Documents
In the French part, just an Identity Card is required, but if you have to visit the neighbouring islands it would be best to have your passport.
Health
No vaccination is required
Average temperatures
22°C winter,
30°C summer

Destination favoured by jet-setters from the world over, the Franco-Dutch island of Saint-Martin is worth visiting above all for its beaches of fine sand and its enchanting lagoon.

Looking like the Saint-Tropez of the Caribbean, Oriental Bay is an under-water nature reserve and offers a splendid panorama over the neighbouring islands of Caye-Verte, Pinel, Tintamarre and Saint Barthelemy.

Airline Companies
Air France, Corsair.
How to get there
From the airport, the road to the north-east leads straight to Oriental Bay.
Best seasons
Between December and April
Accommodation
Several luxury hotels the length of the Bay and several guest houses in the vicinity. You can also rent a villa or an apartment and perhaps have a Hollywood star for a neighbour!
Local cuisine
Accras, soft potatoes, pork colombo, washed down with a delicious fresh fruit juice or rum.
Shopping
Many luxury shops offer tax-free articles for the great delight of the tourists!
What to see
The Pic du Paradis, the highest point on the island (425 meters high), offers a panoramic view over the island; the heavenly small islet of Sandy Island; Grand Case, a typical small village with its wooden houses and colourful hibiscus; the market at Marigot, one of the few places where you can find local products.

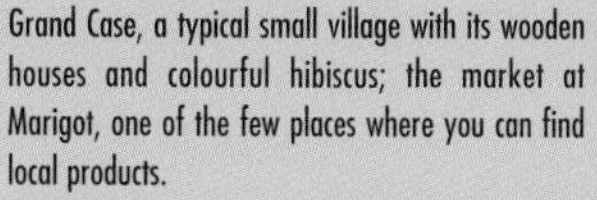

Activities
Sailing, water-skiing, snorkeling, game fishing, parasailing, diving...
Budget
High
Contact
http://www.st-martin.org

 *Luxurious holidays.*

 *A bit sophisticated...*

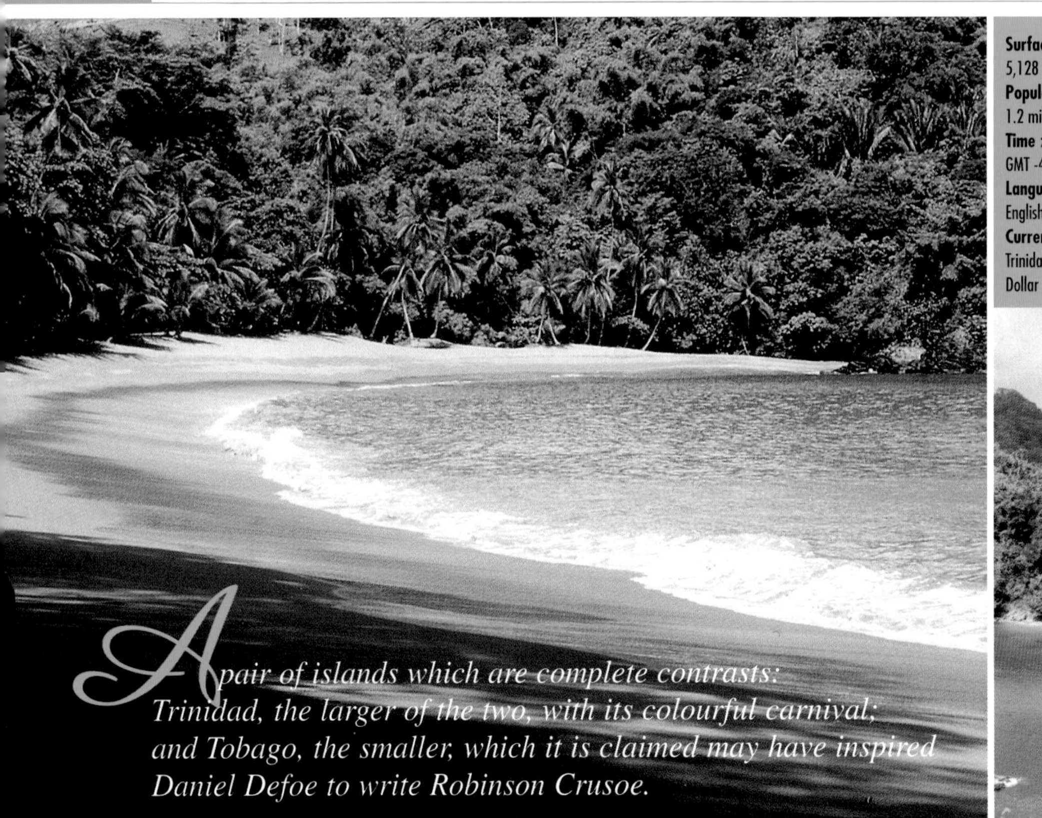

A pair of islands which are complete contrasts: Trinidad, the larger of the two, with its colourful carnival; and Tobago, the smaller, which it is claimed may have inspired Daniel Defoe to write Robinson Crusoe.

Surface area
5,128 km²
Population
1.2 million
Time zone
GMT -4
Language
English, Creole
Currency
Trinidad & Tobago Dollar
Documents
Currently valid passport
Health
You will need an anti-mosquito treatment, notably to avoid the risks of dengue fever.
Average temperatures
25°C winter,
29°C summer

In the north of Tobago, Englishman's Bay is an inlet in a half-moon shape, surrounded by a wild and pristine environment, where nothing happens to trouble the tranquility for bathers.

Airline Companies
Continental Airlines, KLM, British Airways.
How to get there
The beach is accessible by following a dirt road which is off the main road, North Side Road.
Best seasons
In February, during the carnival. The low season from May to December is also very pleasant and a lot less expensive.
Accommodation
No lodging on the site, but there are some B&Bs nearby.
Local cuisine
Brown down (spicy chicken or beef and «ochro» rice served with plantain and potatoes); callaloo (spicy spinach soup); fish, shellfish; tropical fruit...
Shopping
Bamboo vases, dolls, colourful clothes, earrings made from coconuts, copper, straw or leather articles, steelband (the local musical instrument)...
What to see
Caroni Bird Sanctuary, a Nature Park where you can admire the rare birds such as the red ibis; the beach at Manzanilla Beach, with its coconut trees and its swamps; Pitch Lake, an enormous natural tar lake.
Activities
Sailing, snorkeling, fishing, hiking, diving (44 species of coral to discover and lots of manta rays attracted by the abundant plankton).
Budget
High
Contact
http://www.visittnt.com

\+ *A completely empty beach.*

\- *No lodging on the spot.*

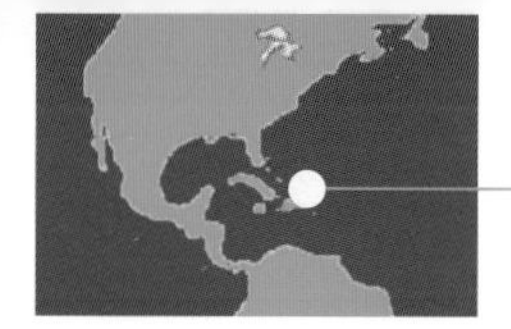

Surface area	**Documents**
430 km²	Currently valid passport
Population	**Health**
17 502	No vaccination is required
Time zone	**Average temperatures**
GMT -4	26°C winter, 32°C summer
Language	
English	
Currency	
Dollar	

Airline Companies
American Airlines, British Airways, Turks & Caicos Airways.

How to get there
No bus, the only way to get to Grace Bay on the island's north-east coast is by taxi, unless you rent a car or a motor-bike.

Best seasons
Avoid the period between August and November, when the warm winds raise the temperatures above 38°C!

Accommodation
Bungalows and comfortable hotels

Local cuisine
The two local specialities are conch, a mollusk prepared in the Creole way or curried, and lobster. Another favourite dish is grits, prepared with peas, dried conch, fish, chicken and vegetables.

Shopping
Mirrors, lamps, bags, straw hats, sculptures from recycled metal...

What to see
South Caicos, the smallest island in the archipelago, where you can admire the wild horses running free; the Conch Bar Caves National Park; Gorgonia's Wall, the not-to-be-missed spot for divers.

Activities
Sailing, water-skiing, snorkeling, bird-watching, Humpback Whale watching, diving, horse-riding...

Budget
High

Contact
http://www.turksandcaicostourism.com

+ *Dive with the Humpback whales and the manta rays.*
- *Sometimes suffocatingly hot.*

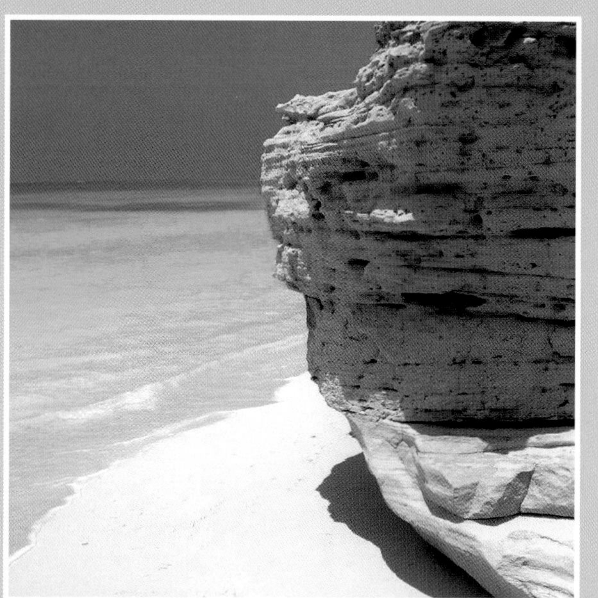

In the continuation of the Bahamas, the Turks and Caicos Islands are above all famous amongst divers for their «Gorgonia's Wall», an under-sea chasm which descends to a depth of over 2000 meters. An asset which puts the destination in the top 10 best diving spots of the planet.

On the small island of Providenciales to the South of the archipelago, the beach at Grace Bay earns its name because the calm and serenity found here carry the visitor a million miles away from civilisation.

VENEZUELA • LOS ROQUES

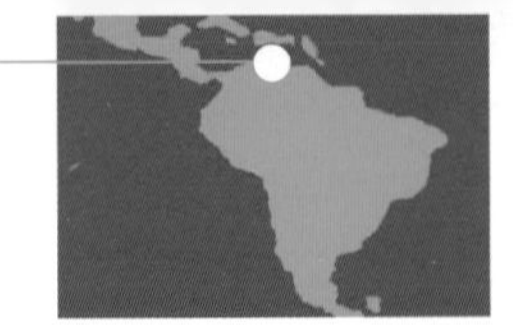

Venezuela, 3000 kilometres of coast overlooking the Caribbean and a dazzling Andean back-country largely covered by the Amazon Forest.

Because of its beauty and its ecological wealth, the Los Roques archipelago – located 168 km north of Caracas - was declared a National Park in 1972. It is on the largest island, Gran Roque, that most of the population live today and where it is easiest to stay.

Surface area
916,050 km²

Population
24.6 million

Time zone
GMT -4

Language
Spanish and American Indian languages

Currency
Bolivar

Documents
Currently valid passport

Health
A series of vaccinations is needed (cholera, dengue fever, hepatitis, yellow fever) as well as an anti-malaria treatment.

Average temperatures
24°C winter,
28°C summer

Airline Companies
Air France, Iberia, Lufthansa, British Airways, KLM, Alitalia.

How to get there
By plane or boat from Caracas.

Best seasons
In the dry season, between December and April.

Accommodation
Because the environment is protected, there are few hotels on Gran Roque. There are however small guest-houses and some villas for rent.

Local cuisine
The national dish, Pabellon Criolo, is prepared from strips of beef, rice, black beans, cheese and fried plantain bananas.

Shopping
Ceramics, pottery, fabrics, rugs, jewelry, Indian baskets, hammocks...

What to see
Gran Roque lighthouse, where you can see the whole island laid out; Francisqui and Crasqui islands, where you can also make the most of the superb beaches.

Activities
Sailing, water-skiing, snorkeling, fishing, hiking, diving on the coral reef...

Budget
Medium

Contact
http://www.venezuelatuya.com

\+ *Explore the small uninhabited islets.*

\- *Difficult to find accommodation.*

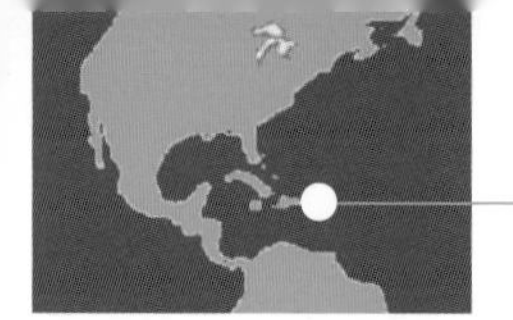

Surface area
350 km²
Population
121 000
Time zone
GMT -4
Language
English, Creole, Spanish and French
Currency
US Dollar
Documents
Currently valid passport
Health
You will need anti-mosquito treatments, notably to avoid the risks of dengue fever.
Average temperatures
24°C winter, 28°C summer

Airline Companies
American Airlines, Delta Airlines.
How to get there
The island of Saint John doesn't have an airport. So you need to fly to its neighbour Saint Thomas then take one of the many ferries which provide connections by sea in the archipelago.
Trunk Bay beach is located in the north-west of the island.
Best seasons
Between December and May
Accommodation
There are many comfortable hotels
Local cuisine
Creole and Western cooking are found together.
Shopping
Duty Free is in force, so the prices of some products might be found to be very attractive.
What to see
Saint John and its National Park, part of which was bought by Rockefeller in the 1950's; Buck Island, a small uninhabited island famous for its seabed; other magnificent beaches such as Hawksnest Bay or Cinnamon Bay; the Annaberg Sugar Mill.
Activities
Sailing, water-skiing, snorkeling, diving, hiking, horse-riding...
Budget
High
Contact
http://www.usvi.net

+ *One of the most beautiful lagoons in the Caribbean.*

- *Over two million tourists each year!*

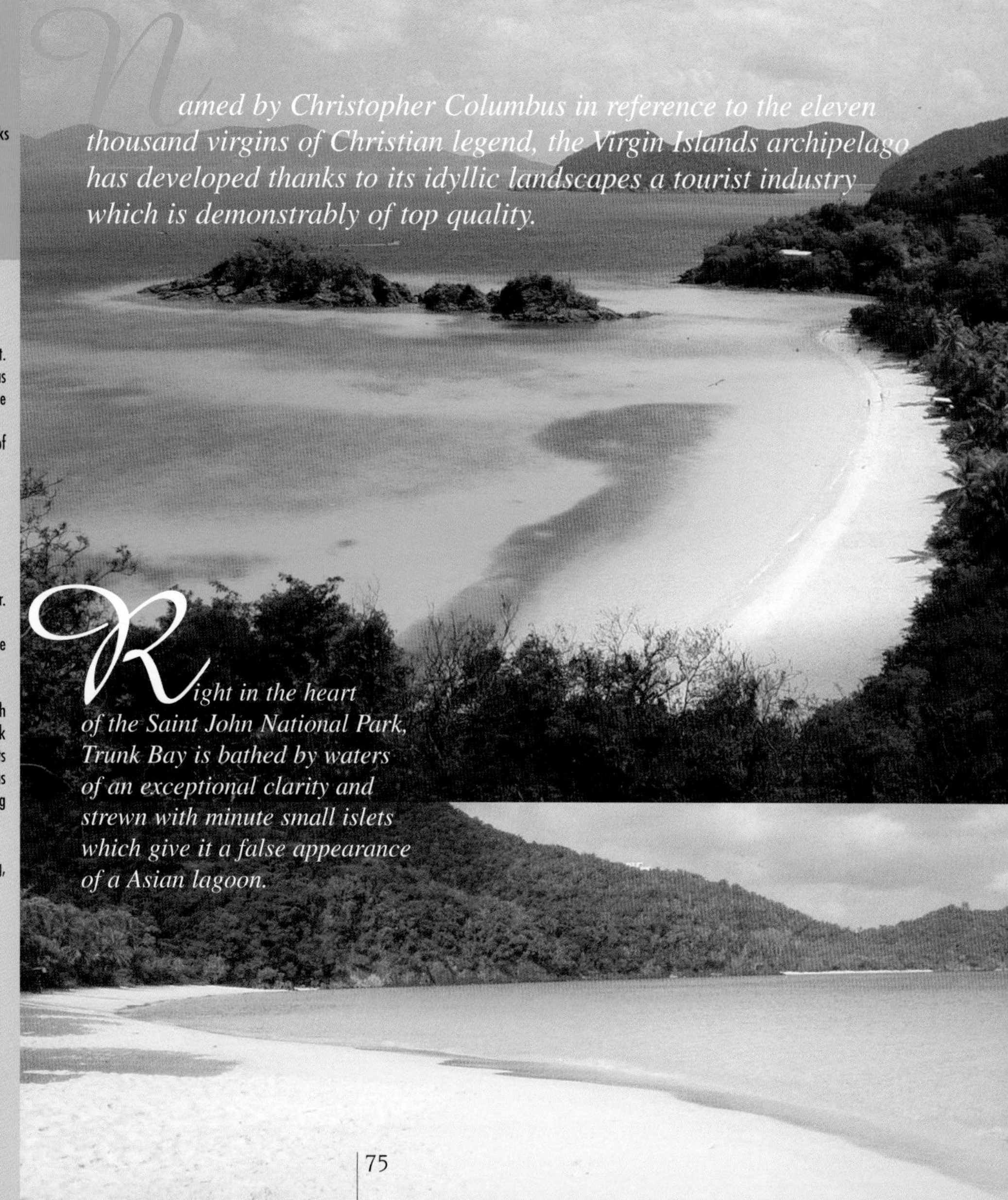

Named by Christopher Columbus in reference to the eleven thousand virgins of Christian legend, the Virgin Islands archipelago has developed thanks to its idyllic landscapes a tourist industry which is demonstrably of top quality.

Right in the heart of the Saint John National Park, Trunk Bay is bathed by waters of an exceptional clarity and strewn with minute small islets which give it a false appearance of a Asian lagoon.

ASIA

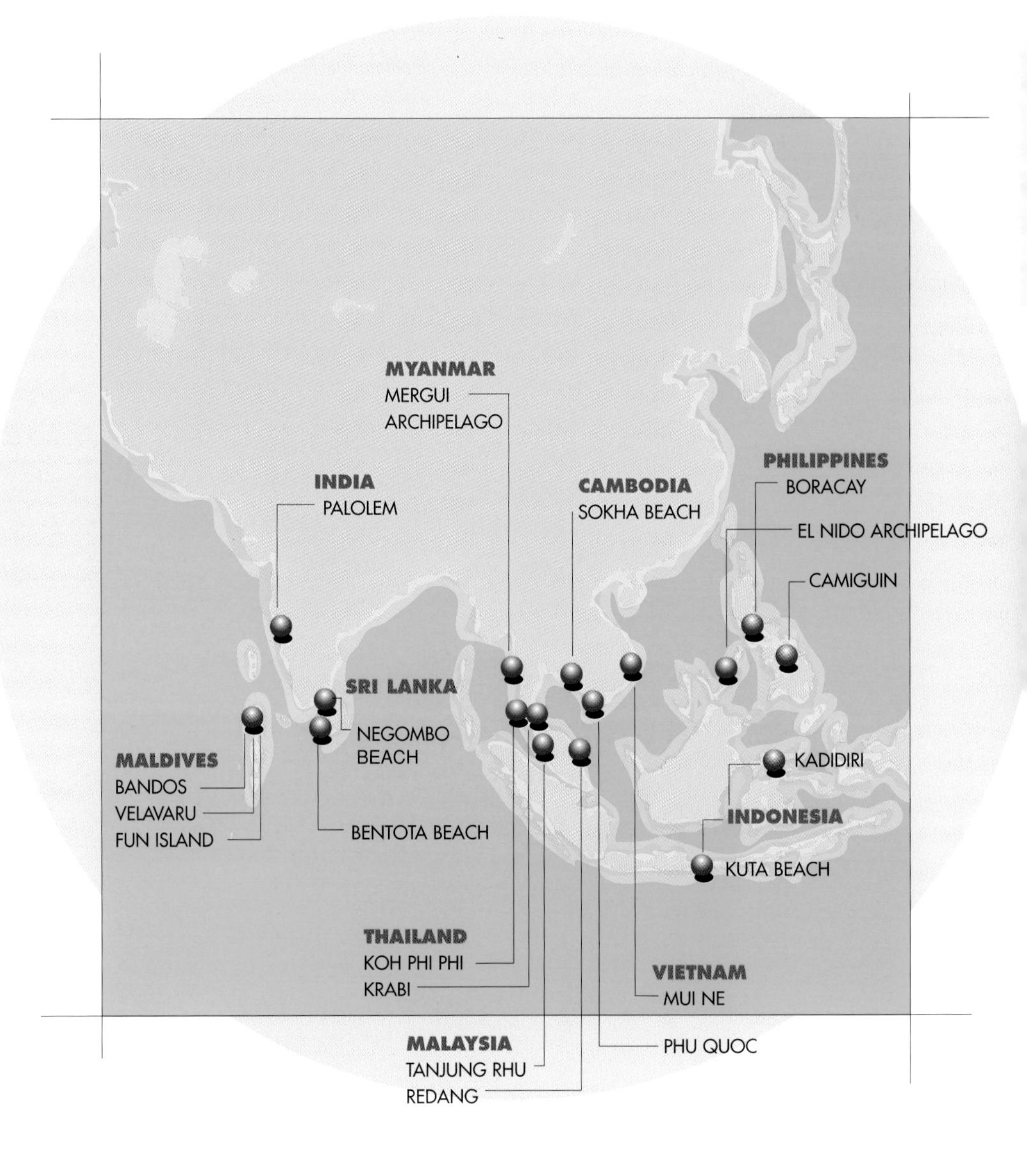
MYANMAR
MERGUI ARCHIPELAGO
INDIA
PALOLEM
CAMBODIA
SOKHA BEACH
PHILIPPINES
BORACAY
EL NIDO ARCHIPELAGO
CAMIGUIN
SRI LANKA
NEGOMBO BEACH
BENTOTA BEACH
MALDIVES
BANDOS
VELAVARU
FUN ISLAND
KADIDIRI
INDONESIA
KUTA BEACH
THAILAND
KOH PHI PHI
KRABI
VIETNAM
MUI NE
PHU QUOC
MALAYSIA
TANJUNG RHU
REDANG

Surface area
181,035 km²
Population
13 million
Time zone
GMT +7
Language
Khmer, English, French
Currency
Riel
Documents
Currently valid passport + Visa valid for one month
Health
Anti-malaria treatment
Average temperatures
30°C winter, 33°C summer

Airline Companies
Thai Airways, Singapore Airlines, Silkair.
How to get there
Royal Air Cambodia provides links between Phnom Penh and Sihanoukville. From there, it is best to take a taxi to the village of Sokha.
Best seasons
Between November and April in the dry season.
Accommodation
There are many hotels around Sihanoukville, ranging from modest to more fashionable, as well as some rooms to rent.
Local cuisine
Samla (a Cambodian soup), trey aing (grilled fish), salads flavoured with coriander, mint and lemon.
Shopping
Scarves (krama), sarongs (fabrics), sculpted wood objects, silver jewelry, copper statuettes (taking any type of antiquities out of the country is of course strictly forbidden).
What to see
Phnom Penh, its French architecture, its National Museum and its Royal Palace; the temples at Angkor; Lake Tonle Sap.
Activities
Sailing, hiking, snorkeling, diving (one of the few diving sites in the country thanks to water that is extremely clear).
Budget
Very good value
Contact
http://www.cambodia-web.net

+ *An authentic beach close to a beautiful fishing village.*

– *The humid heat and the summer monsoons.*

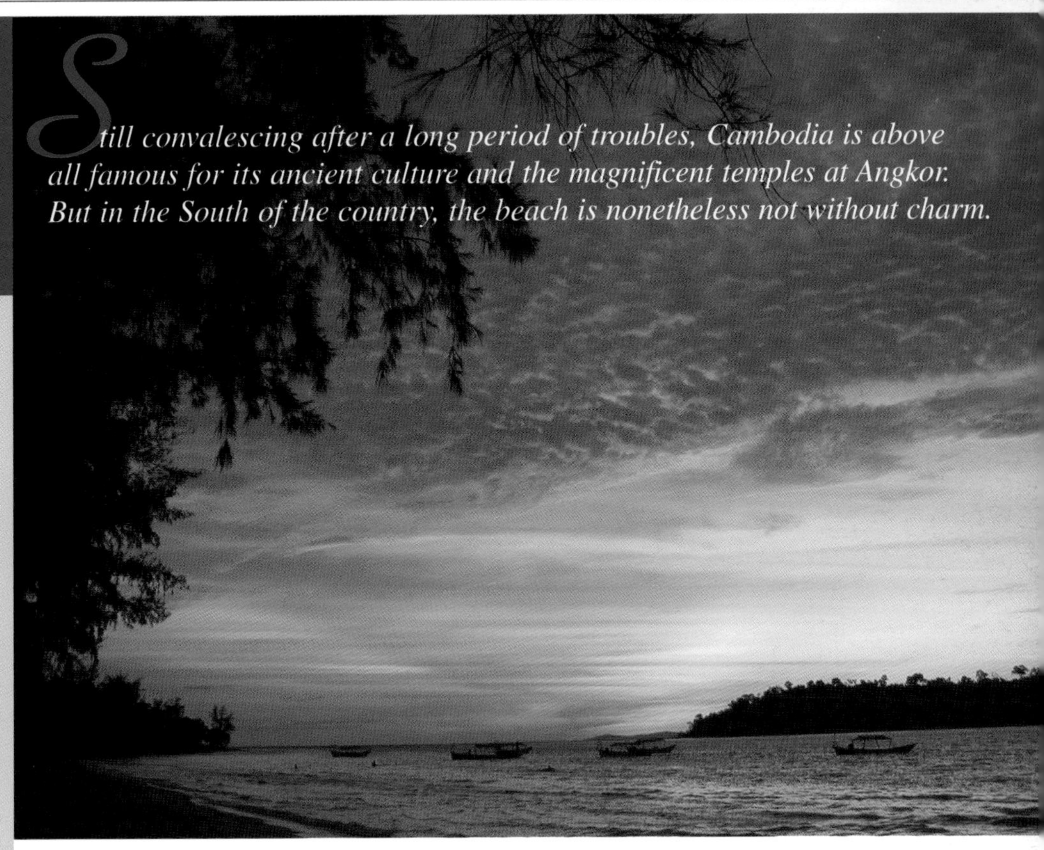

Still convalescing after a long period of troubles, Cambodia is above all famous for its ancient culture and the magnificent temples at Angkor. But in the South of the country, the beach is nonetheless not without charm.

Not far from Sihanoukville, Sohka beach is located along a small peninsula giving onto the Gulf of Thailand, and is used by the fishermen from the neighbouring village as a place to moor their fishing boats.

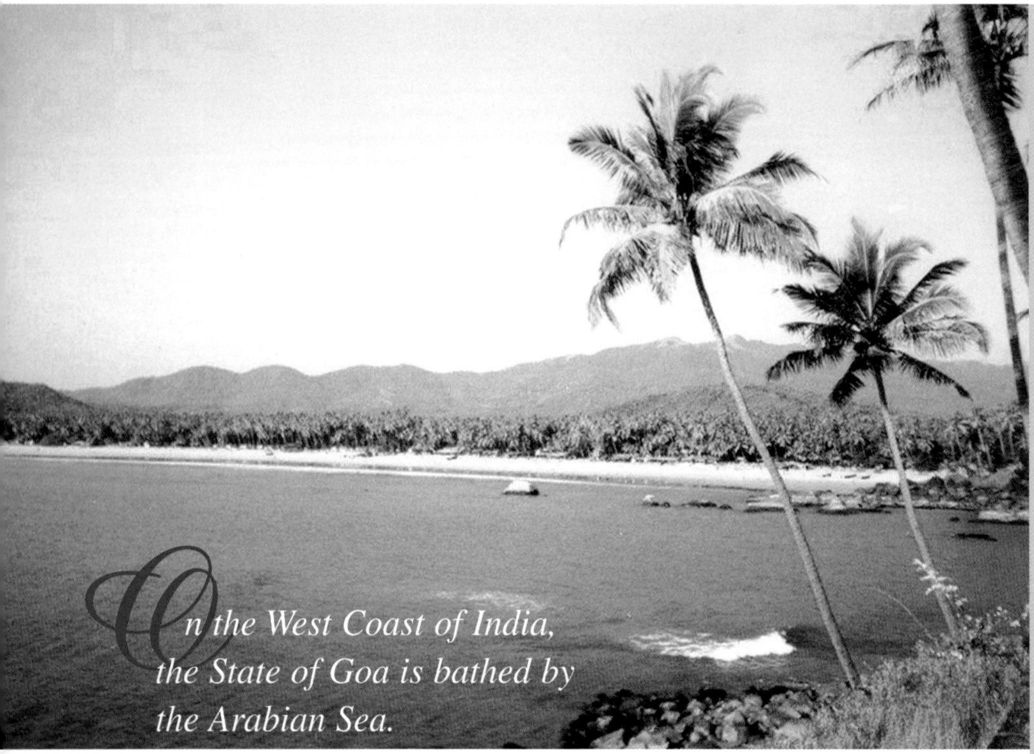

At the extreme South of Goa, Palolem lagoon forms a crescent of white sand more than a kilometre and a half long. At low tide, it is shallow for nearly a kilometre which lets children especially bathe in complete safety.

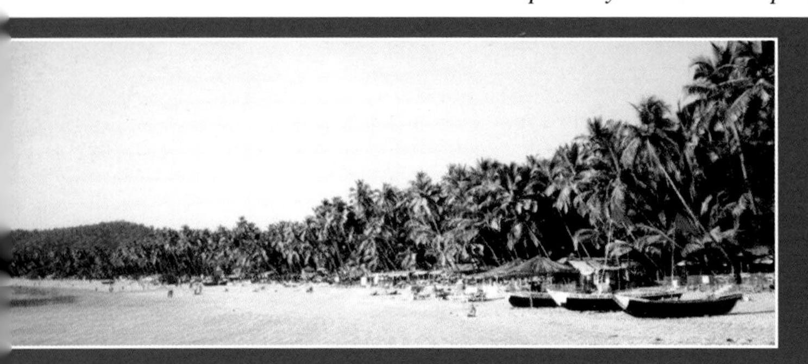

Surface area
3.2 million km²
Population
1 billion
Time zone
GMT + 5:30
Language
Konkani, English
Currency
Indian Rupee
Documents
Passport + Visa

Health
Vaccination against typhoid and hepatitis A and B is recommended, as well as an anti-malaria treatment.
Average temperatures
26°C winter, 30°C summer

Airline Companies
Air France, Air India, Emirates, British Airways, Lufthansa & Alitalia.
How to get there
By bus: from Margao, allow one hour for the journey.
By pousse-pousse: from Chaudi, only 2 kilometres from Palolem.
Best seasons
From November to March. On the other hand, it is best to avoid summer because of the high temperatures and the monsoon.
Accommodation
A camping area close to the beach, rooms and houses to rent at Colomb, to the south of Palolem.
Local cuisine
Fish (castagnole, vivaneau, fish balchao), shellfish (prawns, lobster), curried rice, traditional Indian dishes…
Shopping
Local clothes, jewelry...
What to see
The Shree Mallikarjun temple at Canacona, built in the 16th century.
Activities
Sailing, surfing, beach volley...
Budget
Good value
Contact
http://www.tourindia.com

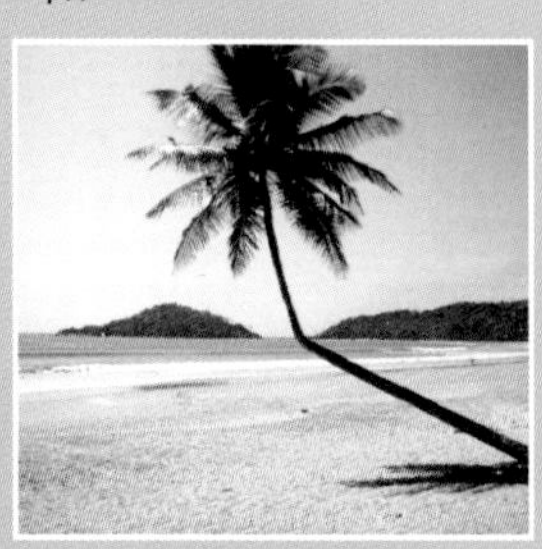

+ *A destination of myth among backpackers.*

− *Some say that in Goa, you're in India without being in India...*

Indonesia, 13,000 islands spread between Asia and the Pacific Ocean where some still keep their share of mystery more than ever.

A sprinkling of modest cabins hidden in the bushy vegetation: Kadidri beach will satisfy the wishes of lovers of nature and tranquility.

Surface area
1,904,400 km²
Population
224 million
Time zone
Between GMT + 7 and GMT +9
Language
Bahasa Indonesia, Javanese, Sudanese, over 400 different languages.
Currency
Indonesian Rupiah

Documents
A currently valid passport is enough, but some islands require a Visa.
Health
Malaria treatment and Hepatitis A vaccination are recommended.
Average temperatures
26°C winter, 27°C summer

Airline Companies
Garuda, Singapore Airlines, Malaysia Airlines.
How to get there
In the north of Sulawesi province, the Togian Islands and Kadidri Island are easily reached by ferry from the town of Ampana. You can also opt for one of the outrigger canoes - a very common mode of transport in the region - which make the trip in about three hours.
Best seasons
The dry season, from May to October.
Accommodation
There isn't much accommodation to be found at Kadidri apart from some bungalows along the beach.
Local cuisine
The national dish - nasi goreng - is made from fried rice mixed with minced meat, shrimps and eggs.
Shopping
Textiles, wooden sculptures, pottery, masks, paintings, baskets, jewelry, puppets, batik...
What to see
The Tanatoraja mountains; the Bada valley and its megaliths, Lake Posso, Lore Lindu Nature Park, the coral reefs surrounding the Togian Islands; the tongkonan (houses on stilts which are typical of the region).
Activities
Surfing, diving, hiking, rafting...
Budget
Not high
Contact
http://www.indonesiatourism.com

+ *A secluded beach that is not overlooked.*
- *Comforts are spartan.*

Bali - Island of the Gods - a land apart edged by spectacular beaches and with a population that has preserved its identity despite the pressures of tourism. A meeting place for surfers and backpackers for a long time, the well-known beach at Kuta blazes into a thousand colours each sunset.

Airline Companies
Garuda, Singapore Airlines, Malaysia Airlines.

How to get there
From Denpasar, take the road south towards Kuta Beach, which you will arrive at in not much more than fifteen minutes.

Best seasons
May to October

Accommodation
There are hotels of all categories around Kuta Beach as well as many losmen (local guest-houses) in the area.

Local cuisine
The national dish - nasi goreng - is made from fried rice mixed with minced meat, shrimps and eggs. At Bali, other local delicacies include crawfish and frog's legs!

Shopping
Textiles, wooden sculptures, pottery, masks, paintings, baskets, jewelry, puppets, batik...

What too see
The terraced green rice paddies; Batur and Agung volcanoes; Bedugui and its temple

Activities
Sailing, water-skiing, surfing, snorkeling, diving, hiking, horse-riding...

Budget
Medium

Contact
http://www.indonesiatourism.com

+ *A legendary beach offering every evening spectacular sunsets.*

- *The island is still suffering from the events of October 2002.*

Surface area
329,750 km²
Population
21 million
Time zone
GMT +8
Language
Malay, Chinese, English, Tamil
Currency
Ringgit
Documents
Currently valid passport

Health
Vaccinations against hepatitis A and typhoid are recommended, as well as an anti-malaria treatment in certain regions.
Average temperatures
23°C winter, 30°C summer

Airline Companies
Malaysian Airlines, British Airways, Lufthansa.
How to get there
By plane: from Kuala Lumpur in 45 minutes
By ferry: from Merang in 40 minutes
Best seasons
May to October
Accommodation
Luxury resorts and water bungalows
Local cuisine
Chinese, Thai, Indian and Malaysian. Some local specialities: satay, meat (beef or chicken) marinated in a spicy sauce and barbecued on small skewers; nasi goreng, fried rice with vegetables and meat; and last but not least rendang, a type of beef curry.
Shopping
Not much to bring back home except for some postcards...
What to see
Enjoy the adventure of a trip in the exuberant jungle
Activities
Sailing, snorkeling, diving, hiking...
Budget
Good value
Contact
http://www.tourism.gov.my

+ *Nature in a pure state and the undersea depths.*

- *Not many activities «off beach».*

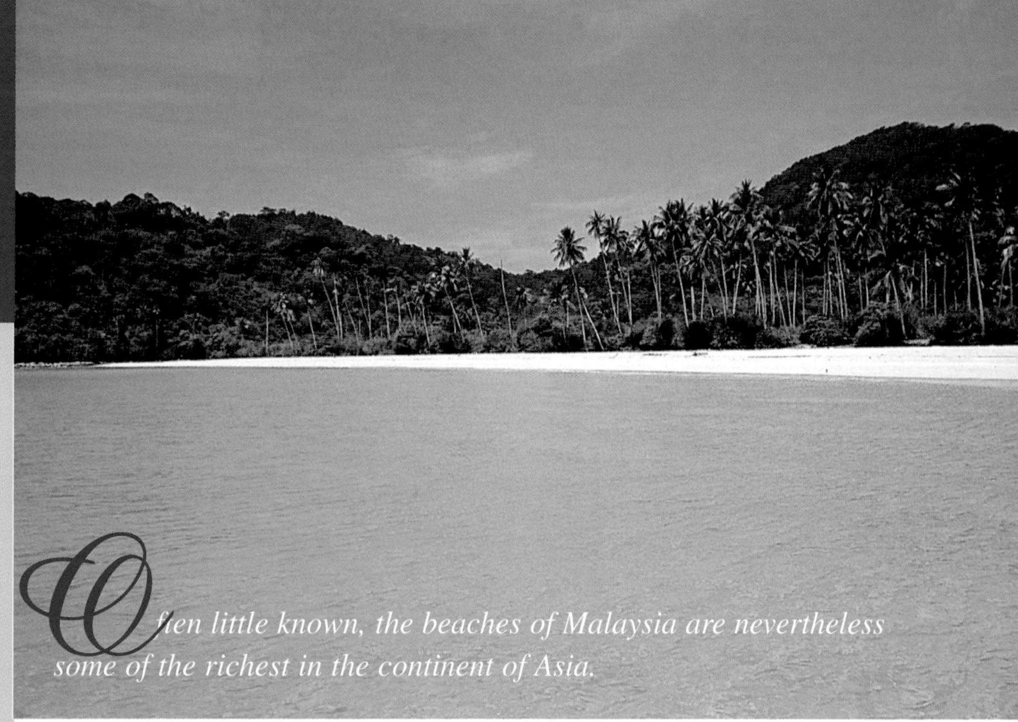

Often little known, the beaches of Malaysia are nevertheless some of the richest in the continent of Asia.

Located on the East of the Malaysian peninsula, Redang Island is a world-famous Marine Nature Park. On shore, magnificent beaches flanked by jungle let you bask in the sun surrounded by the idyllic scenery.

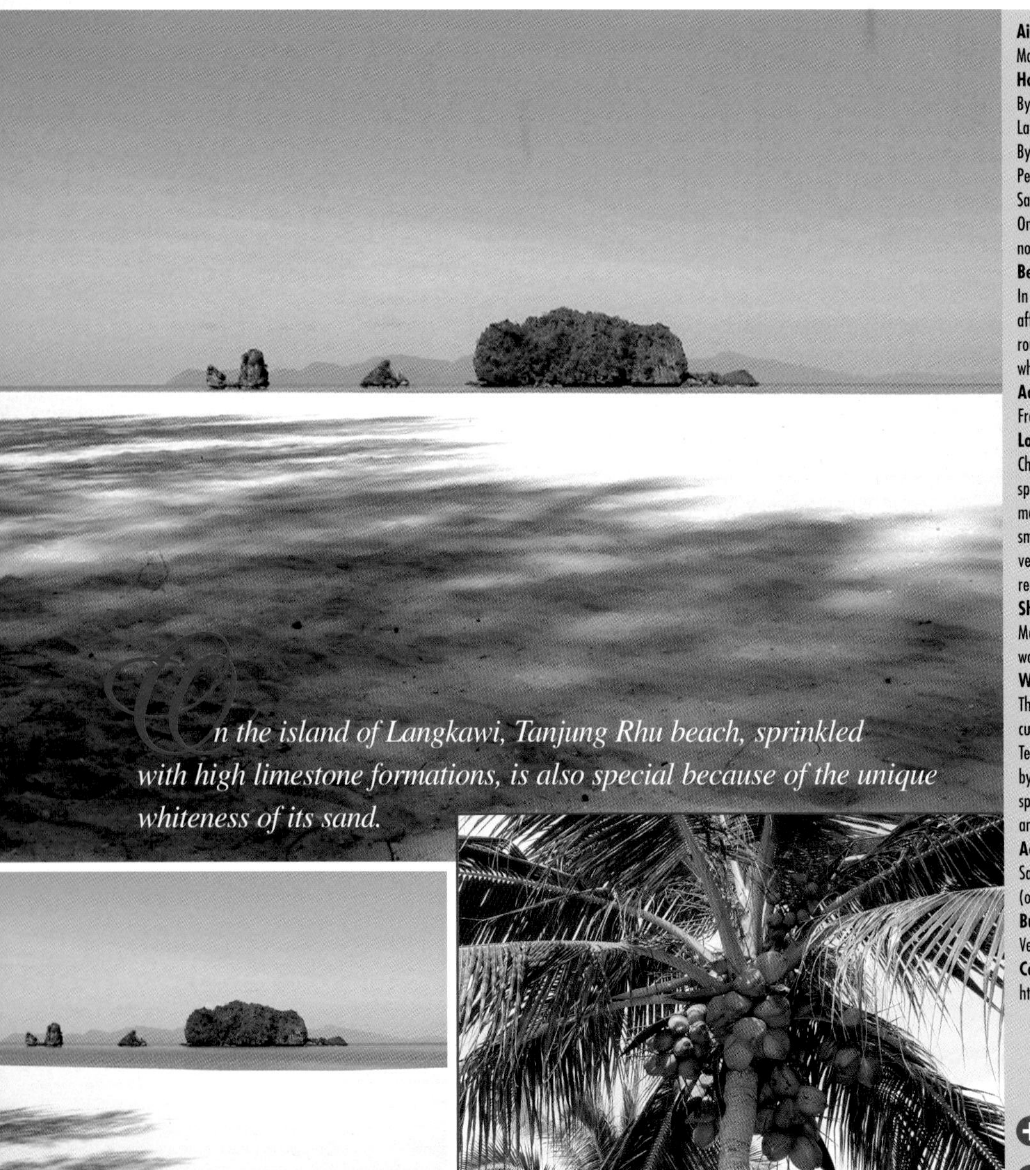

On the island of Langkawi, Tanjung Rhu beach, sprinkled with high limestone formations, is also special because of the unique whiteness of its sand.

Airline Companies
Malaysian Airlines, British Airways, Lufthansa.

How to get there
By plane: Malaysian Airlines has connections to Langkawi from Kuala Lumpur or Penang.
By ferry: there is one daily connection from Penang and another one from Thailand, out of Satun.
Once on the island, Tanjung Rhu beach is on the north coast.

Best seasons
In the West of Malaysia, Langkawi isn't much affected by the monsoon. You can visit all year round, especially between October and May when the showers are less frequent.

Accommodation
From modest bungalow to luxury resort.

Local cuisine
Chinese, Thai, Indian and Malaysian. Some local specialities: satay, meat (beef or chicken) marinated in a spicy sauce and barbecued on small skewers; nasi goreng, fried rice with vegetables and meat; and last but not least rendang, a type of beef curry.

Shopping
Made-to-measure silk clothes, traditional wooden sandals, kites, batiks.

What to see
The tomb of Mahsuri, a princess who laid a curse on the island; the cave of Gua Kelawar; Telaga Tujuh, a set of seven natural basins fed by waterfalls; the Summer Palace, which was specially built in 1999 for the filming of Anna and the King.

Activities
Sailing, water-skiing, fishing, snorkeling, diving (on the magnificent coral reef).

Budget
Very good value.

Contact
http://www.tourism.gov.my

 *Over-development.*

 *A humidity level close to 80 %.*

A 2.5 kilometers of sandy white beach and 1,100 acres of natural wilderness await discovery at Tanjung Rhu Resort. *A place where the wonders of nature harmonise with luxury to create the perfect 'Poetry'. As you settle down for a moment's rest, you will find the rooms an ideal romantic hideaway. Dining is an experience to be savoured. From fine dining to exotic local cuisine, each culminates into a feast for the senses.*

Around the resort, you will never be short of activities, from nite-lit tennis courts, two swimming pools – a salt water chlorinated beach pool and a 60-meter long fresh water pool, non-motorised water sport and spa facilities in our 12 independent villas to fill your languid time.

The myriad charm of the Resort, be it the heavenly juxtaposition of the lush greenery and the various hues of the sea, or the incomparable service and pampering by the staff at the Resort, will make you wish you never had to leave...

Mukim Ayer Hangat, 07000 Langkawi, Kedah Darul Aman, Malaysia.
Tel: 604-959 1033 (24-hour reservations) Fax: 604-959 1899 Email: resort@tanjungrhu.com.my
Managed by Signforce Sdn Bhd (443194D) ISO 9001 : 2000 & ISO 14001 CERTIFIED

The Maldives, many hundreds of coral atolls for a spectacle which exceeds any description...

Located on North Male Atoll, this minute perfectly circular 2km² island is covered with lush tropical vegetation. Ringed by a magnificent coral barrier reef, it is surrounded by many small rings of land just like so many miniature copies.

Airline Companies
Sri Lankan Airlines, Qatar Airways, Emirates

How to get there
By speedboat: allow 20 minutes for the crossing from Male
By traditional boat: 45 minutes

Best seasons
It is balmy all year round in the Maldives, usually between 29° and 32°. However, the dry season from December to April is with doubt the most agreeable period.

Accommodation
Several small bunglaows nestled amidst the lush vegetation.

Local cuisine
The basic cuisine consists of fish and rice. Meat is only prepared for special occasions. You will also find little fruit and vegetables other than in the hotels, which are generally well supplied.

Shopping
Mats, rugs, embroidery, pottery and lacquered vases, silver and gold articles, coral and pearl jewelry...

What to see
Male, the small capital, with its markets, its mosques and its small museum; Fuamulaku, a small island which is unique since it is the only one in the archipelago where fruit such as mangos and pineapples grow; trips to the neighbouring islets.

Activities
Sailing, water skiing, snorkeling, diving (the magnificent coral barrier reef is only 200 meters from shore). You can also watch the turtles coming ashore to lay their eggs on the beaches.

Budget
High

Contact
http://www.visitmaldives.com

+ *One of the best spots for diving in the archipelago.*

− *Sometimes difficult to find accomodation.*

Surface area
298 km²
Population
300 000
Time zone
GMT +5
Language
English, Divehi
Currency
Rufiyaa
Documents
Currently valid passport
Health
Watch out for the tap-water
Average temperatures
The average temperatures vary from 27°C to 29°C year round

Airline Companies
Sri Lankan Airlines, Qatar Airways, Emirates.
How to get there
By seaplane: 40 minutes from Male
Best seasons
It is balmy all year round in the Maldives, usually between 29° and 32°. However, the dry season from December to April is with doubt the most agreeable period.
Accommodation
Fifty bungalows with complete amenities
Local cuisine
The basic cuisine consists of fish and rice. Meat is only prepared for special occasions. You will also find little fruit and vegetables other than in the hotels, which are generally well supplied.
Shopping
Mats, rugs, embroidery, pottery and lacquered vases, silver and gold articles, coral and pearl jewelry...
What to see
Male, the small capital, with its markets, its mosques and its small museum; Fuamulaku, a small island which is unique since it is the only one in the archipelago where fruit such as mangos and pineapples grow; trips to the neighbouring islets.
Activities
Sailing, water-skiing, snorkeling, diving...
Budget
High
Contact
http://www.visitmaldives.com

 *The island isn't much over 1 km²!*

 *Not for hyperactive types!*

Called « Turtle Island » by the Maldivans, Velavaru is a small jewel famed for the emerald colour of its transparent water. It is located in the Dhaalu Atoll.

A carpet of sparkling sand delicately set right next to the ocean. At the heart of South Male Atoll, Fun Island really does live up to its name...

Airline Companies
Sri Lankan Airlines, Qatar Airways, Emirates

How to get there
By speedboat : allow for a 45-minute crossing from Male.
By traditional boat : 3 hours

Best seasons
It is balmy all year round in the Maldives, usually between 29° and 32°. However, the dry season from December to April is with doubt the most agreeable period.

Accommodation
A hundred very comfortable bungalows spread over the island.

Local cuisine
The basic cuisine consists of fish and rice. Meat is only prepared for special occasions. You will also find little fruit and vegetables other than in the hotels, which are generally well supplied.

Shopping
Mats, rugs, embroidery, pottery and lacquered vases, silver and gold articles, coral and pearl jewelry...

What to see
Male, the small capital, with its markets, its mosques and its small museum. Fuamulaku, a small island which is unique since it is the only one in the archipelago where fruit such as mangos and pineapples grow; trips to the neighbouring islets.

Activities
Sailing, water-skiing, snorkeling, diving (in particular, encounters with moray eels, manta rays and grey sharks).

Budget
High

Contact
http://www.visitmaldives.com

+ *The everyday nature of the almost surreal scenery.*

- *You don't meet many Maldivans.*

MYANMAR • MERGUI ARCHIPELAGO

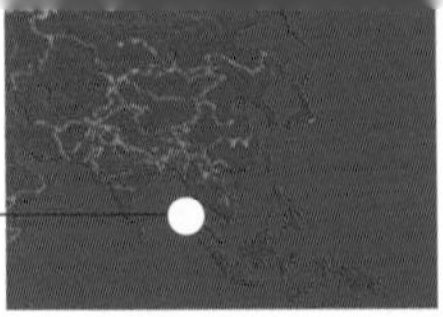

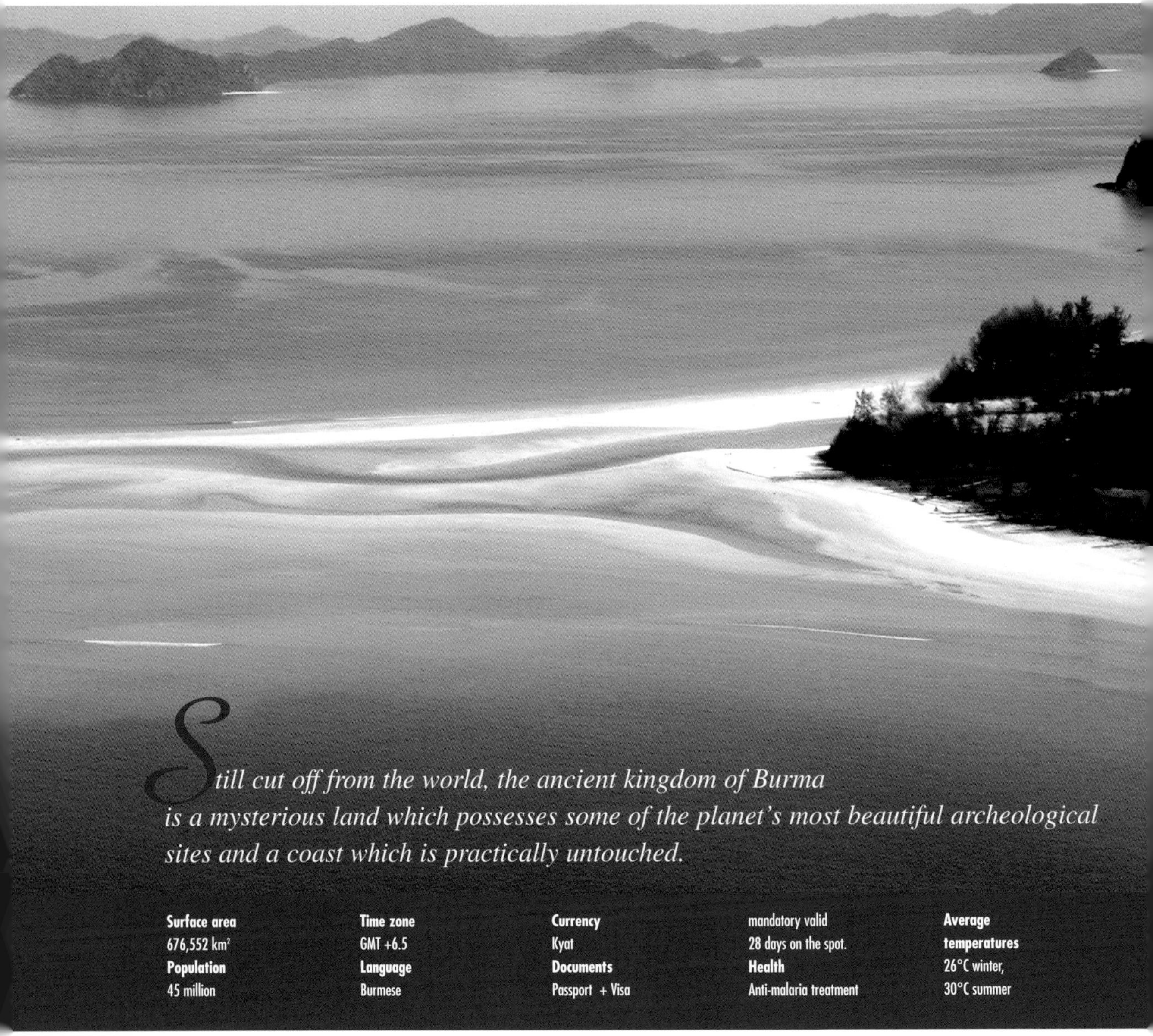

Still cut off from the world, the ancient kingdom of Burma is a mysterious land which possesses some of the planet's most beautiful archeological sites and a coast which is practically untouched.

Surface area
676,552 km^2
Population
45 million

Time zone
GMT +6.5
Language
Burmese

Currency
Kyat
Documents
Passport + Visa mandatory valid 28 days on the spot.
Health
Anti-malaria treatment

Average temperatures
26°C winter,
30°C summer

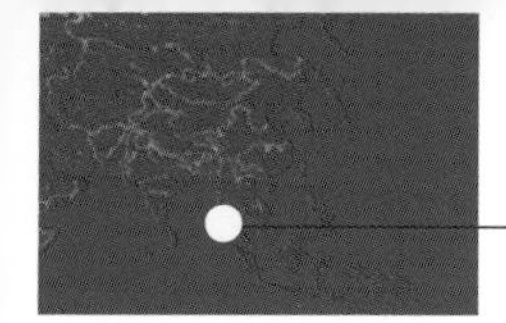

Airline Companies
Thai Airways, Singapore Airlines, Malaysia Airlines, Silk Air.

How to get there
By plane: a small airport at Myeik. The rest of the travel is done by boat.

Best seasons
From December to April, when the heat is less strong and the rains less torrential.

Accommodation
Usually you travel by boat for several days during which you are housed on board.

Local cuisine
The national dish, mohing, is prepared with fish, fish sauce, rice noodles, coriander and eggs. Just like the rest of Asia, fried noodles accompanied by chicken or fish are very popular. And for drinks, tea without sugar.

Shopping
Puppets, embroidered tapestries, lacquer objects, cheerots (small Burmese cigars)...

What to see
The Burma Banks, islands scarely breaking the surface; the many underwater caves scattered through the archipelago; Yangon (ex Rangoon), the capital, bewitching and invaded by the jungle with the dome of Paya Shwedagon, a famous Buddhist temple.

Activities
Snorkeling, diving (for experienced divers, underwater animal life that is matchless, with in particular 7 species of sharks)

Budget
Weak

Contact
http://www.myanmar-tourism.com

+ *A tiny paradise away from any human presence.*

− *A political regime that is against dissent.*

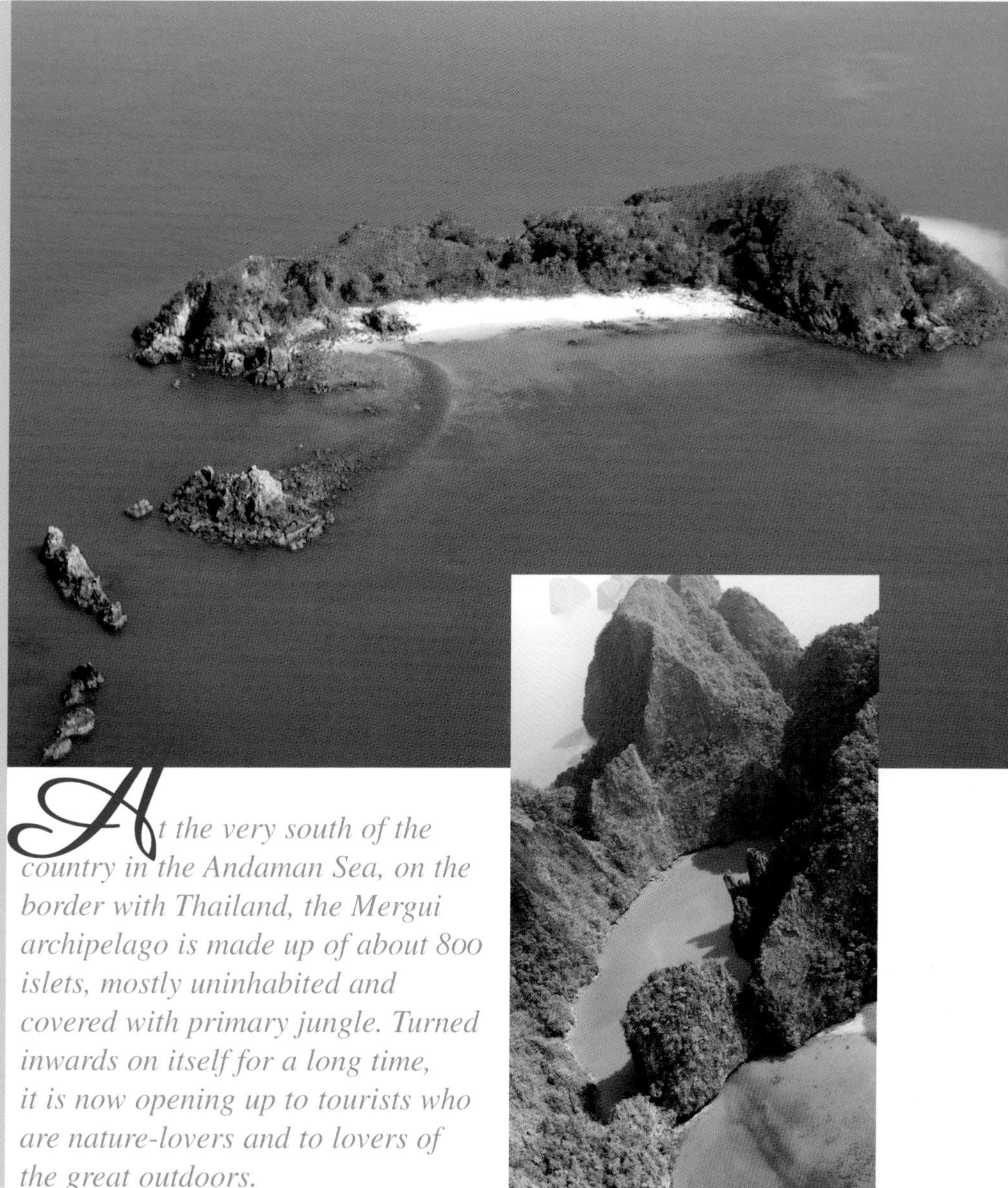

At the very south of the country in the Andaman Sea, on the border with Thailand, the Mergui archipelago is made up of about 800 islets, mostly uninhabited and covered with primary jungle. Turned inwards on itself for a long time, it is now opening up to tourists who are nature-lovers and to lovers of the great outdoors.

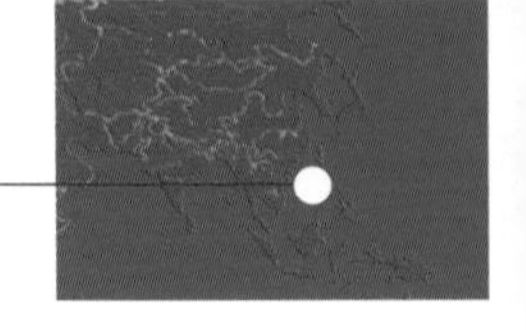

PHILIPPINES • BORACAY

The small island of Boracay (7 km long and only 1 km wide) is famous for the clearness of its water and for its night-life. On the west coast, the superb coral sands of White Beach stretch for over 4 km, while the east coast, which is more exposed to the winds, is the favourite spot for wind-surfers.

The Philippines archipelago forms a labyrinth of over 7,000 islands and islets, many of which still remain uninhabited today. A wild and authentic place, between jungle, volcanoes, rice paddies and idyllic beaches.

Surface area
300,439 km²
Population
77 million
Time zone
GMT +8
Language
Philippine (Tagalog), English

Currency
Philippine peso but the US dollar is accepted everywhere in the tourist industry.
Documents
Currently valid passport. A visa is required for stays of more than 21 days.

Health
No vaccination is required, but an anti-malaria treatment is recommended.
Average temperatures
26°C winter, 29°C summer

Airline Companies
Air France, Cathay Pacific, Thai Airways, Singapore Airlines, Lufthansa.
How to get there
From Manilla or Cebu, there are daily Philippine Airlines flights to Kalibo. From there, take a bus or a «Jeepney» to Caticlan (a trip of 2 hours and 30 minutes), or there are boats which go to Boracay in only fifteen minutes.
Best seasons
During the dry season, mid-November to mid-May, the sky is clear, temperatures are warm and the sea is calm.
Accommodation
The island offers a large range of accommodation, from small rooms to the top class comfort of a luxury hotel.
Local cuisine
Traditional Philippine cuisine is a compromise between Chinese, Malay and Spanish cuisines: meat or fish barbecued on skewers, dishes using coconut milk, «lapu-lapu inihaw» (a local fish which is served most often in a banana leaf).

Shopping
Jewelry, hats, baskets, wooden sculptures, mother-of-pearl.
What to see
The caves in the north, near Yapak, are the home of the giant bats of Boracay; the «Kar-Tir» Seashell Museum at Ilig-Iligan.
Activities
Sailing, water-skiing, snorkeling, canoeing, hiking, VTT, diving...
Budget
Medium
Contact
http://www.tourism.gov.ph

\+ *Waters that are some of the clearest in the world.*

\- *The island is a popular Philippine tourist centre.*

PHILIPPINES • EL NIDO ARCHIPELAGO

Between the China Sea and the Sulu Sea, Palawan island province is the wildest in the Philippines archipelago. Not much opened up to tourism, for a long time it was an ideal location for the South Sea pirates. El Nido Archipelago, a real marine sanctuary sprinkled with pristine beaches and high lime-stone cliffs that reminds some of the very famous Along Bay, only even more wild.

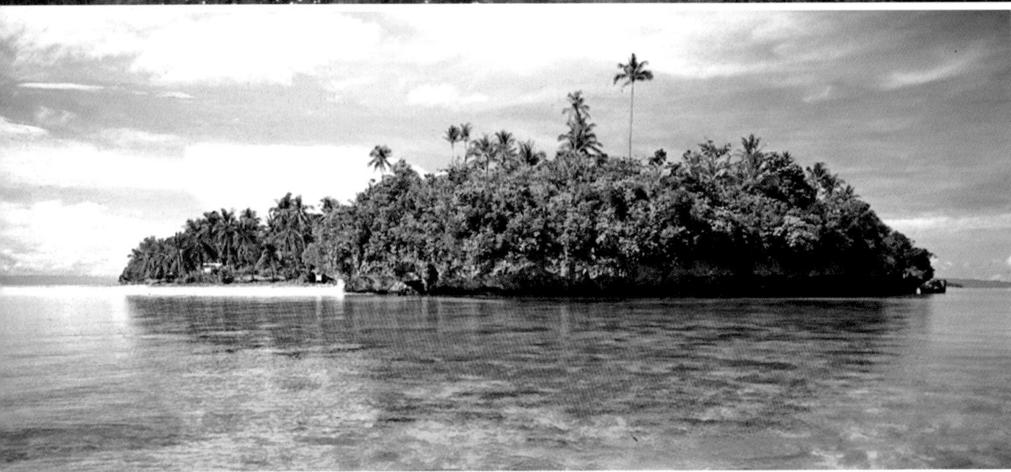

Airline Companies
Air France, Cathay Pacific, Thai Airways, Singapore Airlines, Lufthansa.

How to get there
From Manilla, there are regular Philippines Airlines flights to Puerto Princessa. From there, ferries or air-taxis connect with El Nido and the neighbouring islands.

Best seasons
From mid-December to mid-May, the climate is dry and the wind isn't too strong.

Accommodation
Bungalows, guest-houses and top class resorts.

Local cuisine
Philippine cooking is a compromise between Chinese, Malay and Spanish cuisines: meat or fish barbecued on skewers, dishes using coconut milk, «lapu-lapu inihaw» (a local fish which is served most often in a banana leaf).

Shopping
Objects made from seashells, coral rocks, fabrics, bamboo baskets...

What to see
Calauit Island, an island sanctuary dedicated to protecting nature; Tabon Caves, the most ancient lived-in caverns of Southern Asia; the National Park and underground river at Saint Paul; the unique species of animal life found in the region (leopard cats, varans, pythons).

Activities
Sailing, water-skiing, snorkeling, trekking, horse-riding, diving (the undersea areas contain more than 2000 species of fish).

Budget
Rather high

Contact
http://www.tourism.gov.ph

+ *For those with a soul of explorer or adventurer.*

− *In recent times, the region has had a bad reputation.*

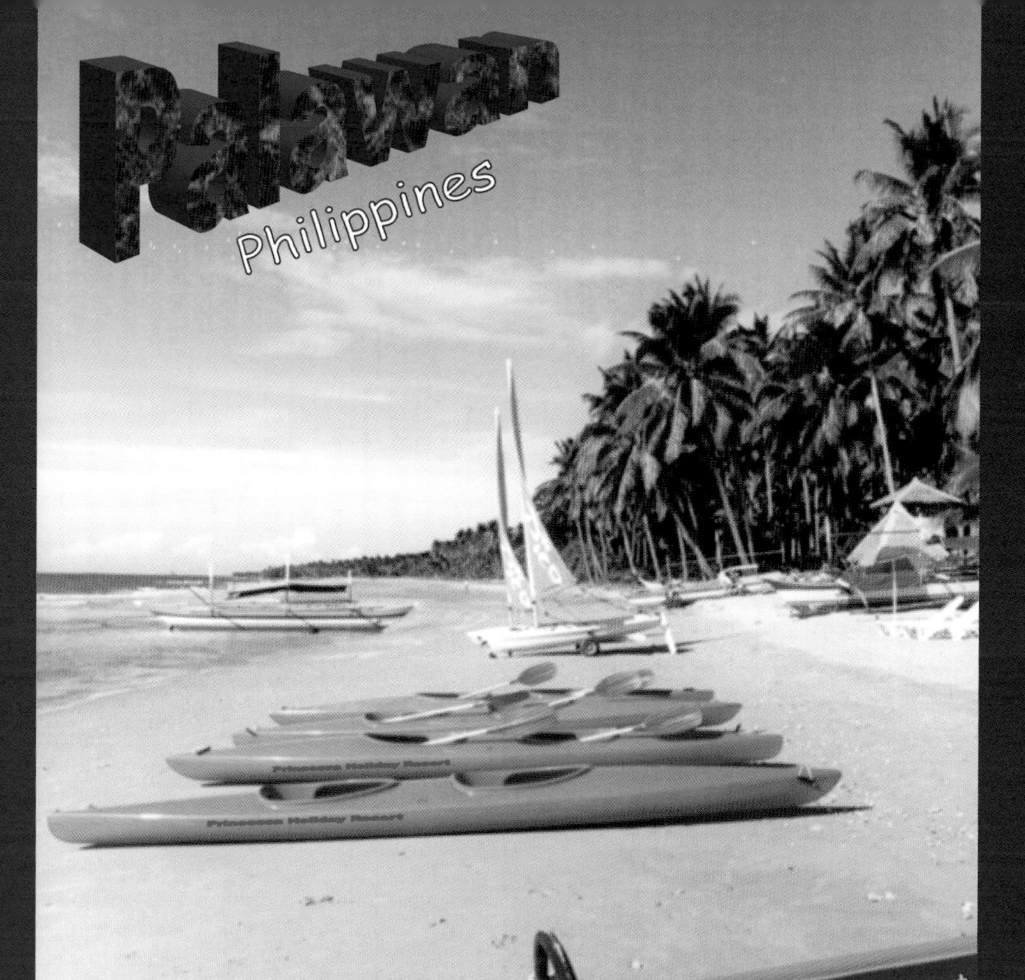
Palawan
Philippines
Princessa Holiday Resort
Princessa Holiday Resort
Princessa Holiday Resort

Nicknamed « the Garden of Eden » by Filippinos, the small volcanic island of Camiguin is bathed by the Bohol Sea. Famous for its natural riches - waterfalls, hot-water springs and lush vegetation - its desert-like beaches are bizarrely stuck at the bases of the volcanoes.

Airline Companies
Air France, Cathay Pacific, Thai Airways, Singapore Airlines, Lufthansa.

How to get there
Take an internal flight (1-1/2 hrs) from Manilla to Cayagan de Oro (Cebu Pacific or PAL). From there, ferries provide the link with Camiguin.

Best seasons
From mid-December to mid-May is the dry season and the temperatures are more pleasant.

Accommodation
Bungalows, small hotels and some cottages for rent.

Local cuisine
Philippine cooking is a compromise between Chinese, Malay and Spanish cuisines: meat or fish barbecued on skewers, dishes using coconut milk, «lapu-lapu inihaw» (a local fish which is served most often in a banana leaf).

Shopping
Baskets, silverware, pottery...

What to see
The ruins of the church of Old Catarman destroyed in 1871 by a volcanic eruption; Ardent Springs, a hot-water spring where you can bathe even at night time; Katibasawan Falls, waterfalls that measure over 50 meters high; the small circular road which goes round the island.

Activities
Sailing, snorkeling, trekking, diving (the sea bed looks just like the moon surface because of the volcanic rocks).

Budget
Very good value

Contact
http://www.tourism.gov.ph

+ *The magnificent turbulent landscapes.*

- *Top class comfort.*

Surface area
65,610 km²

Population
18.7 million

Time zone
GMT +6

Language
Sinhala, Tamil, English

Currency
Sri Lankan Rupee

Documents
Currently valid passport

Health
No vaccination is required, but an anti-malaria treatment is strongly advised.

Average temperatures
Average temperatures stay between 27°C and 29°C all year round.

Airline Companies
Sri Lankan Airlines, Singapore Airlines, Emirates

How to get there
From Colombo, follow the main road along the west coast for about 70 km.

Best seasons
The two monsoon periods which affect the country are in December to January and May to September. The high season in February-March is the most pleasant, but it is also most crowded with tourists.

Accommodation
Many hotels and some guest-houses on the seashore.

Local cuisine
Rice and curry, lamprai (rice mixed with vegetables and meat and then cooked in a banana leaf), sambol (coconut and finely chopped onion spiced with red chilli pepper), acawuapura (crispy fritters), spices. The fish, crab and shrimps are also excellent, not to mention the national drink: tea.

Shopping
Local handicrafts made out of sculpted wood, coconuts or lacquered, multi-coloured masks, pottery, baskets, batiks, leather goods, precious stones (watch out for the rip-offs).

What to see
The mosque at Beruwela, the oldest in the country.

Activities
Sailing, snorkeling, fishing, diving, water-skiing on the Bentota river.

Budget
Not high

Contact
http://www.srilankatourism.org

South of India, between the Gulf of Bengal and the Arabian Sea, Sri Lanka - previously called Ceylan - is also known as the « Pearl of the Indian Ocean ».

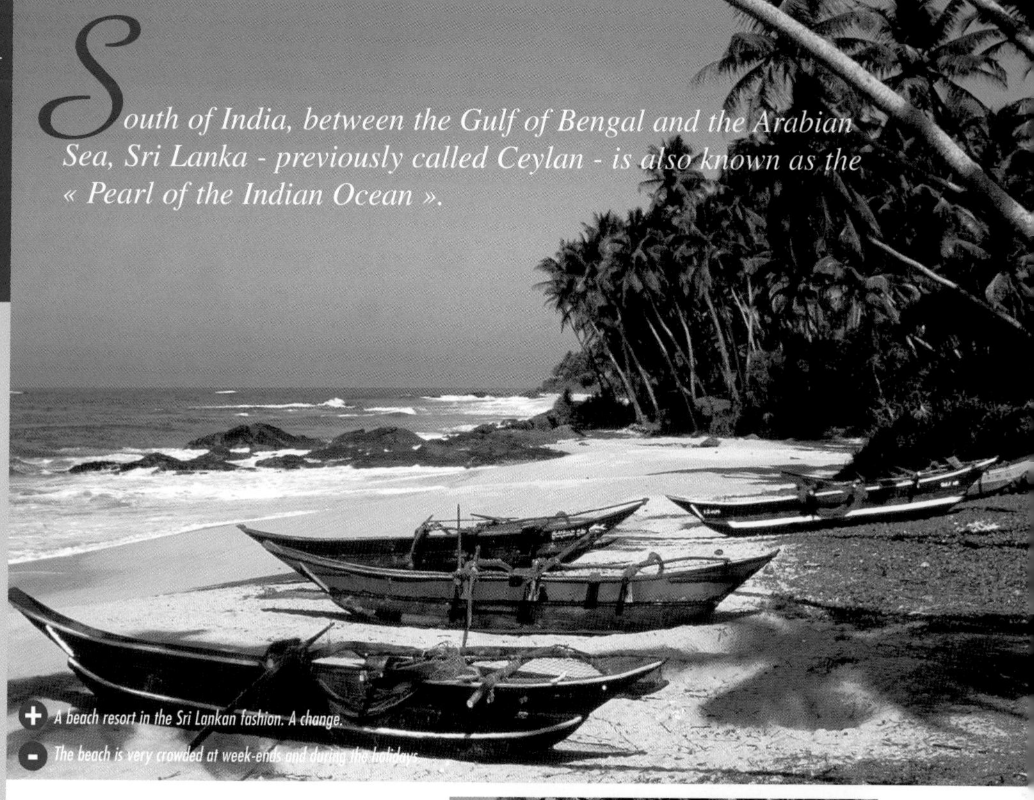

+ A beach resort in the Sri Lankan fashion. A change.

- The beach is very crowded at week-ends and during the holidays.

South of Colombo, the lagoon at Bentota offers a magnificent sight with its dusting of small islands and its beautiful beach dotted by coconut trees.

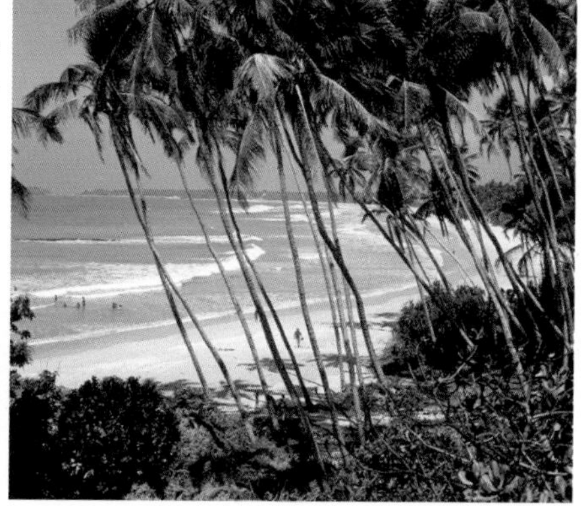

Negombo, located 30 km north of the capital Colombo, is sometimes called « Little Rome » because of its churches in the gothic style. But above all it is famous for its large beach of pale sand, washed by the emerald-coloured waves of the Indian Ocean.

Airline Companies
Sri Lankan Airlines, Singapore Airlines, Emirates.

How to get there
From Colombo, allow half an hour to get to Negombo by road.

Best seasons
The two monsoon periods which affect the country are in December to January and May to September. The high season in February-March is the most pleasant, but it is also most crowded with tourists.

Accommodation
Hotels and guest-houses in town and along the beach.

Local cuisine
Rice and curry, lamprai (rice mixed with vegetables and meat and then cooked in a banana leaf), sambol (coconut and finely chopped onion spiced with red chilli pepper), acawuapura (crispy fritters), spices. The fish, crab and shrimps are also excellent, not to mention the national drink: tea.

Shopping
Local handicrafts made out of sculpted wood, coconuts or lacquered, multi-coloured masks, pottery, baskets, batiks, leather goods, precious stones (watch out for the rip-offs).

What to see
The churches and the Portugese Fort from the XVIIth century; the market; Colombo, the capital.

Activities
Sailing, snorkeling, fishing, diving.

Budget
Not high

Contact
http://www.srilankatourism.org

+ *The country's cultural wealth, as well as the beauty of its beaches.*

- *Tourists are not welcomed in the north of the country.*

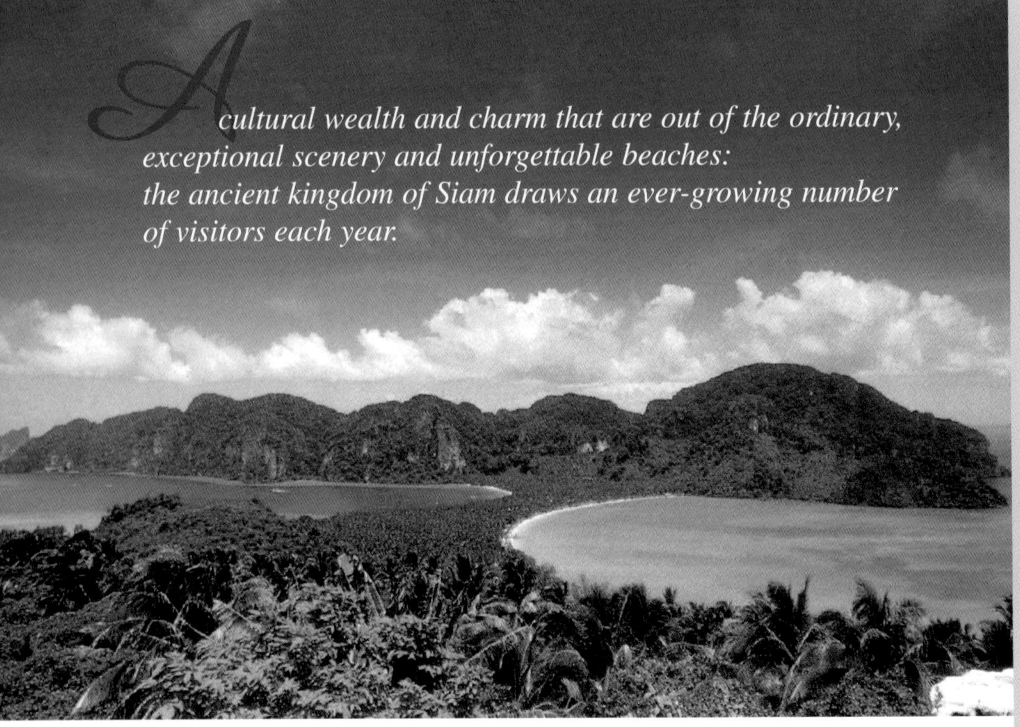

A cultural wealth and charm that are out of the ordinary, exceptional scenery and unforgettable beaches: the ancient kingdom of Siam draws an ever-growing number of visitors each year.

The Koh Phi Phi archipelago consists of two principal islands, only one of which is inhabited: Koh Phi Phi Don. Here there are no roads, no cars: travel is by foot or by boat only. A true paradise indeed...

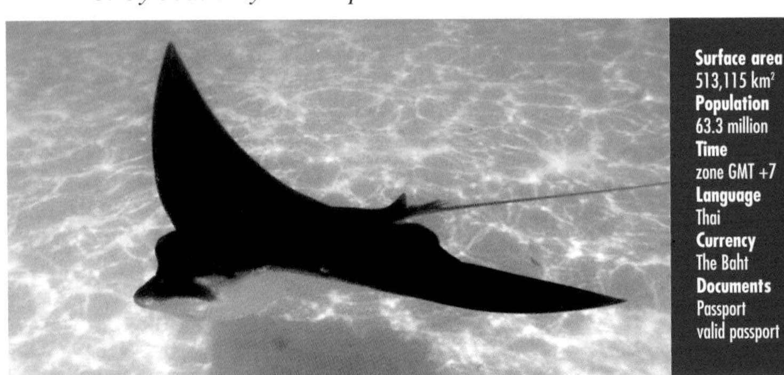

Surface area
513,115 km²
Population
63.3 million
Time
zone GMT +7
Language
Thai
Currency
The Baht
Documents
Passport
valid passport

Health
Some vaccinations such as Hepatitis A and typhoid are advised. Treatment against dengue fever and malaria is recommended outside of the large towns.
Average temperatures
27°C winter,
30°C summer

Airline Companies
Air France, Thai Airways, British Airways, Lufthansa.

How to get there
There are lots of daily connections by boat from Krabi and Phuket. Allow about 2 hours for the crossing.

Best seasons
From October to April in the dry season. From December, tourist numbers and prices start rising..

Accommodation
On Koh Phi Phi Don, there are delightful water bungalows as well as small guest-houses in the village. In the high season, it can sometimes be difficult to find a room.

Local cuisine
The Thai cuisine is rich and very varied: fried dishes (rice, vegetables, beef, chicken), soups, fried noodles, fish and seafood (shark, many coloured crabs...), teas, spices, fruit (pineapple, lychee, durian...). On the island, small Thai places rub shoulders with restaurants serving Western food.

Shopping
Clothes at low prices, jewelry, bamboo furniture and Thai handicrafts, spices and teas.

What to see
The Koh Phi Phi Don view-point, from the top of which there is an exceptional panoramic view; Maya Bay Beach, on the neighbouring island of Koh Phi Phi Lay, used in the film The Beach; Bamboo Beach on the island of that name; 1 hour by boat, the Koh Lanta National Park.

Activities
Sailing, water-skiing, snorkeling, climbing, hiking, Thai massages, diving (leopard sharks are to be found nearby).

Budget
Medium

Contact
http://www.tat.or.th

 *A corner of paradise, Thai-style.*

 *The long-boats are sometimes noisy.*

Some people enjoy big resort with all its grandeur and magnitude of services. Then there are others...

For those others may we offer
an exclusive 31-seaview-rooms hideaway
and the only boutique habitat right in front of Patong Beach.
If the idea of having your mind tunes
to the rhythm of peace and tranquility appeals to you...
if a place where you can simply close your eyes
and let all the roughness of life seeps out of you and
if you think you can enjoy a simple Thai hospitality then...
welcome to Avantika, let us spoil your spirit.

AVANTIKA...a place where peace touches you

A V A N T I K A

Airline Companies
Air France, Thai Airways, British Airways, Lufthansa.

How to get there
By road: 800 km south of Bangkok.
By plane: Thai Airways offers regular flights between Bangkok and Krabi.
By train: 12 hours from Bangkok.

Best seasons
From October to April in the dry season. Be aware that the region is affected by frequent tropical storms and has the highest rainfall levels in the whole country.

Accommodation
Bungalows and hotels of all categories.

Local cuisine
The Thai cuisine is rich and very varied: fried dishes (rice, vegetables, beef, chicken), soups, fried noodles, fish and seafood, fruit (pineapple, lychee, durian...).

Shopping
Clothes at low prices, jewelry, bamboo furniture and Thai handicrafts, teas, spices.

South of Bangkok, this small coastal province which is also the site of a National Park is known for its coastline strewn with strange limestone isles, some of which are honeycombed by sea caves.

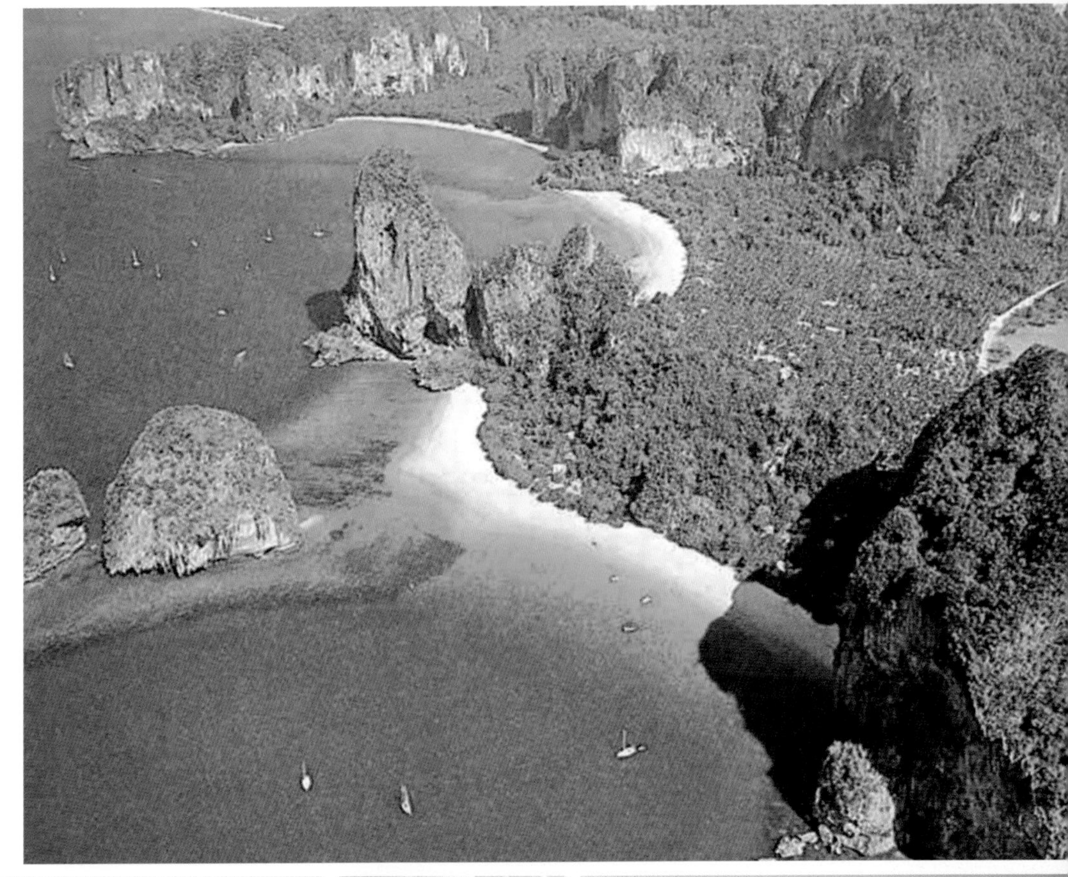

What to see
The large number of pre-historic caves in the region; the temples ; the seashell graveyard; the island of Koh Phi Phi; the Koh Lanta National Park; the island of Kao Tapoo, which was used in 1974 in a James Bond film (The Man With The Golden Gun).

Activities
Sailing, water-skiing, snorkeling, climbing, hiking, Thai massages, safaris by 4WD or on the back of an elephant, diving (the luckiest divers might see some manta rays).

Budget
Not high

Contact
http://www.tat.or.th

\+ *The coast and its rock formations.*

\- *Recently, hotels are springing up like mushrooms...*

Basically a coastal nation, Vietnam is edged by the China Sea and the Gulf of Tonkin.

Surface area
332,000 km²
Population
79 million
Time zone
GMT +7
Language
Vietnamese
Currency
Dong
Documents
Passport + Visa
Health
No vaccination is required but an anti-malaria treament is advisable
Average temperatures
27°C winter, 30°C summer

Airline Companies
Air France, Vietnam Airlines.
How to get there
By bus or by car: from Phan Thiet, the nearest town, count on about a half-hour's drive.
Best seasons
From November to April to avoid the summer monsoon.
Accommodation
Some hotels and guest-houses close to the beach.
Local cuisine
Nuoc mam (a condiment made from pickled fish), ban canh (a clear soup served with large rice-paste noodles, balls of fish and pork, and seasoned with coriander), seafood dishes...
Shopping
Local handicrafts, lacquer objects, silk, embroidered clothes, tea, spices, traditional Vietnamese hats.
What to see
Ho Chi Minh City (its pagodas, its Chinese quarter and its buildings from the Colonial era); Da Lat and its surrounding area (especially the Valley of Love).
Activities
Sailing, VTT, hiking...
Budget
Good value.
Contact
http://www.vietnamtourism.com

Mui Ne is a small fishing village located about 200 km north-east of Ho Chi Minh City. Its beach is famous for the enormous golden dunes, which give you a strange feeling of being in the Sahara.

+ *The dunes of Mui Ne are worth the trip.*
- *It gets very crowded at week-ends.*

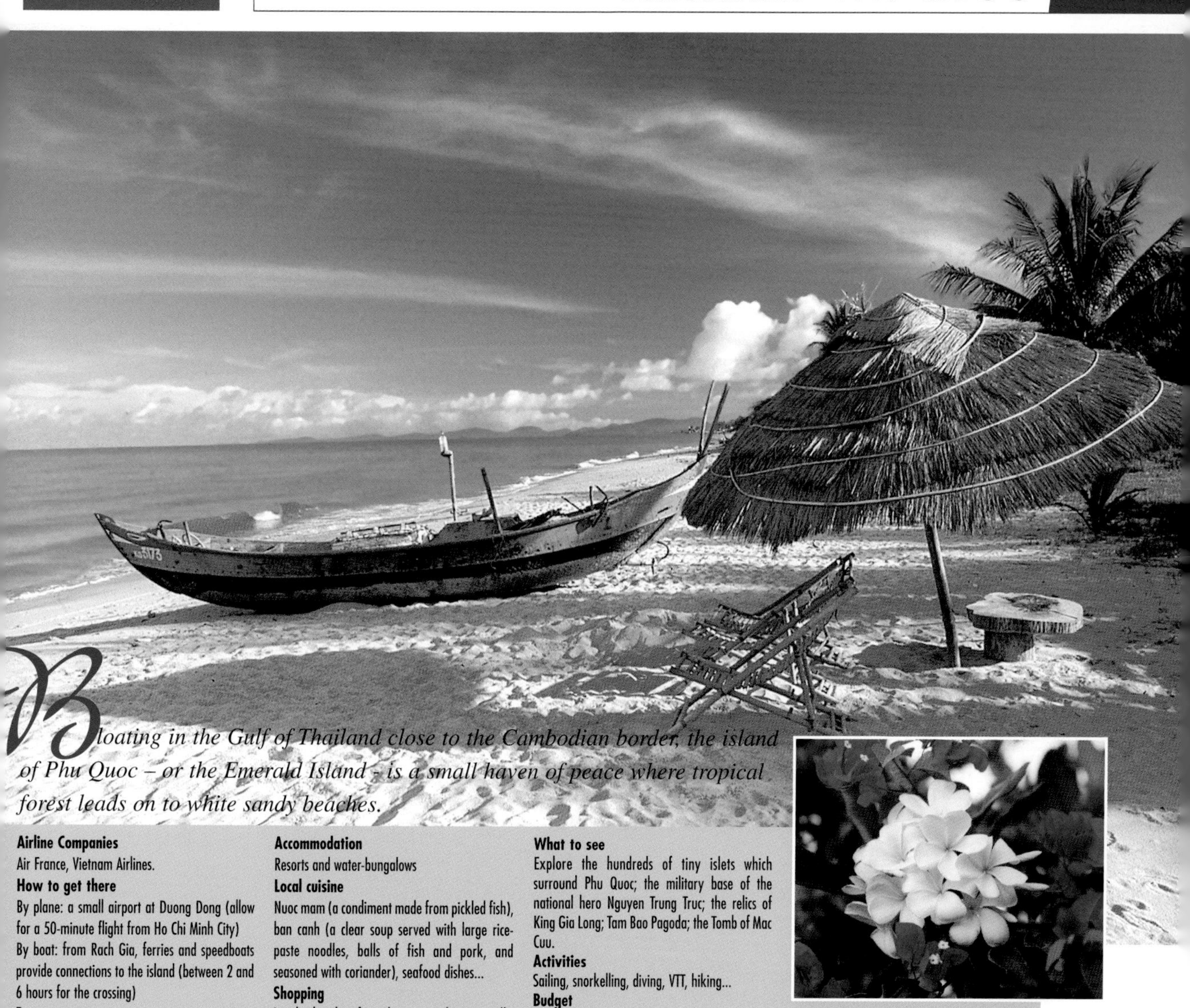

Floating in the Gulf of Thailand close to the Cambodian border, the island of Phu Quoc – or the Emerald Island – is a small haven of peace where tropical forest leads on to white sandy beaches.

Airline Companies
Air France, Vietnam Airlines.

How to get there
By plane: a small airport at Duong Dong (allow for a 50-minute flight from Ho Chi Minh City)
By boat: from Rach Gia, ferries and speedboats provide connections to the island (between 2 and 6 hours for the crossing)

Best seasons
From November to April to avoid the summer monsoon.

Accommodation
Resorts and water-bungalows

Local cuisine
Nuoc mam (a condiment made from pickled fish), ban canh (a clear soup served with large rice-paste noodles, balls of fish and pork, and seasoned with coriander), seafood dishes...

Shopping
Local handicrafts, lacquer objects, silk, embroidered clothes, tea, spices, traditional Vietnamese hats.

What to see
Explore the hundreds of tiny islets which surround Phu Quoc; the military base of the national hero Nguyen Trung Truc; the relics of King Gia Long; Tam Bao Pagoda; the Tomb of Mac Cuu.

Activities
Sailing, snorkelling, diving, VTT, hiking...

Budget
Good value.

Contact
http://www.vietnamtourism.com

+ *Away from the traditional tourist trails.*

– *A bit remote from the rest of the country.*

EUROPE

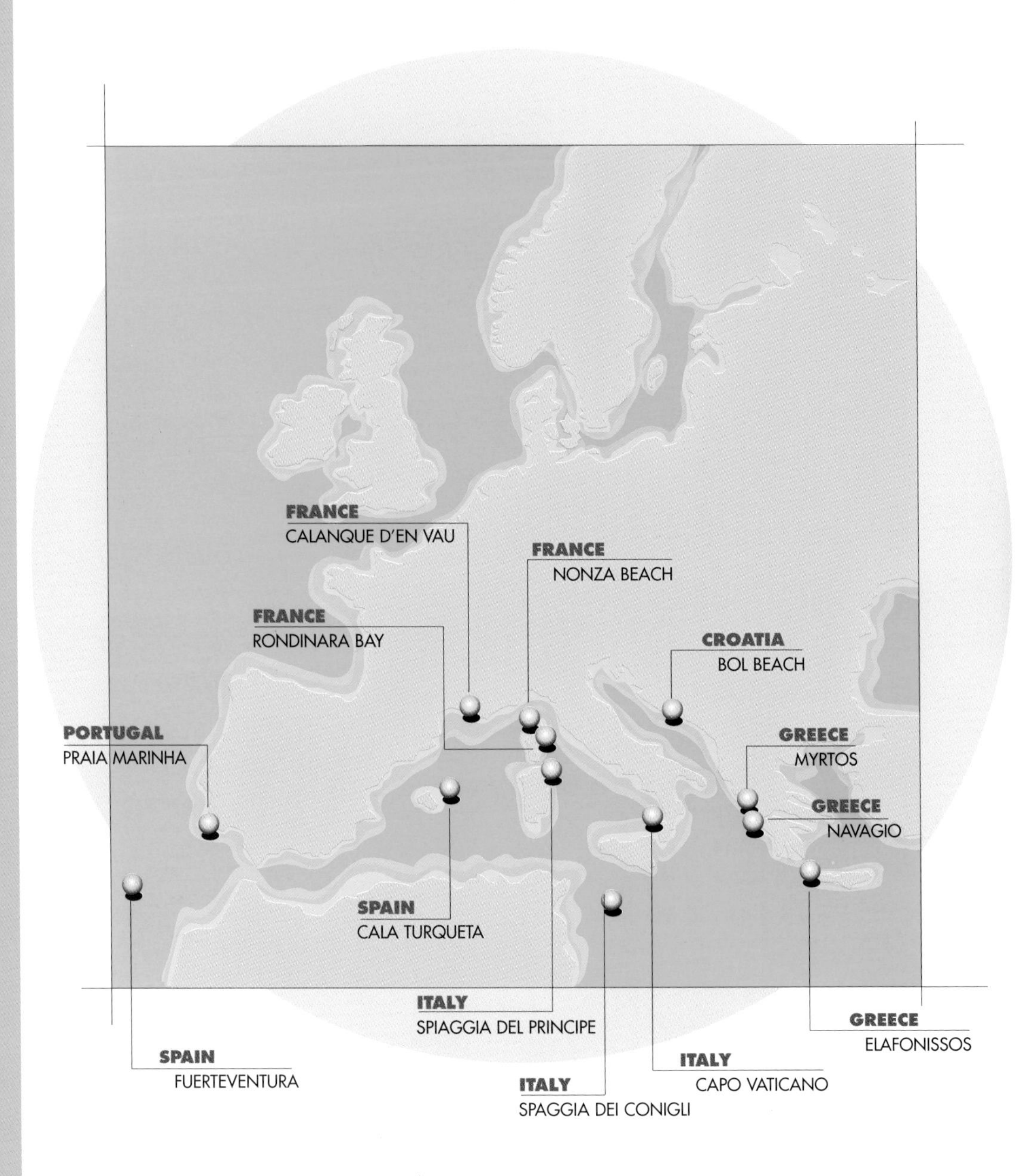
FRANCE
CALANQUE D'EN VAU
FRANCE
NONZA BEACH
FRANCE
RONDINARA BAY
CROATIA
BOL BEACH
PORTUGAL
PRAIA MARINHA
GREECE
MYRTOS
GREECE
NAVAGIO
SPAIN
CALA TURQUETA
ITALY
SPIAGGIA DEL PRINCIPE
GREECE
ELAFONISSOS
SPAIN
FUERTEVENTURA
ITALY
CAPO VATICANO
ITALY
SPAGGIA DEI CONIGLI

CROATIA • BOL

Surface area
56,691 km²

Population
4.8 million

Time zone
GMT +1

Language
Croatian

Currency
Kuna

Documents
Currently valid passport

Health
No vaccination is required

Average temperatures
12°C winter, 29°C summer

Airline Companies
Croatia Airlines, British Airways, Lufthansa, Alitalia.

How to get there
From Split, a ferry makes several daily trips to the island. Once you get to Bol village, follow the directions to Zlatni Rat.

Best seasons
May to October

Accommodation
Camp sites, hotels of all categories and vacation rentals in the village.

Local cuisine
Prsut (dried ham), prosek (the local aperitif), ready-to-eat fish and seafood in the local olive oil.

Shopping
Embroidery, copper or hand-sculpted wooden objects, bottles of water or the local wines in unusual forms…

What to see
Blaca, a XVIth century monastery built on the sides of a mountain; west of Bol there are the Dragon's Caves; Split, the well-known medieval city.

Activities
Sailing, water-skiing, snorkeling, diving (the Adriatic seabed is still not well known despite the richness of the marine animal- and plant-life and the presence of a large number of wrecks...).

Budget
Medium

Contact
http://www.htz.hr

\+ *Over 11 hours sunshine in summer !*

\- *The beach is the victim of its own success in the high season.*

Naturally turned to face the sea with a 5,835 km shore and nearly 1200 islands, Croatia is a colourful countryside with an outstanding coastline.

Brac is the largest island in Dalmatia and perhaps also the most spectacular. An ancient haunt of pirates, the small village of Bol is famous for its beach, which is thought to be the most beautiful in the Adriatic, and for its small houses made of white chalk which sparkle in the sunshine.

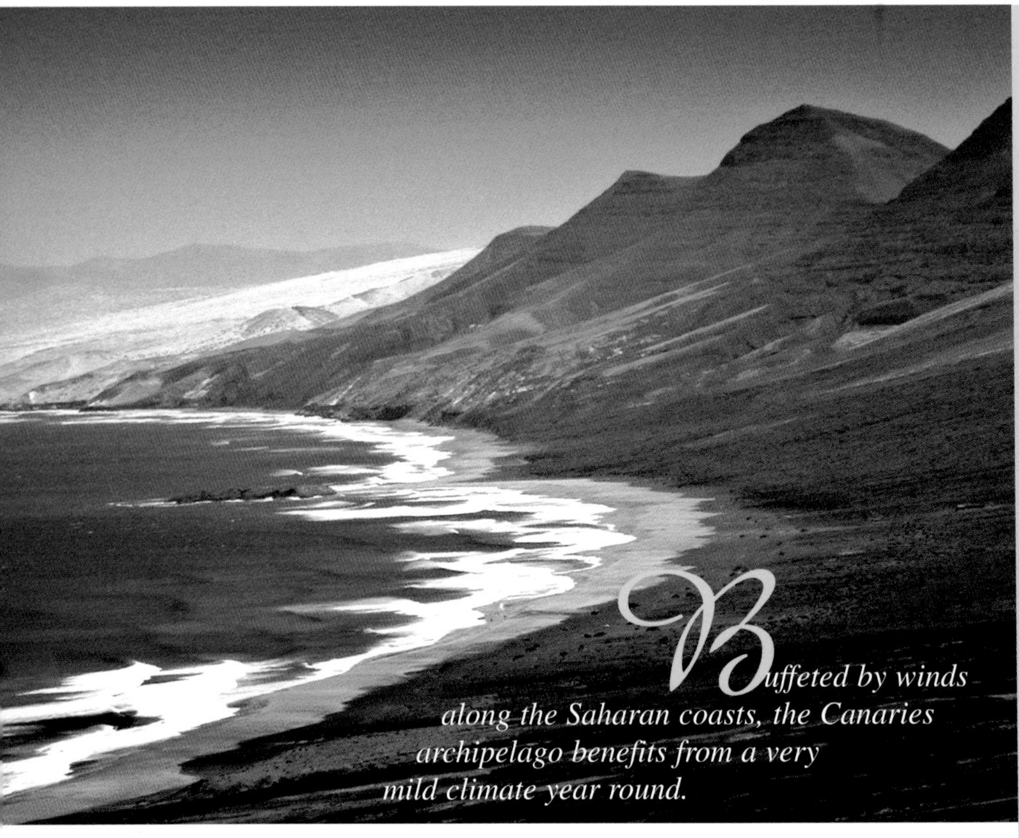

Buffeted by winds along the Saharan coasts, the Canaries archipelago benefits from a very mild climate year round.

If Fuerteventura is above all famous amongst surfers for the quality of its waves and its hundreds of golden beaches, its brilliant red volcanic soils and its small villages of white chalk also make this a destination which is outstanding and only three hours from the bustling urban centre.

Surface area
505,000 km²
Population
41 million
Time zone
GMT
Language
Spanish
Currency
Euro

Documents
Identity card
Health
No vaccination needed
Average temperatures
19°C winter, 27°C summer (Canaries)

Airline Companies
Iberia, British Airways, Lufthansa, Alitalia.

How to get there
By plane: Fuerteventura has its own airport. Internal flights serve the whole of the Canaries archipelago.
By Ferry: Regular connections let you get to the neighbouring islands.

Best seasons
The Canaries enjoys clement weather all year round. Winter is the most popular tourist season, and thus is the dearest, especially during the Christmas and February breaks: it is therefore better to come and visit during autumn or spring.

Accommodation
Hotels of all categories, guest-houses, rural camping is tolerated.

Local cuisine
Gofio (bread made from wheat, barley, maize and chickpeas), papas arrugadas (potatoes cooked in salt and served with a spicy sauce), queso majorero (goat's-milk cheese), fish, shellfish, seafood…

Shopping
Pottery, embroidery, baskets woven from palm-leaves...

What to see
At Puerto del Rosario, Pago de Casillas del Angel church in the colonial style; the small villages in the white chalk typical of the Canaries.

Activities
Sailing, surfing, horse-riding, VTT, diving (especially Lobos island).

Budget
Medium

Contact
http://www.spain.info

\+ *Only three hours from London, you can swim even in winter.*

\- *The sometimes spectacular waves.*

Airline Companies
Iberia, British Airways, Lufthansa, Alitalia.

How to get there
From Es Castell, take the road towards Ferreries, then follow Santa Caldana right to Cala Turqueta.

Best seasons
May to October

Accommodation
Camp sites, hotels or rental villas

Local cuisine
Calderata de langosta (crayfish soup), oliaiga (fish prepared with baked potatoes and aubergines), honey and fig cake, squid, cheeses...

Shopping
Pottery, woven baskets, abarcas (sandals)...

What to see
La Ciutadella, at the very west of the island; the remains of the Basilica de Son Bou destroyed in the IXth century; Monte Toro, the highest mountain on the island; the different prehistoric sites.

Activities
Sailing, snorkeling, horse-back tours, diving...

Budget
Medium

Contact
http://www.spain.info

\+ *Water so clear you would swear you were in the Caribbean !*

\- *The inlet is a bit packed in the middle of summer.*

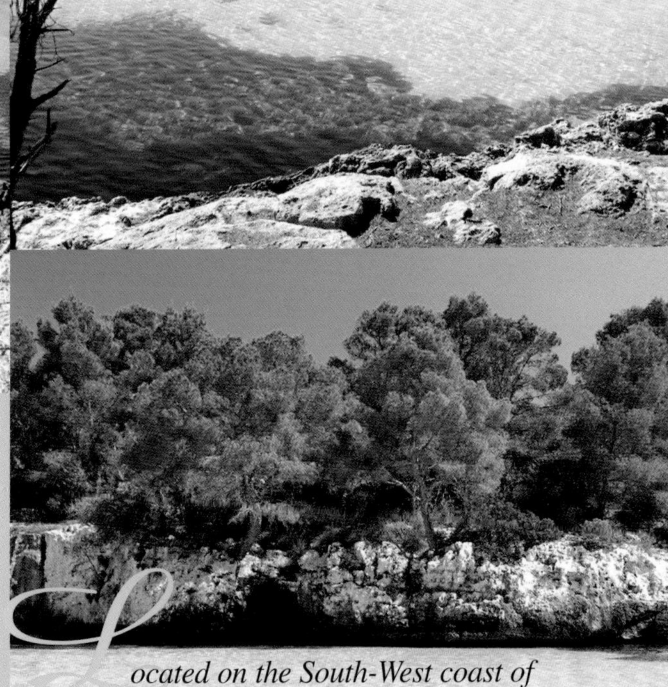

Located on the South-West coast of Minorca in the Balearic archipelago, Cala Turqueta is a typical Mediterranean inlet bathed in turquoise waters.

Outlined by high limestone cliffs and long needles of rock, Calanque d'En Vau is quite simply out of this world. But it needs to be so spectacular because it takes a walk of several hours before you get there.

Airline Companies
Air France, Easyjet, British Airways, Lufthansa, Alitalia.

How to get there
By land: from the village of Cassis, go past the creeks of Port-Miou and Port-Pin, then follow the Gardiole footpath which drops down to the beach across the Vallon d'En-Vau. Count on a walk of 2 to 3 hours.
By sea: by speedboat leaving from the port of Cassis (a 30-minute journey).

Best seasons
May to October

Accommodation
Hotels of all categories at Cassis and Marseilles, guest-houses...

Local cuisine
Provencal cooking is featured: bouillabaisse, seafood, aioli, daube a la provencal, calissons, everything to be washed down with pastis and the local wines…

Shopping
Provencal handicrafts, ceramics, fabrics, olive oil...

What to see
The extraordinary vista from the top of the valley; the neighbouring creeks of Port-Miou and Port-Pin, the species of rare birds which nest in the cliffs (Bonelli's Eagle, Peregrine Falcon, Eagle Owl...)

Activities
Sailing, snorkeling, sea-canoeing, climbing, paragliding, hiking, diving

Budget
Medium

Contact
http://www.tourisme.fr

Surface area
550,000 km²

Population
60 million

Time zone
None

Language
French

Currency
Euro

Documents
Identity card

Health
No vaccination is required

Average temperatures
12 °C winter,
26 °C summer
on the Mediterranean coast

\+ *It's in Provence and nowhere else.*

\- *For experienced hikers...*

On Corsica, twenty kilometres from Bonifacio, Rondinara Beach is an astonishing bay nestled in a pristine natural environment and washed by clear water. In the low season, the tourists give way to the cattle who come enjoy the peace of this superb scenery.

Airline Companies
Air France

How to get there
By plane: the simplest way is to fly to the airport at Figari
By Ferry: regular connections from Marseilles, Toulon and Nice
Leaving Figari, take the N198 to half-way between Bonifacio and Porto-Vecchio. From there, a small winding deserted road leads right to La Rondinara by way of the hamlet of Suartone.

Best seasons
May to October

Accommodation
A camp site close to the beach and hotels of all categories at Bonifacio and Porto-Vecchio.

Local cuisine
Bouillabaisse, bacon and vegetable soup, boar stew, prisuttu (dried ham), figatelli, stuffed aubergines a la sartenaise, Corsican cheeses, canistrellis (almond biscuits)...

Shopping
Corsican handicrafts, wooden sculptures, polyphony recordings...

What to see
The Lavezzi islands 10 km from Bonifaccio; the mountainous formation of Bavella.

Activities
Sailing, water-skiing, snorkeling, VTT, hiking, diving (with, close by, the Bouches de Bonifacio, the Reserves at the Lavezzi and Cerbicales islands as well as several submerged wrecks).

Budget
Rather high unless you are camping

Contact
http://www.tourisme.fr

\+ *Only one hour away from the big city.*

\- *Avoid the high season between July 14 and August 15.*

Clinging to the Cap Corse mountain, the pictuesque village of Nonza floats above the Bay of Saint Florent. Its charcoal grey shingle beach and unobstructed view make it one of the most bewitching sites on the Island of Beauty.

Airline Companies
Air France.

How to get there
By plane: the simplest way is to fly to Bastia.
By ferry: regular connections from Marseilles, Toulon and Nice. To get to Nonza from Bastia (33 km), take the D81 heading west to Patrimonio, then the D80 heading North. From the village, you can reach the beach on foot in fifteen minutes or by car in a couple of minutes.

Best seasons
May to October

Accommodation
Some houses to rent in the village of Nonza, camp sites and hotels at Saint Florent.

Local cuisine
Bouillabaisse, bacon and vegetable soup, boar stew, prisuttu (dried ham), figatelli, stuffed aubergines a la sartenaise, Corsican cheeses, canistrellis (almond biscuits)…

Shopping
Corsican handicrafts, wooden sculptures, polyphony recordings…

What to see
The old Genoese tower perched 150 metres above the sea; the church; the ruins of the convent; the Miraculous Fountain.

Activities
Sailing, snorkeling, paragliding, hiking, diving (in the heart of the Nonza Nature Reserve).

Budget
Medium

Contact
http://www.tourisme.fr

\+ *The beauty of the landscape between sea and mountain.*

\- *Take care on the small roads of Cap Corse !*

GREECE • MYRTOS

Greece, land of myth, with its necklace of islands strung out like so many pearls in the Mediterranean.

Kafalonia, the largest of the Ionian islands, lies to the west of the Greek peninsula. Shaped like a half-moon, the magnificent beach at Myrtos lies hidden underneath steep cliffs, from the top of which you can get a superb view over the bay.

Airline Companies
Air France, Olympic Airways, British Airways, Lufthansa, Alitalia.

How to get there
By plane : some direct flights from Athens
By ferry : A regular connetion from Patras
Once you get to Argostoli, take the road which goes North, towards Assos. Myrtos beach is a short distance away from the village.

Best seasons
May to October

Accommodation
A camp site at Argostoli and some hotels round the island.

Local cuisine
Pasteli (honey and sesame cakes), mezze, salad with kefalotiki (the local goat's cheese), Kefalonia muscat, moussaka, papoutsaki, fish, octopus, lobster...

Shopping
Nougat, olive oil, ceramics, jewelry...

What to see
Mount Ainos where a unique species of fir native to the island grows; the natural fissure filled with sea-water, between Sami and Argostoli; the village of Fiskardo and its houses of many colours.

Activities
Sailing, snorkeling, diving (highly regulated in Greece in order to protect the marine animals and plants).

Budget
Medium.

Contact
http://www.gnto.gr

Surface area
132,914 km²

Population
11 million

Time zone
GMT +2

Language
Greek

Currency
Euro

Documents
Identity card

Health
No vaccination is needed, but take care with the medicines you bring with you: codeine is forbidden.

Average temperatures
15°C winter, 27°C summer

\+ *An explosion of colours !*

\- *Not an ounce of shade...Don't forget a parasol !*

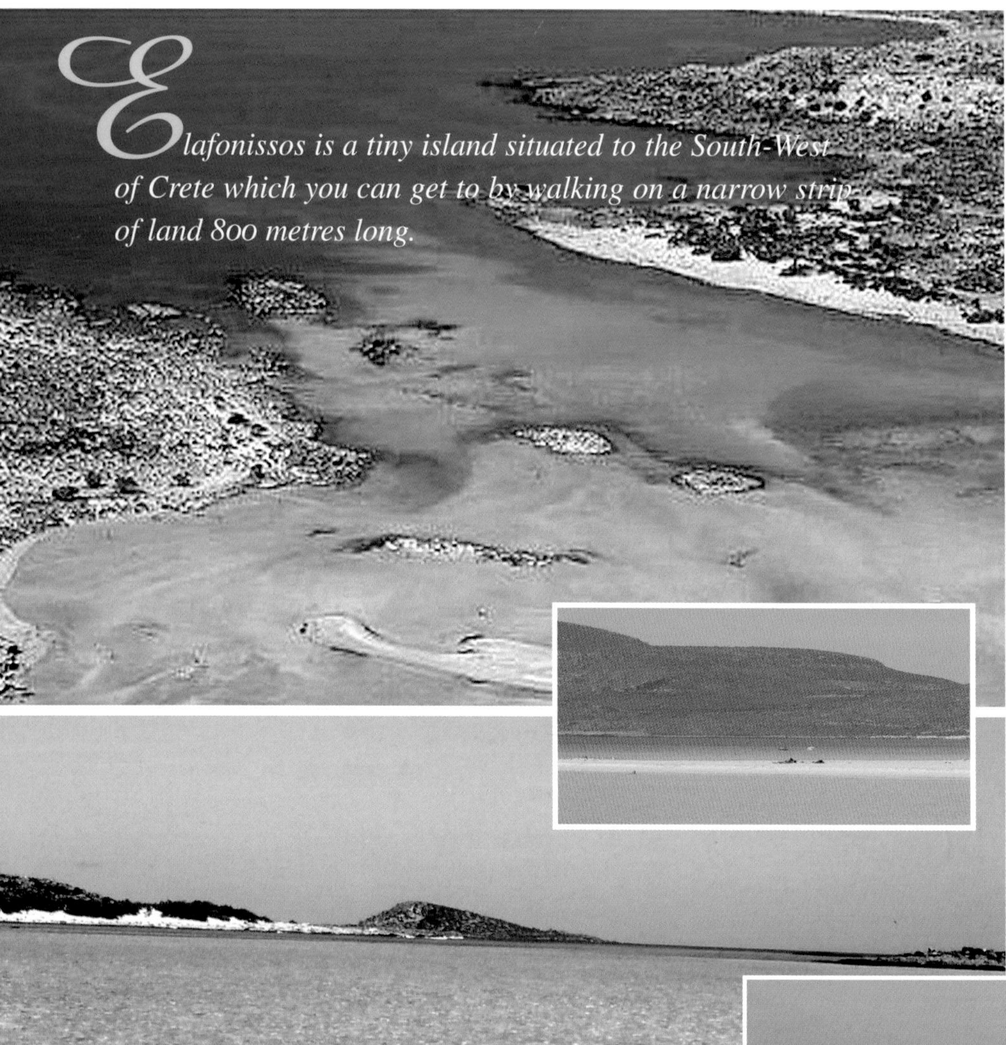

Elafonissos is a tiny island situated to the South-West of Crete which you can get to by walking on a narrow strip of land 800 metres long.

Airline Companies
Air France, Olympic Airways, British Airways, Lufthansa, Alitalia.

How to get there
On the coast road, about 6 km before Neapoli, follow the sign-posts towards Elafonissos. From there, you can take a ferry but when the weather is calm it is very easy to get to the island on foot.

Best seasons
May to October

Accommodation
Camp sites and small hotels in the area.

Local cuisine
Pasteli (honey and sesame cakes), mezze, salad with kefalotiki (the local goat's cheese), local wine, moussaka, papoutsaki, fish, octopus, lobster...

Shopping
Nougat, olive oil, ceramics, jewelry...

What to see
Built on a rock plunging down to the sea, the Monastery of Chrysoskalitissa can be reached by pilgrims taking a curving stairway of 90 steps (legend has it that the last step is made of gold, but only the true believers can see it).

Activities
Admire the superb seashells, take photos of this enchanting and unusual place...

Budget
Medium.

Contact
http://www.gnto.gr

\+ *An unusual very protected spot.*

\- *Inaccessible in bad weather.*

ꟷREATE YOUR OWN MAGIC ON THE ISLAND OF MIRACLES

LA CRETE

Villa Arhanes

creta maris

silva maris

ꟷrt with extraordinary scenery : the beautiful blue-green of the sea, a pristine beach, temperate ꟷys. Add the flamboyance of Zorba the Greek, that life-loving creation of Nikos Kazantzakis, a native of Crete. Good wines; endless feasts. Starting to get the picture?
Can you almost hear the music of the bouzouki?
Take these ingredients that are at the soul of this Greek island, add the beauty, charm and warmth of any of the Maris hotels and you have an unforgettable experience.

creta maris

The Maris Hotels group operates seven distinctive properties on the most beautiful holiday locations of Crete island and consists of :
ꟷeta Maris Hotel, a 5 star beachfront facility with 547 rooms. It provides 68 Conference Halls ꟷring the largest conference hall in the area. ✓Terra Maris Hotel, a 5 star «Ultra All-Inclusive» ꟷllness and Golf Resort with 146 rooms. ✓Silva Maris Hotel, a 4 star beachfront facility with 312 rooms. ✓Bella Maris Hotel, a 5 star beachfront facility with 159 rooms.
ꟷndia Maris Hotel, a 5 star beachfront facility with 257 rooms. ✓Villa Arhanes, a newly restored ꟷnal Cretan mansion converted into 6 attractive apartments, for people who are nature oriented. ꟷdou Villas, set in an organic farm with 8 apartments. ✓«Thalasso» Thalassotherapy Centres within the pleasant environment of the Hotels Candia Maris and Creta Maris.
ꟷris Hotels' Private Football Pitches for professional or amateur training. Every guest will find ꟷedients for an unforgettable experience. While the natural beauty of Crete and the quality ꟷice of the Maris Hotels would suffice to create the ideal environment, a variety of activities are ꟷlable to please even the most discerning of clients. --- or you can design your own custom ꟷram --- to create your own magic on the Island of Miracles --- Crete.

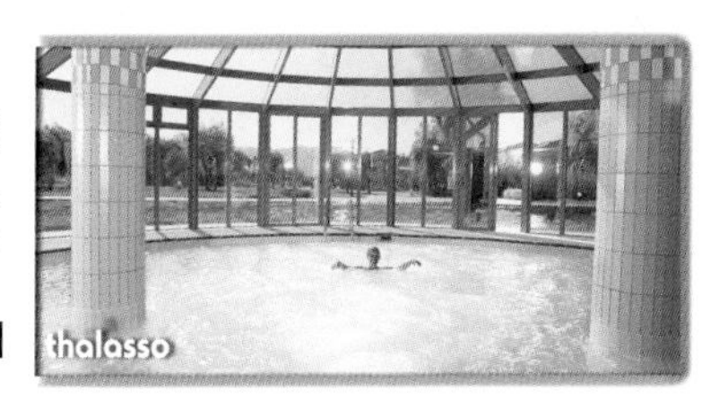

thalasso

For more immediate information on all of the Maris Hotels :
Central Sales & Reservation Office, Dimokratias 15, 71306, Heraklion, Crete, Greece
+30 2810 343110, Fax+30 2810 346088, E-mail: maris@maris.gr, http://www.maris.gr

creta maris Conference Centre

Short hop from the island of Zanta – to the south of Kefalonia –, the wreck at Navagio is discretely hidden at the foot of an immense cliff. Here it isn't sand, just water so blue it looks unreal and large scarlet pebbles which are reflected even in the waves. Surroundings which are perfect for the sea turtles which have been coming here to lay their eggs for nearly 400 years.

GREECE • NAVAGIO

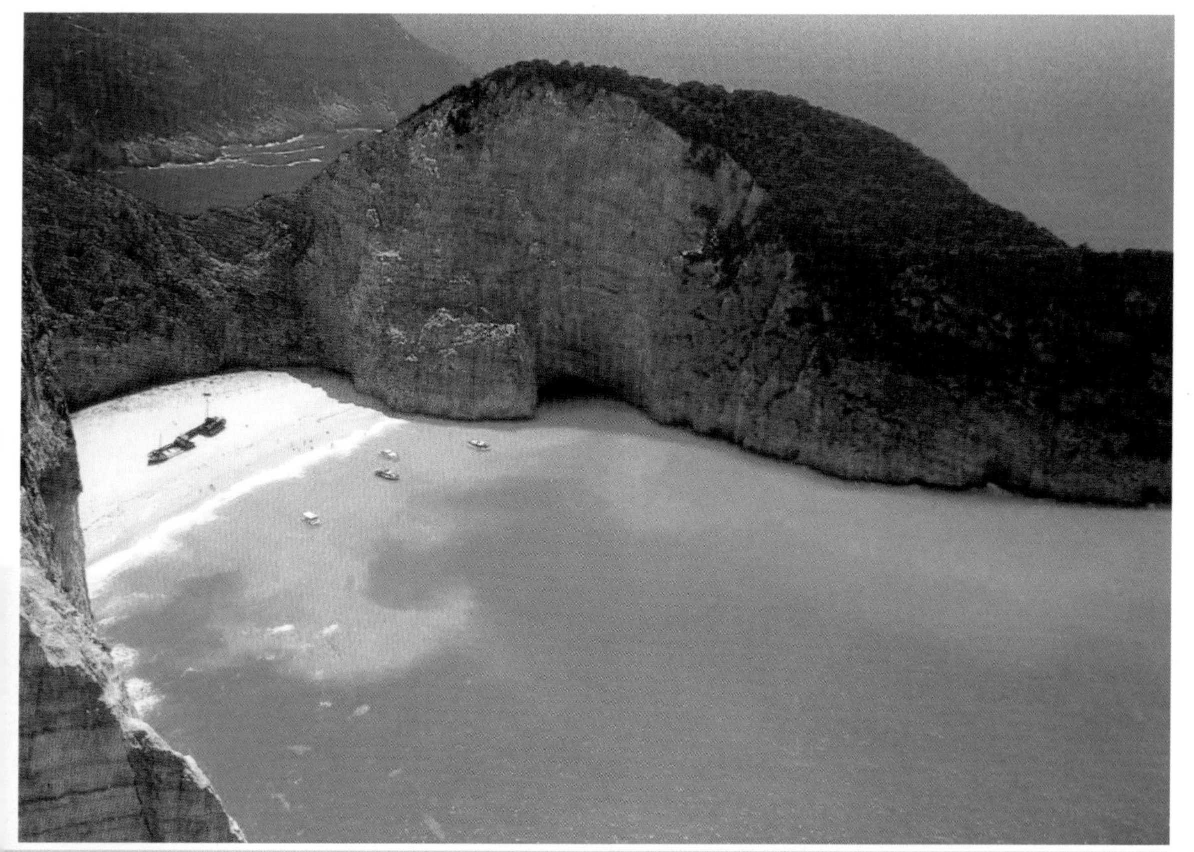

Airline Companies
Air France, Olympic Airways, British Airways, Lufthansa, Alitalia.

How to get there
At Zakinthos, the island's capital, it is easy to hire a boat (with its captain) to go to the beach at Navagio. Don't hesitate to negotiate the price of the trip...

Best seasons
May to October.

Accommodation
No accommodation there, but you can find a place very easily at Zakinthos (camp sites, hotels and vacation rentals).

Local cuisine
Pasteli (honey and sesame cakes), mezze, salad with kefalotiki (the local goat's cheese), local wine, moussaka, papoutsaki, fish, octopus, lobster...

Shopping
Nougat, olive oil, ceramics, jewelry...

What to see
The Byzantine Museum at Zakinthos; the Church of Saint Nikolao; Vassiliki, a picturesque village where you can listen to bouzouki.

Activities
Snorkeling, underwater diving (interesting excursions because of the Caretta turtle found on the island and the many submerged caverns to visit).

Budget
Medium.

Contact
http://www.gnto.gr

+ *The Mediterranean's most beatiful inlet.*

- *The cost of hiring a boat...*

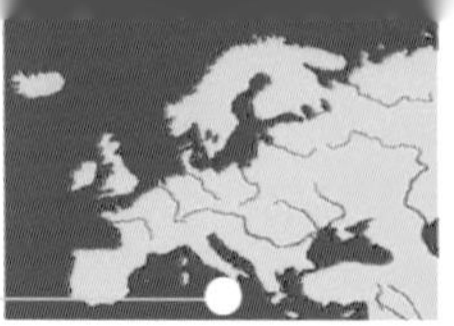

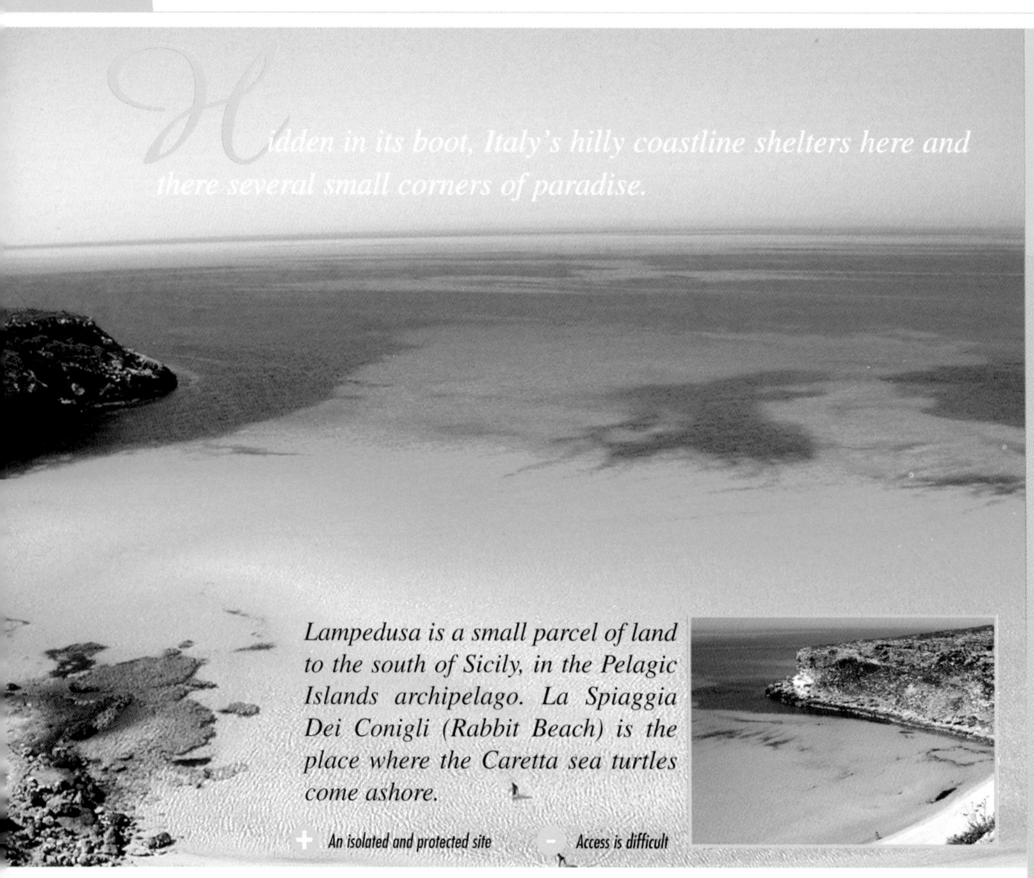

Hidden in its boot, Italy's hilly coastline shelters here and there several small corners of paradise.

Lampedusa is a small parcel of land to the south of Sicily, in the Pelagic Islands archipelago. La Spiaggia Dei Conigli (Rabbit Beach) is the place where the Caretta sea turtles come ashore.

\+ An isolated and protected site

\- Access is difficult

Surface area	**Documents**
302,000 km²	Identity card
Population	**Health**
57.5 million	No vaccination needed
Time zone	**Average temperatures**
GMT +1	12°C winter, 25°C summer
Language	
Italian	
Currency	
Euro	

Airline Companies
Alitalia, Air France, British Airways, Lufthansa.

How to get there
By plane: daily flights provide connections with Palermo and the main Italian cities.
By ferry: from Agrigento in Sicily.
The beach is quite far from the village of Tabaccara. Several buses make the trip, but it is better to get there by car. Take the road south-east, then turn left and head towards the beach for a good fifteen minutes.

Best seasons
May to October

Accommodation
Some small hotels, a camp site at La Roccia and apartments for rent.

Local cuisine
Fish in olive oil and salt, babalucis (small snails cooked in a tomato sauce), silures de Ghedafi (stuffed squid), ricotta prepared on the island in Spring.

Shopping
Lampedusan ceramics, olive oil…

What to see
The small Rabbit Island, which you can reach by swimming because of fairly shallow water for 150 meters.

Activities
Sailing, water-skiing, snorkeling, diving (thanks to the exceptionally clear waters which give 40- to 50-meters visibility), watching the sea turtles lay their eggs.

Budget
Rather high

Contact
http://www.enit.it

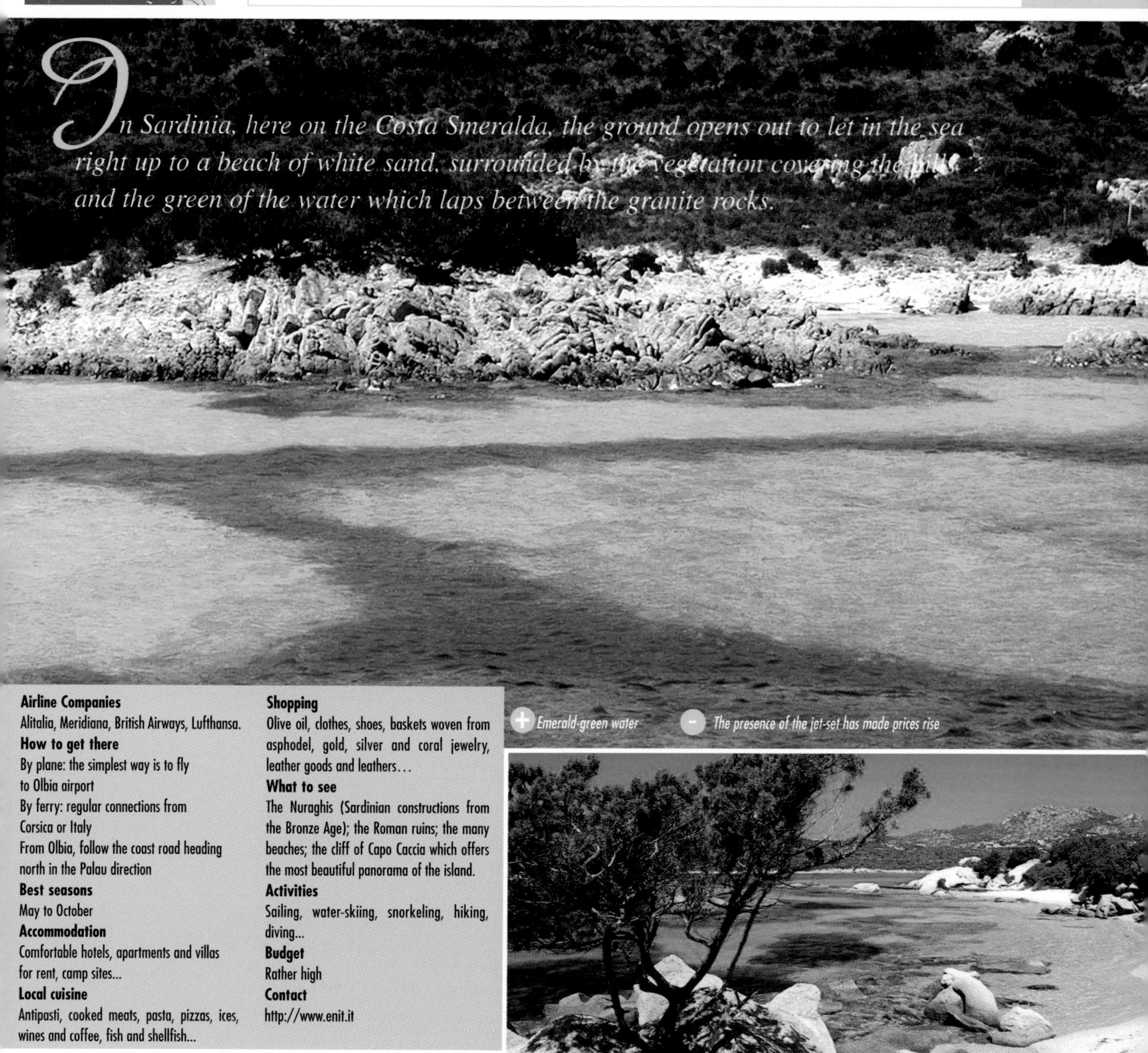

In Sardinia, here on the Costa Smeralda, the ground opens out to let in the sea right up to a beach of white sand, surrounded by the vegetation covering the hills and the green of the water which laps between the granite rocks.

Airline Companies
Alitalia, Meridiana, British Airways, Lufthansa.

How to get there
By plane: the simplest way is to fly to Olbia airport
By ferry: regular connections from Corsica or Italy
From Olbia, follow the coast road heading north in the Palau direction

Best seasons
May to October

Accommodation
Comfortable hotels, apartments and villas for rent, camp sites...

Local cuisine
Antipasti, cooked meats, pasta, pizzas, ices, wines and coffee, fish and shellfish...

Shopping
Olive oil, clothes, shoes, baskets woven from asphodel, gold, silver and coral jewelry, leather goods and leathers…

What to see
The Nuraghis (Sardinian constructions from the Bronze Age); the Roman ruins; the many beaches; the cliff of Capo Caccia which offers the most beautiful panorama of the island.

Activities
Sailing, water-skiing, snorkeling, hiking, diving...

Budget
Rather high

Contact
http://www.enit.it

+ *Emerald-green water*

- *The presence of the jet-set has made prices rise*

Nestled between two rocky outcrops, Capo Vaticano and its azure-blue lagoon are among the most beautiful spots in Calabria.

Airline Companies
Air France, Alitalia, British Airways, Lufthansa.

How to get there
By plane: fly to Lamezia Terme airport, only one hour from Capo Vaticano.
By train: Take a train to Tropea station.
By car: Take the A3 motorway towards Salerno-Reggio Calabria, exit at Pizzo then follow the coast to Tropea and Capo Vaticano.

Best seasons
May to October

Accommodation
Comfortable hotels, apartments and villas for rent nearby

Local cuisine
Antipasti, cooked meats, pasta, pizzas, ices, wines and coffee, fish and shellfish...

Shopping
Olive oil, clothes, shoes, gold, silver and coral jewelry, leather goods and leathers…

What to see
Sicily; the Eolian Islands; more to the north, Abruzzo National Park where you might be lucky and see the bears, wolves and lynx; Naples, Pompei and, in Calabria itself, the Sila massif.

Activities
Sailing, water-skiing, snorkeling, diving, hiking ...

Budget
Rather high

Contact
http://www.enit.it

\+ *The gentle Calabrian way of life.*

\- *Prices tend to skyrocket during the summer season.*

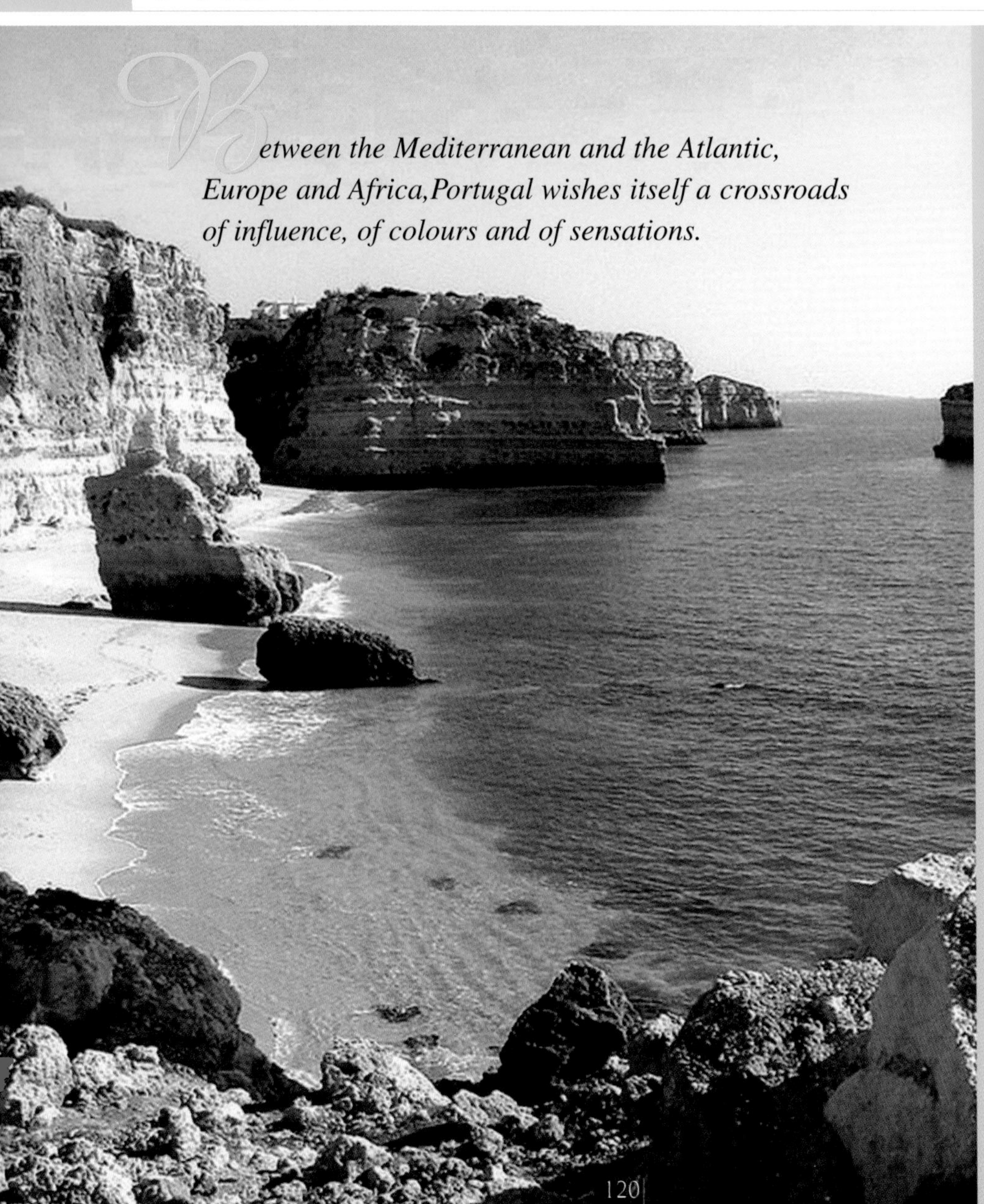

Between the Mediterranean and the Atlantic, Europe and Africa,Portugal wishes itself a crossroads of influence, of colours and of sensations.

Surface area
36,030 km²
Population
10 million
Time zone
GMT +1
Language
Portugese
Currency
Euro

Documents
Identity card
Health
No vaccination is required
Average temperatures
14°C winter, 22°C summer

Airline Companies
Air France, TAP, Alitalia, British Airways, Lufthansa.

How to get there
From Faro, it is best to hire a car or to take a bus to Benagil.

Best seasons
May to October

Accommodation
All categories of hotels, guest-houses, campsites...

Local cuisine
Grilled sardines, cod croquettes, cabbage and potato soup, fish and shellfish. To drink, the delicious wines from Porto.

Shopping
Earthenware, lace, pottery, Port...

What to see
The coast with its 150 km of inlets; Cape Saint Vincent and its high cliffs; the villages with their white houses and the Moorish architecture.

Activities
Sailing, surfing, hiking, VTT, canyoning, horse-riding, diving (some underwater canyons and wrecks are nearby).

Budget
Medium

Contact
http://www.portugal.org

+ *Unique scenery.*

- *The water is a bit cool...*

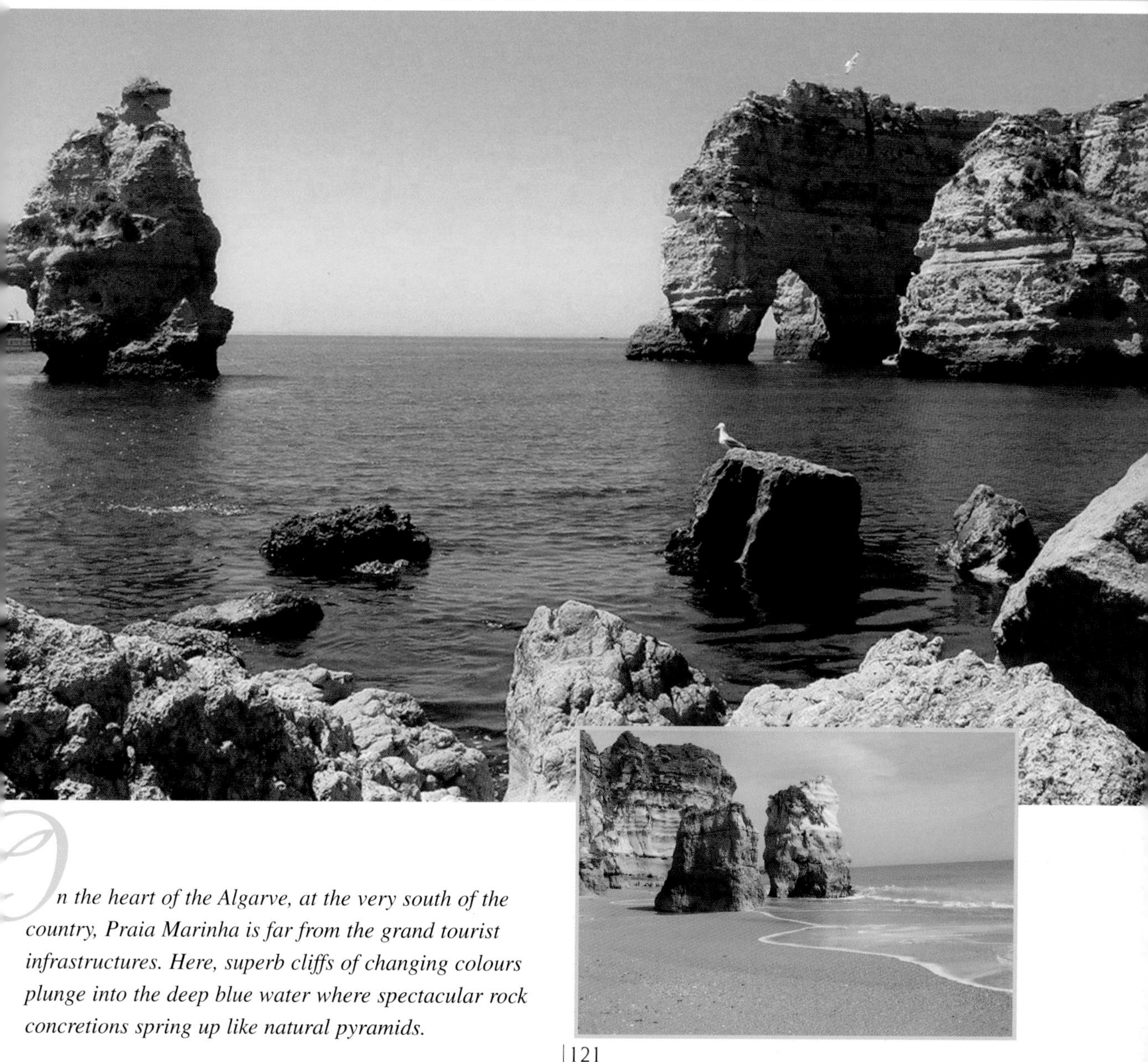

In the heart of the Algarve, at the very south of the country, Praia Marinha is far from the grand tourist infrastructures. Here, superb cliffs of changing colours plunge into the deep blue water where spectacular rock concretions spring up like natural pyramids.

OCEANIA

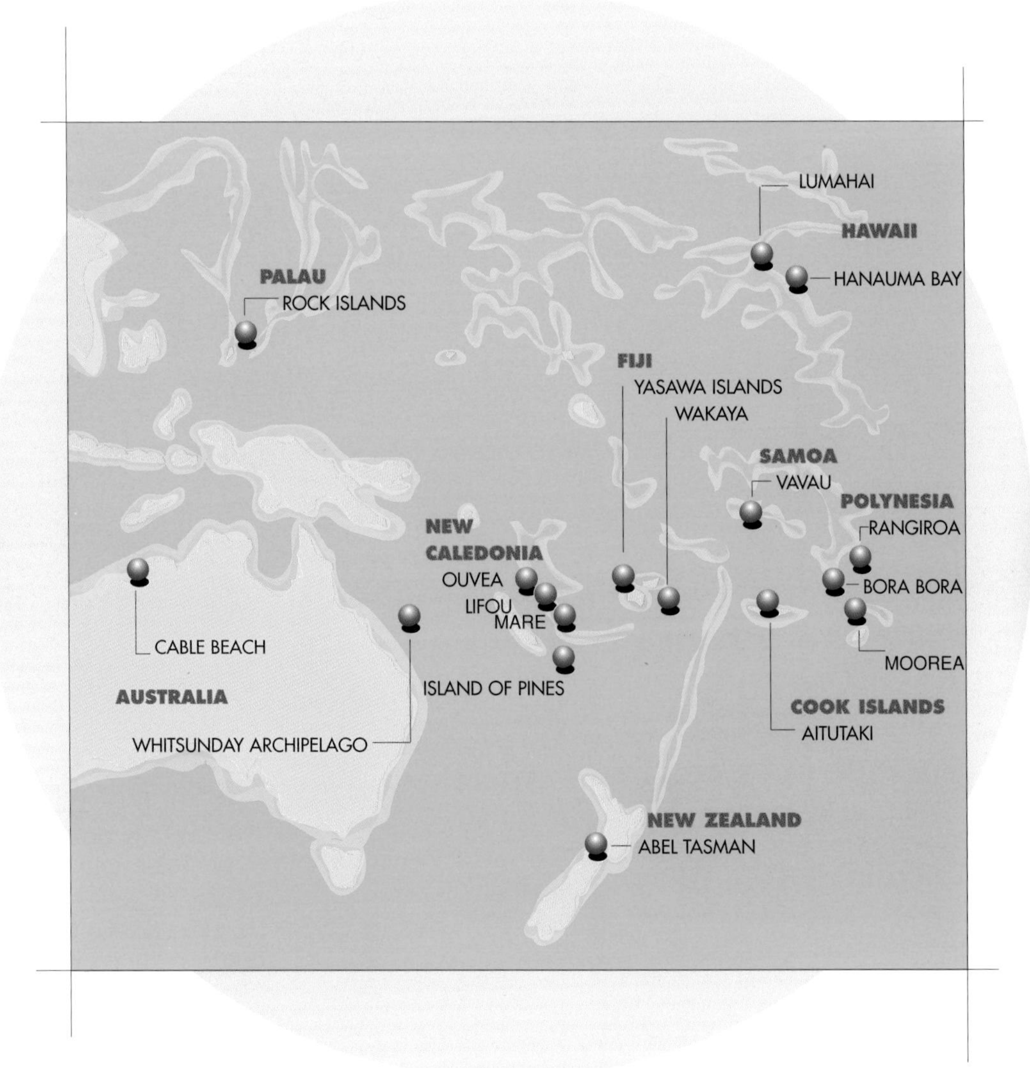

LUMAHAI
HAWAII
HANAUMA BAY
PALAU
ROCK ISLANDS
FIJI
YASAWA ISLANDS
WAKAYA
SAMOA
VAVAU
POLYNESIA
RANGIROA
BORA BORA
MOOREA
NEW CALEDONIA
OUVEA
LIFOU
MARE
ISLAND OF PINES
CABLE BEACH
AUSTRALIA
WHITSUNDAY ARCHIPELAGO
COOK ISLANDS
AITUTAKI
NEW ZEALAND
ABEL TASMAN

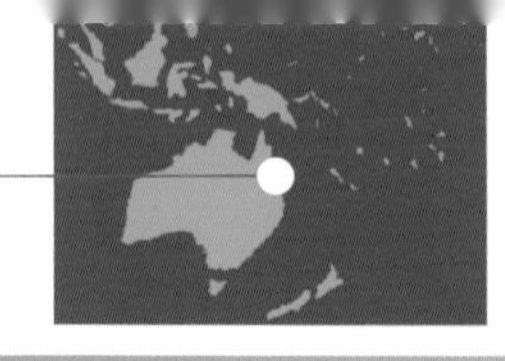

An island the size of a continent, unusual landscapes and a culture 40 thousand years old: welcome to Australia.

AUSTRALIA • WHITSUNDAYS ARCHIPELAGO

Surface area
7,682,300 km²
Population
19 million
Time zone
From GMT +8 to GMT+10
Language
English, aboriginal languages
Currency
Australian dollar
Documents
Currently valid passport +
Visa (ETA - electronic travel authority)
Health
No vaccination is required however watch out for loiasis, a viral illness transmitted by mosquitoes.
Average temperatures
11°C winter,
23°C summer (Sydney)

In the north-east of the country, the Whitsundays archipelago is made up of 160 small lush islets sometimes joined to each other by endless sandbanks of an almost unreal whiteness. Offshore, the fabulous Australian Barrier Reef of coral and the unique animal life found there have made this a paradise for divers and yachtsment.

Airline Companies
Qantas, British Airways, Singapore Airlines, Malaysian Airlines, Cathay Pacific, Thai Airways, Lufthansa.
How to get there
By plane: the best way is to take an internal flight to Prosperpine or Hamilton Island.
By bus: go from Brisbane or Cairns to Airlie Beach or Shuttle Harbour, from where you take a boat to the Whitsundays.
Best seasons
May to October The water is always between 24°C and 27°C all the year.
Accommodation
All categories of hotels, motels, B&Bs, camp-sites, resorts...
Local cuisine
Aboriginee bush cooking is very popular (braised kangaroo tail samosas, emu pate, eucalyptus-smoked game) but of course the fish and seafood have pride of place in the archipelago.
Shopping
Aboriginee handicrafts (didgeridoos, boomerangs, bark paintings...), dotted paintings, batiks, sculptures, jewelry (opals and pearls)...
What to see
Navigate the islands and explore the archipelago: and so satisfy your thirst for adventure!
Activities
Sailing, water-skiing, snorkeling, fishing, parasailing, diving (excursions to the longest coral barrier reef in the world).
Budget
Rather high
Contact
http://www.australia.com

+ *160 island paradises to explore.*

- *Look out for the sharks !*

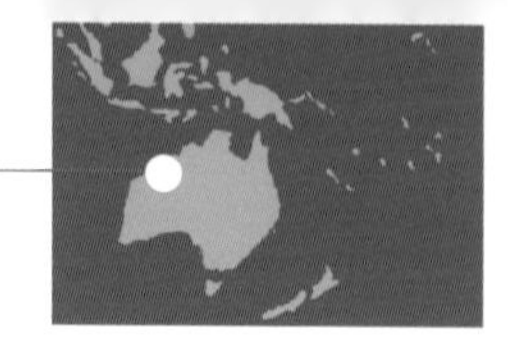

In the North-West, on the edge of the Indian Ocean, its 22 km of white sand has made Cable Beach one of the wildest and most popular destinations of the Australian continent.

+ Unforgettable sunsets

- A very strong tide

Airline Companies
Qantas, British Airways, Singapore Airlines, Malaysian Airlines, Cathay Pacific, Thai Airways, Lufthansa.

How to get there
By plane: the best way is to take an internal flight to Broome.
By bus or by car: if you don't mind long journeys.

Best seasons
In the Broome area, the Australian summer means rains and tropical heat. From April to October, you can visit the region while the climate is milder.

Accommodation
From the Inn for backpackers through to luxury hotels, as well as the B&Bs, motels and even a camp site near the beach.

Local cuisine
Broome has a lot of Indonesian, Thai, Chinese and Japanese restaurants. Local specialities include lots of fish and seafood (eels, salmon, oysters, mussels, crawfish, barramundis…), not to forget the famous Bush dishes (braised kangaroo-tail samosas, emu pate, eucalyptus-smoked game).

Shopping
Pearls, precious stones, Aboriginal handicrafts (didgeridoos, boomerangs, bark paintings..)…

What to see
At Broome, the Chinatown area, the Indiginous Art galeries and the Crocodile Park; the Bird Observatory at Roebuck Bay.

Activities
Sailing, surfing, camel-back rides on the beach, fishing, VTT, diving (two hours journey from Broome, the site at Rowley Shoals is famous for its coral gardens).

Budget
Medium

Contact
http://www.australia.com

Surface area
18,274 km²

Population
832 500

Time zone
GMT +12

Language
English, Hindi, Fijian

Currency
Fiji dollar

Documents
A free 4-week visa is given to tourists carrying a currently valid passport.

Health
Anti-malaria treatment

Average temperatures
26°C winter, 29°C summer

Airline Companies
Air New Zealand

How to get there
By plane: small planes provide connections in the archipelago.
By boat: many ferries make the crossing from Nadi

Best seasons
The dry season, from May to October.

Accommodation
A number of luxury hotels on Turtle Island, Waya Island, Tavewa Island and Yasawa Island.

Local cuisine
Kakoda (fish with coconut and lime), cassava (tapioca baked in the oven with coconut milk, cane sugar and banana), tropical fruit...

Shopping
Local handicrafts (plates, statuettes, pottery...), mother-of-pearl jewelry, pearls, decorated musical instruments, paintings on wood, spices...

What to see
Suva, the capital on Viti Levu with its cathedral, its museum and its market; Navala, one of the most picturesque villages in the archipelago.

Activities
Sailing, water-skiing, snorkeling, rafting, hiking, horse riding, bird watching, diving (among the most beautiful seabeds in Melanesia).

Budget
Rather high

Contact
http://www.bulafiji.com

Somewhere in the South Pacific, north-east of New Caledonia, the Fiji archipelago - once known as the « Cannibal Islands » - is made up of 332 small atolls of soft coral, all as charming and as beautiful as anything.

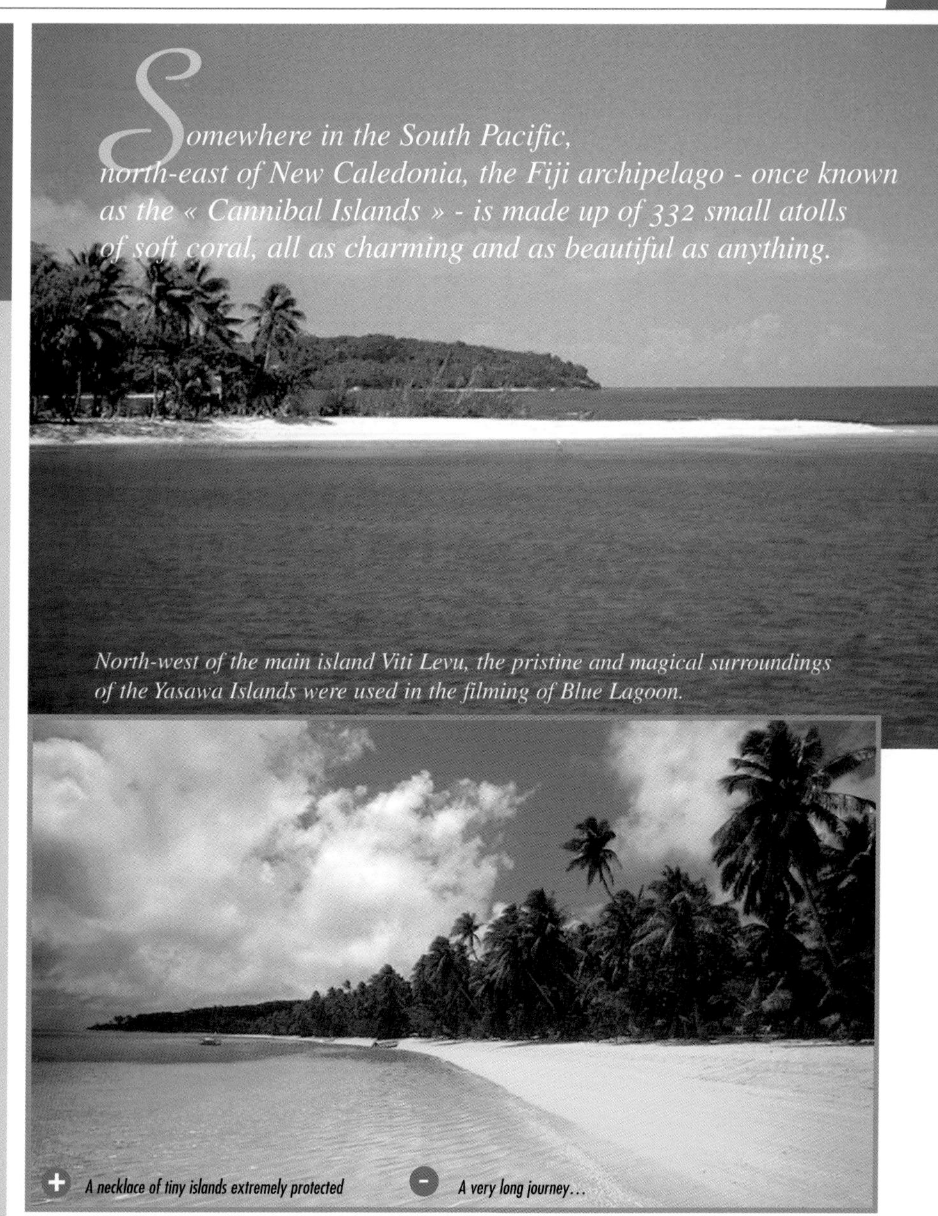

North-west of the main island Viti Levu, the pristine and magical surroundings of the Yasawa Islands were used in the filming of Blue Lagoon.

+ *A necklace of tiny islands extremely protected*

- *A very long journey...*

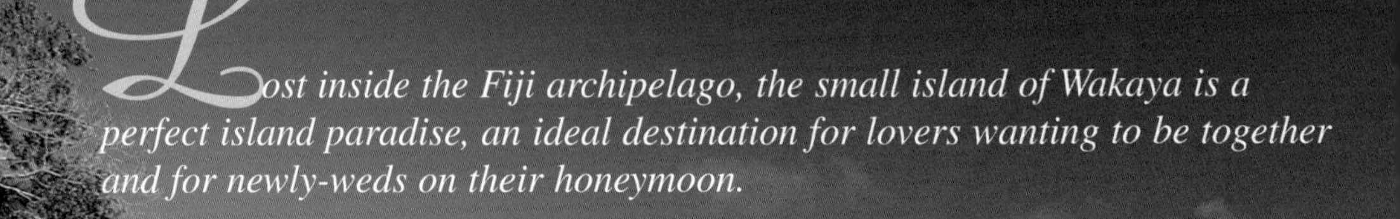

Lost inside the Fiji archipelago, the small island of Wakaya is a perfect island paradise, an ideal destination for lovers wanting to be together and for newly-weds on their honeymoon.

+ *You are all alone...*
- *There is only one hotel*

Airline Companies
Air New Zealand.
How to get there
From Nadi International Airport, count on a 40-minute flight.
Best seasons
The dry season, from May to October.

Accommodation
A top class hotel.
Local cuisine
Kakoda (fish with coconut and lime), cassava (tapioca baked in the oven and grilled with coconut milk, cane sugar and banana) tropical fruit...

Shopping
Local handicrafts (plates, statuettes, pottery...), mother-of-pearl jewelry, pearls, decorated musical instruments, paintings on wood, spices...
What to see
Suva, the capital on Viti Levu with its cathedral, its museum and its market; Navala, one of the most picturesque villages in the archipelago.
Activities
Sailing, water-skiing, snorkeling, diving...

Budget
Very high
Contact
http://www.bulafiji.com

Surface area
16,600 km²
Population
1.2 million
Time zone
GMT -10
Language
English and Hawaian
Currency
Dollar
Documents
Currently valid passport

Health
Vaccination against both Hepatitis and typhoid recommended. Preventative anti-mosquito treatment against dengue fever.
Average temperatures
22°C winter, 28°C summer

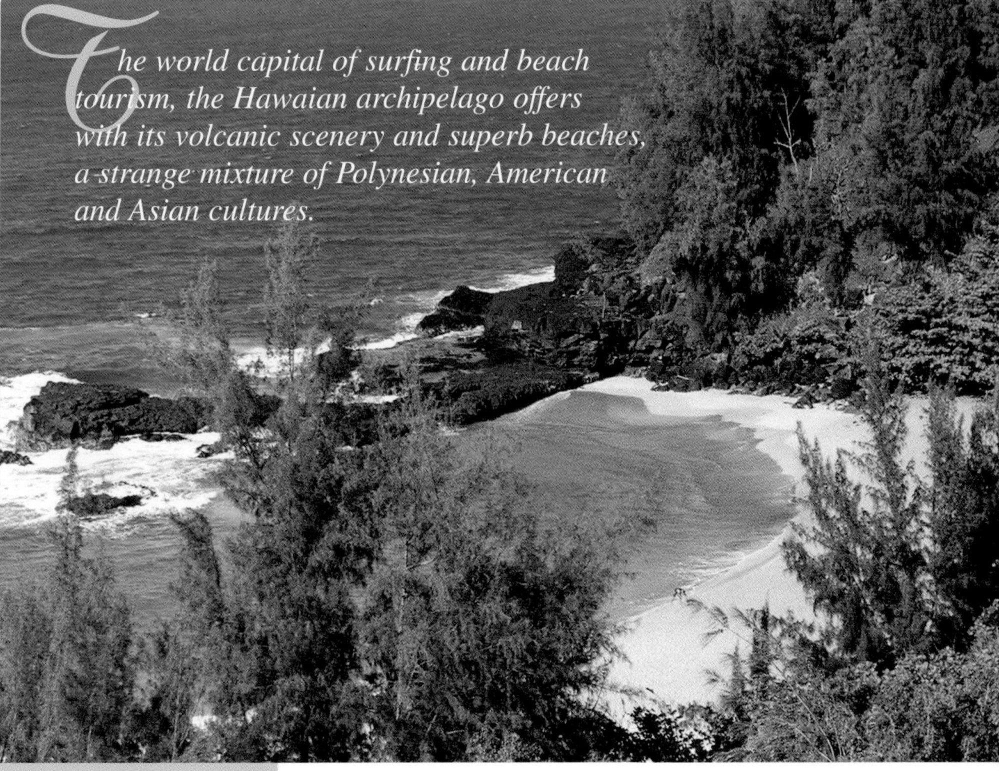

The world capital of surfing and beach tourism, the Hawaian archipelago offers with its volcanic scenery and superb beaches, a strange mixture of Polynesian, American and Asian cultures.

Airline Companies
United Airlines
How to get there
Follow the A59 heading north to the town of Hanalei, then turn left after the market and take the small track which goes down to the beach.
Best seasons
Throughout the year, even if the prices are more affordable from April to October.
Accommodation
No accommodation immediately next to the beach, but the island offers a vast choice of hotels of all categories and B&Bs.
Local cuisine
Malihini (chicken stewed in coconut milk with pieces of pineapple), laulaus (pieces of salted fish, pork, beef and taro cooked in ti leaves), salmon lomi-lomi (a mixture of smoked salmon, tomatoes and shallots served with crushed ice), taro (local vegetable), wild pig, ignames, breadfruit…
Shopping
Fabric made from beaten bark, patchwork, necklaces of shells or flowers, surf-boards...
What to see
Hanakapi'ai Falls, breathtaking waterfalls wahich were named after a Hawaian princess; Queen's Bath, a natural swimming pool carved out of a lava hollow; Waimea Canyon, the biggest canyon in the Pacific.
Activities
Sailing, surfing, water-skiing, snorkeling, hiking, fishing, diving...
Budget
Rather high
Contact
http://www.visit.hawai.org

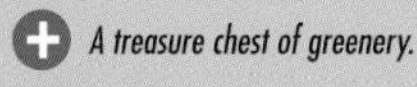

+ *A treasure chest of greenery.*

- *Currents are sometimes dangerous.*

At the North-west point on the island of Kauai - which the Hawaians call the Garden Island - Lumahai beach is sheltered at the foot of magnificent cliffs down which tumbles lush vegetation that is reflected in the blue ocean.

On the island of Oahu, Hanauma Bay is a spectacular beach nestled in an ancient volcanic crater open to the ocean. Declared an underwater National Park, she is a delight for divers.

Airline Companies
United Airlines

How to get there
From Waikiki, head east to Hawai Kai then take the A72 which leads to Hanauma Bay.

Best seasons
Throughout the year, even if the prices are more affordable from April to October.

Accommodation
Bungalows, hotels of all categories and B&B.

Local cuisine
Malihini (chicken stewed in coconut milk with pieces of pineapple), laulaus (pieces of salted fish, pork, beef and taro cooked in ti leaves), salmon lomi-lomi (a mixture of smoked salmon, tomatoes and shallots served with crushed ice), taro (local vegetable), wild pig, ignames, breadfruit…

Shopping
Fabric made from beaten bark, patchwork, necklaces of shells or flowers, surf-boards...

What to see
North of Hanauma Bay is Diamond Head lighthouse, built on the extinct volcano of the same name in 1899; the Blowhole, a lava tube into which sea water is driven until being thrown violently up into the sky like a geyser; Dole Pineapple, a pineapple plantation at Kamehameha which preserves the ancient agricultural traditions.

Activities
Sailing, surfing, water-skiing, snorkeling, hiking, fishing, diving...

Budget
Rather high

Contact
http://www.visit.hawai.org

+ *A curved-out beach in a volcano.*
- *Watch out for the jelly fish and the slippery and sharp lava rocks !*

Discovered in 1777 by Captain James Cook, these 15 islands are scattered over more than 2 million km² between Samoa and Tahiti like so many pieces of paradise on earth...

Surface area
2 million km²
Population
18 000
Time zone
GMT -10
Language
Maori, English
Currency
New Zealand dollar
Documents
The Cook Islands are an autonomous territory of New Zealand A passport is all you need for stays of under three months.
Health
No vaccination is required
Average temperatures
24°C winter, 29°C summer

Airline Companies
Air New Zealand.
How to get there
It takes over 33 hours flying – via New Zealand - to get to Rarotonga, the capital of the Cook Islands. Air Rarontonga then flies to Aitutaki island in under an hour.

Best seasons
June to October
Accommodation
Resorts and bungalows with complete amenities
Local cusine
Mitiore (fermented seafood with coconut), tiopu kuru (breadfruit with chicken, pork and coconut),

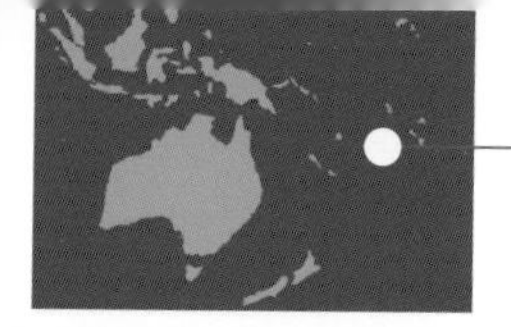

With a triangular shape, Aitutaki Atoll - called the blue lagoon by by the native people - consists of 3 volcanic islets and 12 coral islets. It is, on its own, emblematic of the Cook Islands archipelago.

+ *One of the world's most beautiful lagoons.*

- *The flight is never-ending.*

ika mata (raw fish with coconut), traditional salad with papaya...

Shopping

Black pearls, wood or stone sculptures in the Polynesian style, «rito» hats, tivaivai (patchwork)...

What to see

The town of Rarotonga; the church and market at Arutanga; One Foot Island.

Activities

Sailing, snorkeling, fishing, excursions to neighbouring islands, diving (on the coral reef to the East of the atoll)...

Budget

Rather high

Contact

http://cook-islands.com

*Lost in the vast Pacific Ocean,
New Caledonia is a subtle mix of Melanesia, Asia and France.*

Surface area
18,578 km²
Population
220 000
Time zone
GMT +11
Language
French and 24 Kanak languages
Currency
Pacific Franc
Documents
No visa required for European Union nationals.
Health
No vaccination resuired
Average temperatures
19°C winter, 26°C summer

NEW CALEDONIA • ISLAND OF PINES

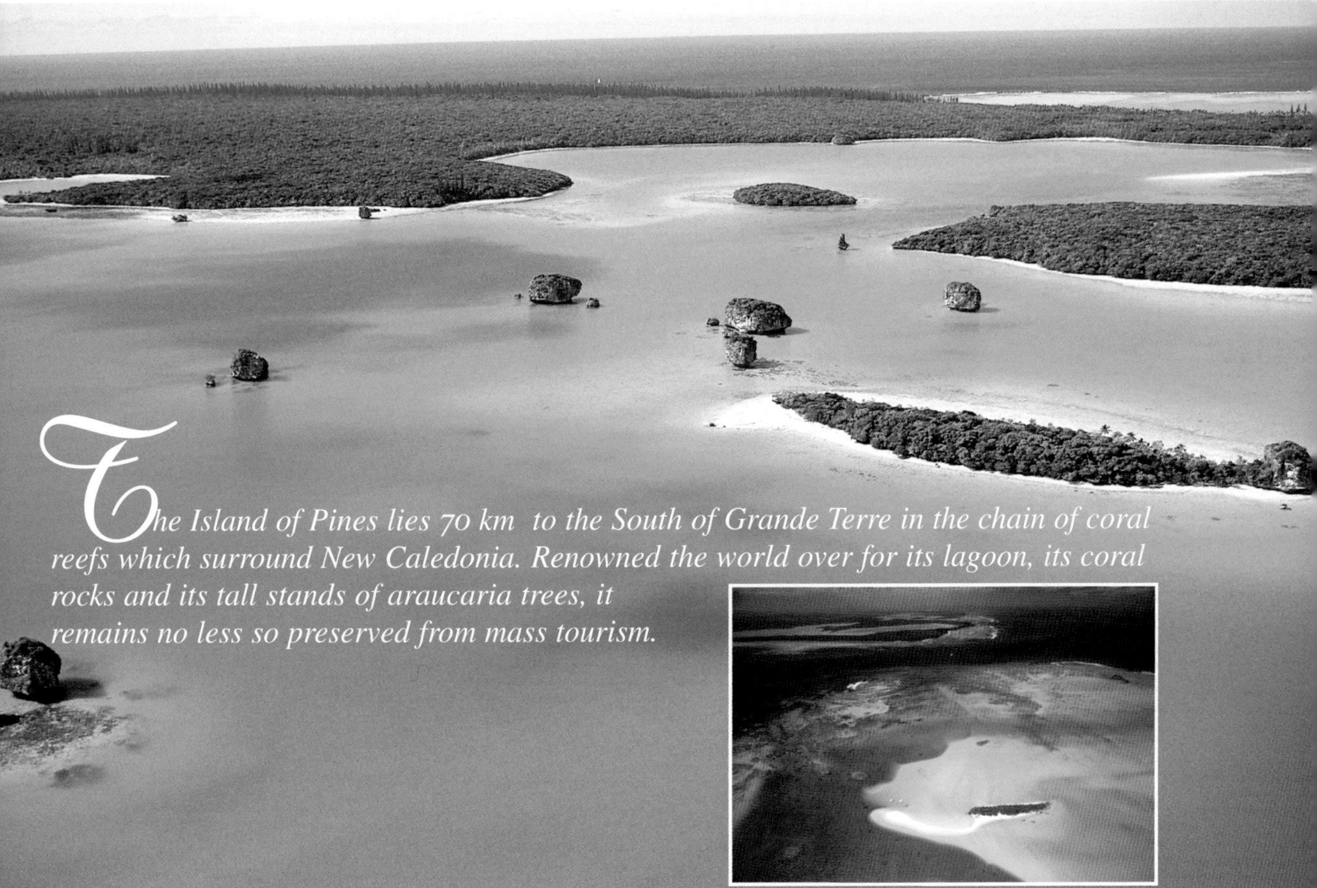

The Island of Pines lies 70 km to the South of Grande Terre in the chain of coral reefs which surround New Caledonia. Renowned the world over for its lagoon, its coral rocks and its tall stands of araucaria trees, it remains no less so preserved from mass tourism.

Airline Companies
Air France, Qantas, Air New Zealand.

How to get there
By plane: the island is served by daily connections from Noumea (allow for a half-hour flight).
By boat: a catamaran links Noumea and the Island of Pines in 2 hours 15 minutes.

Best seasons
Avoid the rainy season between January and April

Accommodation
Camp-sites, B&B, bungalows and hotels offering full amenities in a typically Melanesian decor.

Local cuisine
«Bulime» snails, bougna (meat, fish or vegetables cooked in banana leaves and cocnut milk), igname, taro, crayfish, fish, coconut crab, banana, coconut…

Shopping
Wooden sculptures, hand-painted fabrics, polished shells, Caledonian stones, local music CDs, vanilla...

What to see
The caves of Oumagne, Ouatchia and La Troisieme; Pic Nga (262 m); the ruins of the old prison; on Grande Terre, the Jean-Marie Tjibaou Centre.

Activities
Sailing, snorkeling, diving (the New Caledonian seabed is one of the most lavish in the whole world). The favourite activity of the island is above all the canoe trip.
From Saint Joseph Bay, near the village of Vao, you can take a day trip out to visit the islets in Upi Bay, or else to visit Oro Bay and its celebrated natural swimming pool.

Budget
Rather high.

Contact
http://www.nouvellecaledonietourisme-sud.com

+ *If paradise still existed…*

− *A very remote destination.*

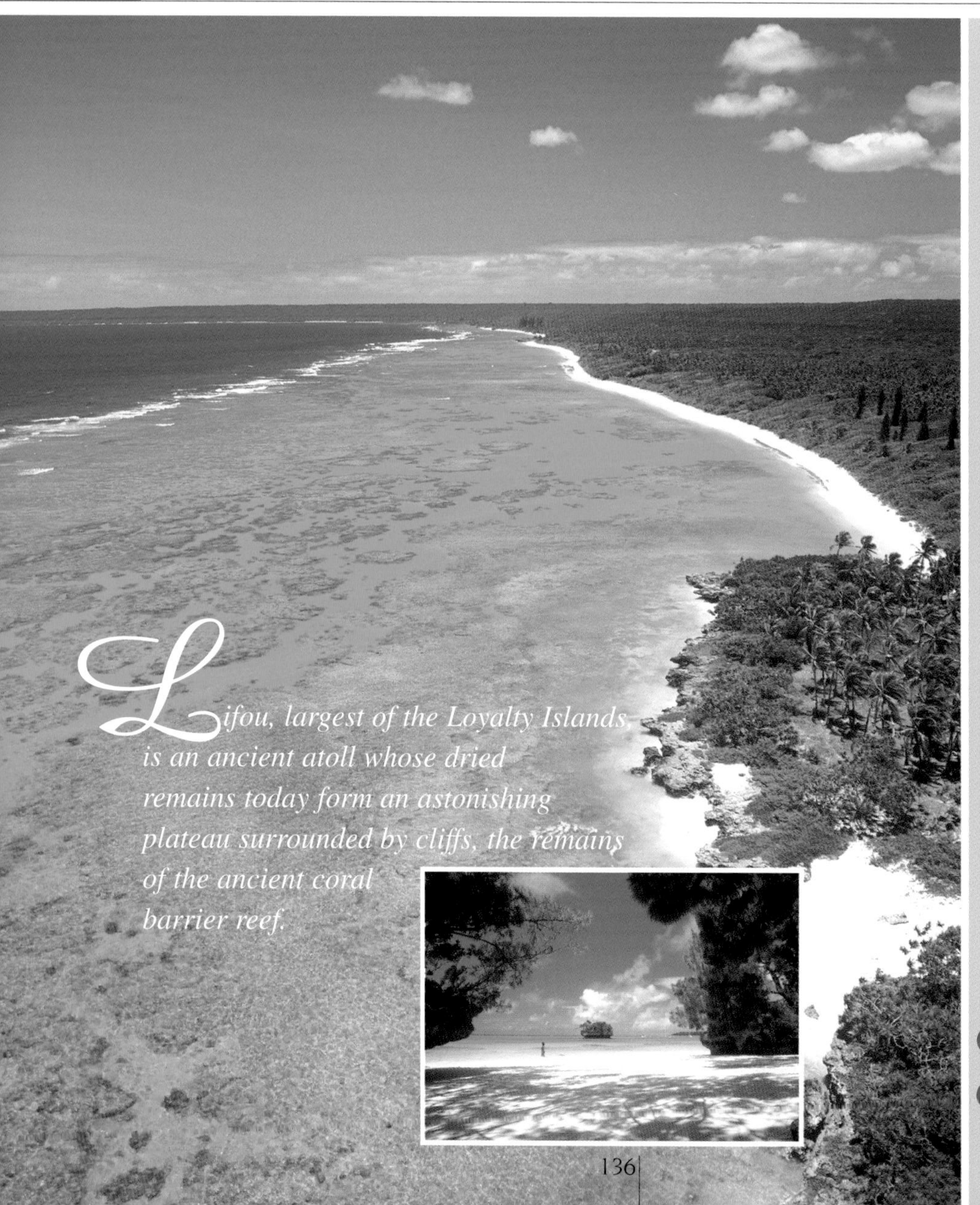

Lifou, largest of the Loyalty Islands, is an ancient atoll whose dried remains today form an astonishing plateau surrounded by cliffs, the remains of the ancient coral barrier reef.

Airline Companies
Air France, Qantas, Air New Zealand.

How to get there
By plane:
from Noumea the flight takes 35 minutes.
By boat:
from Port Moselle (4-1/2 hours journey).

Best seasons
Avoid the rainy season between January and April.

Accommodation
There is a de-luxe hotel, but you can also rent a place in one of the ravishing Melanesian huts.

Local cuisine
«Bulime» snails, bougna (meat, fish or vegetables cooked in banana leaves and cocnut milk), igname, taro, crayfish, fish, coconut crab, banana, coconut…

Shopping
Wooden sculptures, hand-painted fabrics, polished shells, Caledonian stones, local music CDs, vanilla...

What to see
The high plunging cliffs at Joking, in the north of Lifou; the Hermit Crab trail (the Hmelek tribe); the caves (Quajo in Qanono, Xodre, the Devil's Cave); the vanilla plantations.

Activities
Sailing, snorkeling, game fishing, hiking, diving (the New Caledonian seabed is one of the most lavish in the whole world).

Budget
Prices lower if you choose to stay in a B&B.

Contact
http://www.loyalty-islands.com

+ *The scenery out of a post card and the Kanak culture.*

- *You need authorisation to visit some tribal areas.*

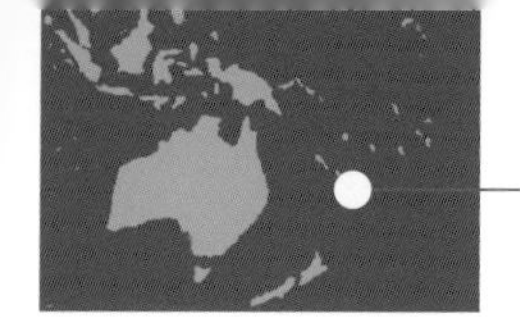

Mare, with a population of 7,000, is renowned for its hospitality and its easy living. Advantages which, added to the pristine scenery, make it a not-to-be-missed part of any visit to the Loyalty Islands.

Airline Companies
Air France, Qantas, Air New Zealand.
How to get there
By plane:
from Noumea the flight takes 35 minutes
By boat:
from Grande Terre, allow for a journey of 5 hours.
Best seasons
Avoid the rainy season between January and April

Accommodation
Hotels, comfortable bungalows and some guest-houses.
Local cuisine
«Bulime» snails, bougna (meat, fish or vegetables cooked in banana leaves and cocnut milk), igname, taro, crayfish, fish, coconut crab, banana, coconut…
Shopping
Wooden sculptures, hand-painted fabrics, polished shells, Caledonian stones, local music CDs...
What to see
The Karnak tribes and their traditions; the Bone Hole, a cave surrounded by banyan roots; the Natural Aquarium, a water hole set back from the sea where you can admire the many colured fish.
Activities
Sailing, snorkeling, game fishing, hiking, diving (the New Caledonian seabed is one of the most lavish in the whole world).

Budget
Medium
Contact
http://www.loyalty-islands.com

+ *The friendly and welcoming people.*

- *The inter-island transfers end up by adding to costs.*

A magic lagoon and unbelievably turquoise water, Ouvea owes its unusual arced shape to the upheaval of the atoll that itused to be.

NEW CALEDONIA • OUVEA

Airline Companies
Air France, Qantas, Air New Zealand.

How to get there
By plane: from Noumea.
By boat: from Grande Terre,
allow 7-1/2 hours travelling.

Best seasons
Avoid the rainy season between January and April.

Accommodation
A de-luxe hotel or some rooms in local houses.

Local cuisine
«Bulime» snails, bougna (meat, fish or vegetables cooked in banana leaves and cocnut milk), igname, taro, crayfish, fish, coconut crab, banana, coconut…

Shopping
Wooden sculptures, hand-painted fabrics, polished shells, Caledonian stones, local music CDs...

What to see
Fayaoue beach with its 25 km of sand and coconut trees; the Blue Hole of Anawa, where sea water and fresh water do not mix and which acts as a swimming pool for the island's children; the grey cliffs of Lekine which plunge into the bay.

Activities
Sailing, snorkeling, game fishing, hiking, diving (resplendant waters filled with multi-coloured corals and slow-moving turtles).

Budget
Rather high.

Contact
http://www.loyalty-islands.com

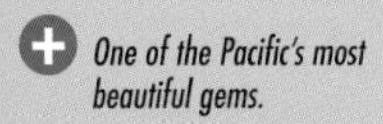

+ *One of the Pacific's most beautiful gems.*

- *You have to book in advance if you want to find a place.*

NEW ZEALAND • ABEL TASMAN

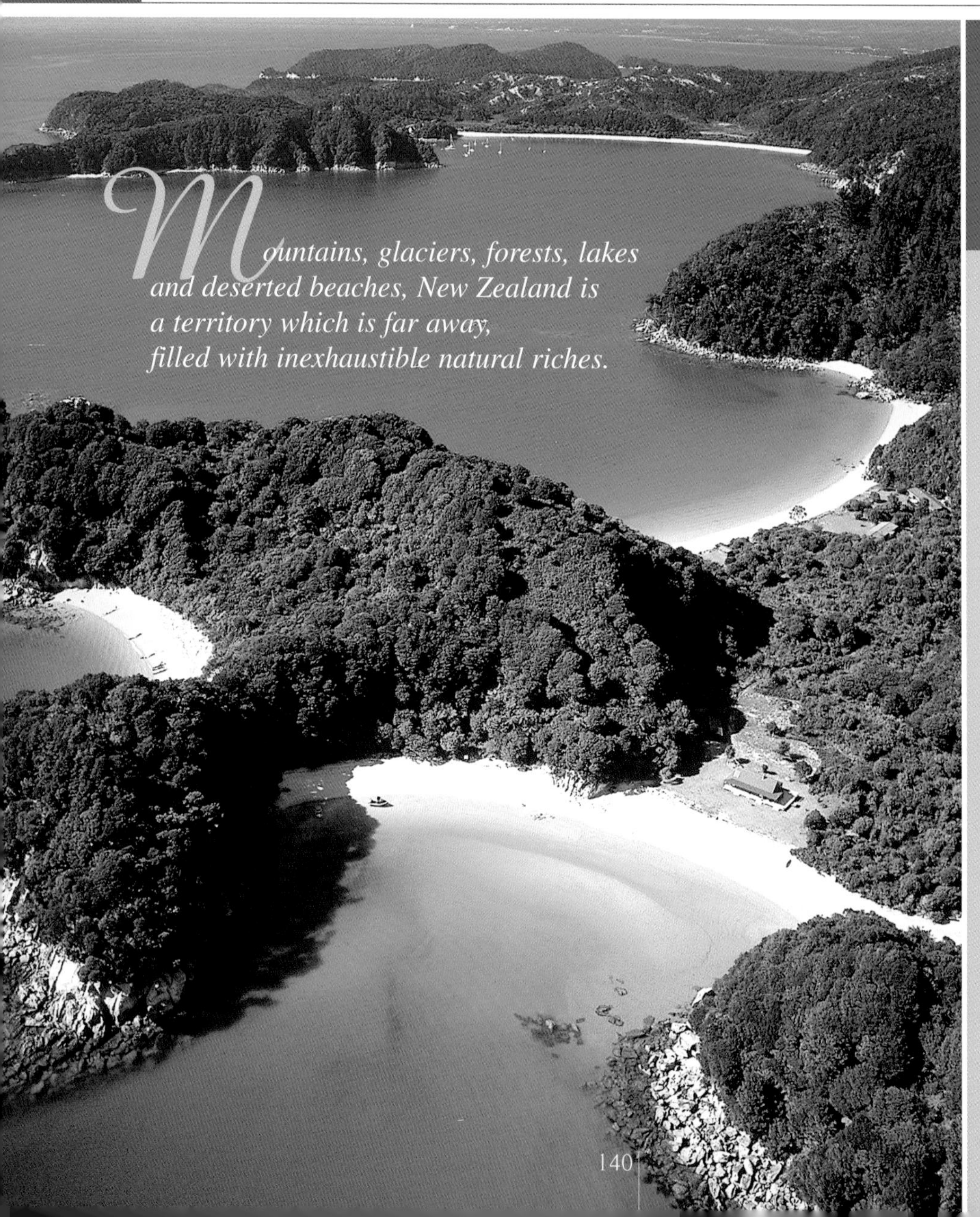

Mountains, glaciers, forests, lakes and deserted beaches, New Zealand is a territory which is far away, filled with inexhaustible natural riches.

Surface area
270,534 km²
Population
3.8 million
Time zone
GMT +12
Language
English and Maori
Currency
New Zealand dollar
Documents
Currently valid passport
Health
No vaccination is required
Average temperatures
12°C winter, 21°C summer

Airline Companies
Air New Zealand, British Airways.
How to get there
By plane: from Wellington, take a flight to Nelson (allow for a 30-minute flight)
By ferry: regular connections leave from Picton
Best seasons
December to February
Accommodation
Hotels of all categories, camp-sites, motels and B&B around Nelson.
Local cuisine
Dishes based on lamb, beef or pork, kumara (a natural sweet potato), kiwis, salmon, local wines...
Shopping
Maori handicrafts, jewelry, pottery, baskets, sheepskins...
What to see
Parallel the Park along the coast road; climb Takaka Hill, a hill which verges on 900 metres in height; at Nelson, Founder's Park and the Cathedral.
Activities
Sailing, snorkeling, fishing, diving, paragliding, VTT, climbing, rafting, hiking...
Budget
Medium.
Contact
http://www.tourisminfo.govt.nz

 *The beaches rimmed by the bush.*

 *The cost of the trip.*

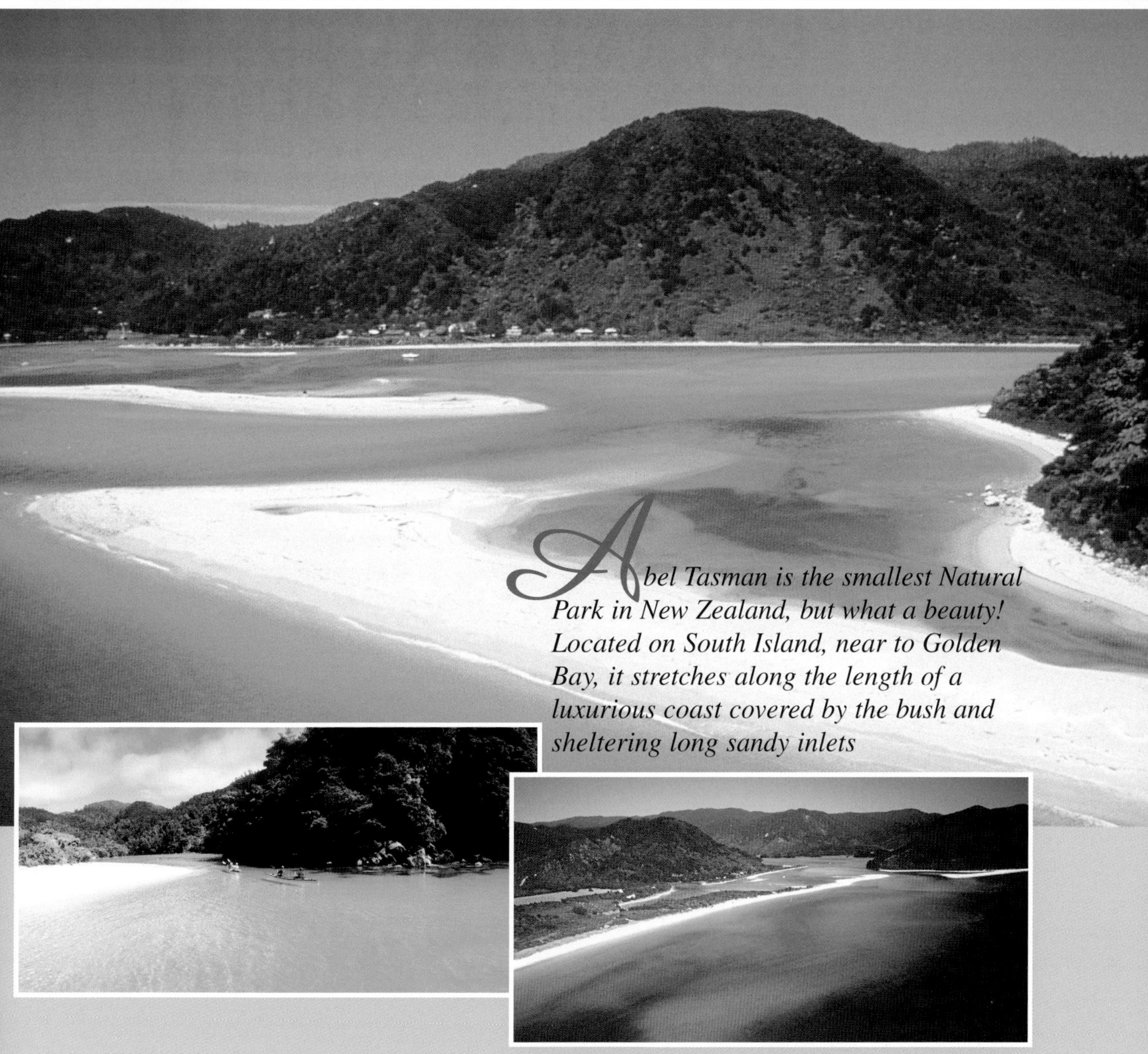

Abel Tasman is the smallest Natural Park in New Zealand, but what a beauty! Located on South Island, near to Golden Bay, it stretches along the length of a luxurious coast covered by the bush and sheltering long sandy inlets

Discovered by the Spaniards in the XVIth century, then settled by the English, it was sold to Germans and was occupied by the Japenese during the Second World War, Palau is today a tiny independant state in the heart of Micronesia (500 km to the east of the Philippines), with unprecedented ecological riches both on land as well as under the sea.

Surface area
460 km²
Population
18 400
Time zone
GMT +9
Language
English, Palauan
Currency
US Dollar
Documents
A free 4-week visa is given to tourists carrying a currently valid passport.
Health
No vaccination is required but an anti-mosquito treatment against dengue fever is recommended.
Average temperatures
28°C all year round

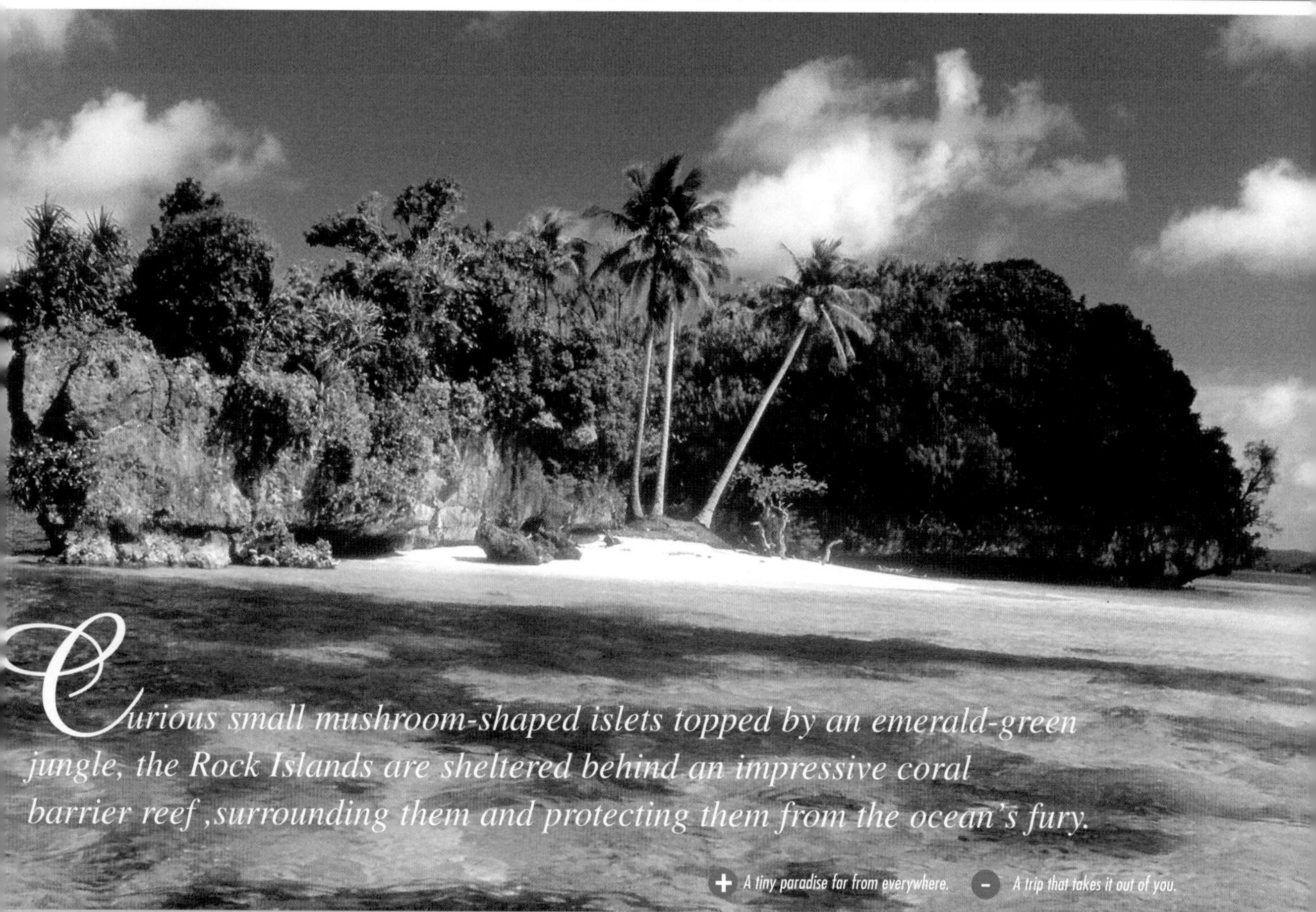

Curious small mushroom-shaped islets topped by an emerald-green jungle, the Rock Islands are sheltered behind an impressive coral barrier reef ,surrounding them and protecting them from the ocean's fury.

+ *A tiny paradise far from everywhere.*
- *A trip that takes it out of you.*

Airline Companies
Cathay Pacific, Thai Airways, Singapore Airlines Air France via Manilla and Eva Air.

How to get there
Boats make the trips between islets of Palau, especially the diving clubs, who propose excursions in the Rock Islands.

Best seasons
It is hot all year round, even if February and March are the driest months. From June to August it is more humid and there are risks of typhoons.

Accommodation
Most of the hotels are found in the capital Koror, but you can find charmining small bungalows on the northern and southern islets.

Local cuisine
Cooking based on the dried meat of tapioca (copra), sweet potatoes, fish and coconut, with sometimes a few Japanese influences.

Shopping
Baskets and bags woven from the leaves of the coconut trees, jewelry...

What to see
Belau (the old name for Palau) National Museum; the Palau International Coral Reef Center, where you can make the most of the seabed while staying dry thanks to the enormous aquariums which let the local marine species be admired; and finally an airplane graveyard in the north of the island, where many planes dating from the last World War can be seen.

Activities
Sailing, water-skiing, snorkeling, fishing, parasailing, diving (Palau's coral reefs are home to more than 1400 species of fish and 400 varieties of coral and sea anemones. There are many wrecks in the area as well, to the great delight of the divers).

Budget
High

Contact
http://www.visit-palau.com

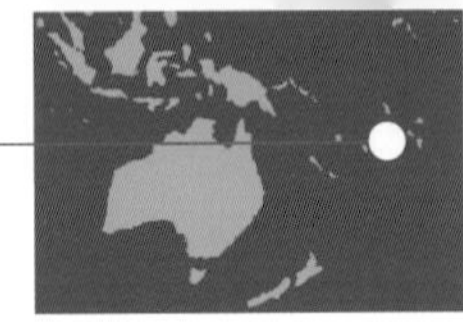

Polynesia, a sacred land which has always evoked the myth of an earthly paradise, and doesn't stop enthralling us by its beauty and the feelings it generates.

Surface area
The whole of the territory covers 4 million km², but the land above sea-level represents only 4,000 km².
Population
230 000
Time zone
GMT -10
Language
French, Tahitan
Currency
Pacific Franc
Documents
Currently valid passport (except transit to the USA)
Health
No vaccination is required
Average temperatures
25°C all year round

Airline Companies
Air France, Air New Zealand, Air Tahiti Nui.

How to get there
By plane: several flights each day between Tahiti and Bora Bora (about 45 mins).
By boat: a fast catamaran links Tahiti and Bora Bora in 7 hours.

Best seasons
May to October, the southern summer, when the climate is less stifling.

Accommodation
Ranging from private rooms to luxury hotels, including guest-houses and camp-sites.

Local cuisine
On the menu you will find above all fish and seafood (swordfish, crayfish, varo...) as well as all sorts of tropical fruit (mangos, bananas, papayas, lemons, guavas, uru (breadfruit)). Traditional dishes are prepared in a special oven, the Ahimaa, in which the food cooks gently wrapped in banana leaves. The national dish - raw fish marinated in lemon juice and coconut milk - is superb.

Shopping
Pareos, floral shirts, ukuleles, tikis (sacred statuettes), mother-of-pearl jewelry, shell necklaces, beauty products based on monoi, local spirits, vanilla, surf boards... And for those who want to bring back a souvenir they will never loose, the art of tatooing is very popular.

What to see
Island tour by 4WD or canoe; visit the Lagoonarium; the Maraes archaological site; the lush Faanui valley, the handicraft centre of Vaitape.

Activities
Sailing, water-skiing, game fishing, hiking, VTT, horse riding, snorkeling, diving (the lagoon at Bora Bora is an enormous aquarium: thousands of species all live together there, including sharks as you get closer to the coral barrier reef...).

Budget
High

Contact
http://www.tahiti-tourisme.com

 *Dream become reality.* — *The no1 destination in Polynesia.*

Born many thousands of years ago from the geological convulsions of the Pacific, Bora Bora island is without doubt one of the most photographed places in the world. 270 km north-west of Tahiti, it is immediately recognisable by its crystal-clear lagoon and the majestic silhouette of its volcano which contrasts with the delicacy of the atoll.

Between Tahiti and Bora Bora, Moorea is a small triangular island edged by idyllic beaches whose steep peaks are reflcted majestically in the tranquil waters of its lagoon.

Airline Companies
Air France, Air New Zealand, Air Tahiti Nui.

How to get there
By plane: from Tahiti by Air Tahiti or Air Moorea.
By ferry: allow 35 minutes.
On the island itself, hiring a vehicle is recommended.

Best seasons
May to October, during the Southern winter.

Accommodation
Camp sites, farés (bungalows), hotels of all categories and bed-&-breakfast to immerse yourself in the Polynesian way of life.

Local cuisine
On the menu you will find above all fish and seafood (swordfish, crayfish, varo...) as well as all sorts of tropical fruit (mangos, bananas, papayas, lemons, guavas, uru (breadfruit)). Traditional dishes are prepared in a special oven, the Ahimaa, in which the food cooks gently wrapped in banana leaves. The national dish - raw fish marinated in lemon juice and coconut milk - is superb.

Shopping
Pareos, floral shirts, ukuleles, tikis (sacred statuettes), mother-of-pearl jewelry, shell necklaces, beauty products based on monoi, local spirits, vanilla, surf boards... And for those who want to bring back a souvenir they will never loose, the art of tattooing is very popular.

What to see
Cook and Opunohu bays; Afareaitu waterfall; the Saddle of the Three Coconuts; the ascent of 900-meter high Rotui.

Activities
Sailing, water-skiing, game fishing, hiking, VTT, horse riding, snorkeling, excursions by glass-bottomed boat or by canoe, swimming with dolphins, whale watching, diving.

Budget
High

Contact
http://www.tahiti-tourisme.com

 *A true Garden of Eden.*

 *The thousands of insistent mosquitos.*

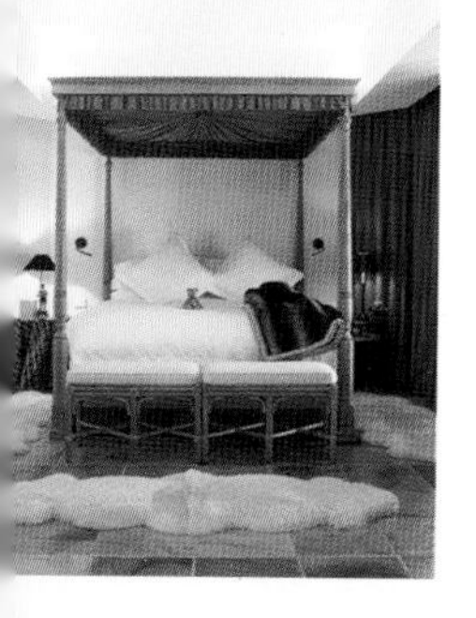

The Art of Splendid Indulgence

Experience the golden sand beaches of the world renowned Abel Tasman National Park. At the end of each day... it's only 25 minutes drive to the luxurious serenity and splendid indulgence that is Paratiho.

Airline Companies
Air France, Air New Zealand, Air Tahiti Nui.

How to get there
By plane: from Paeete allow a 55-minute flight

Best seasons
May to October, during the Southern winter.

Accommodation
Some luxury hotels with bungalows overlooking the sea and a handful of more modest guest-houses.

Local cuisine
On the menu you will find above all fish and seafood (swordfish, crayfish, varo...) as well as all sorts of tropical fruit (mangos, bananas, papayas, lemons, guavas, uru (breadfruit)). Traditional dishes are prepared in a special oven, the Ahimaa, in which the food cooks gently wrapped in banana leaves. The national dish - raw fish marinated in lemon juice and coconut milk - is superb.

Shopping
Pareos, floral shirts, ukuleles, tikis (sacred statuettes), mother-of-pearl jewelry, shell necklaces, beauty products based on monoi, local spirits, vanilla, surf boards...
And for those who want to bring back a souvenir they will never loose, the art of tattooing is very popular.

What to see
Paio Motu islet with its bird sanctuary; Tiputa Pass where you can watch the dolphins frolic.

Activities
Sailing, water-skiing, game fishing, hiking, VTT, horse riding, snorkeling, diving (Rangiroa is a place with a world-wide reputation where you can admire the impressive specimens of white and black sharks as well as the giant rays).

Budget
Very high.

Contact
http://www.tahiti-tourisme.com

+ *The not-to-be-missed Polynesian stopover for diving enthusiasts.*

− *An expensive stay.*

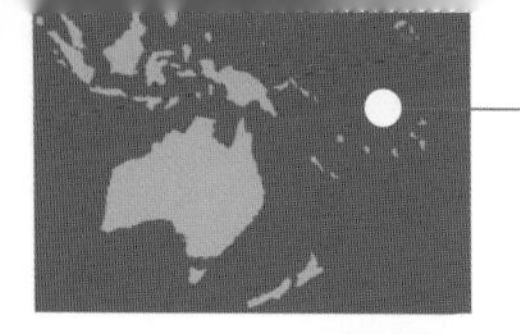

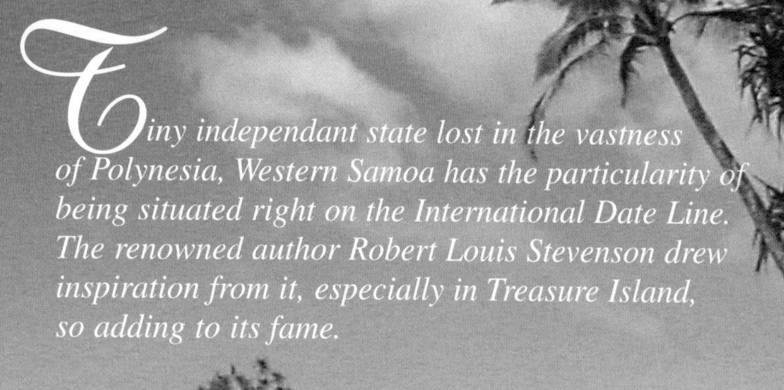

Tiny independant state lost in the vastness of Polynesia, Western Samoa has the particularity of being situated right on the International Date Line. The renowned author Robert Louis Stevenson drew inspiration from it, especially in Treasure Island, so adding to its fame.

Surface area
2,935 km²
Population
179 000
Time zone
GMT -11
Language
Samoan and English
Currency
Tala
Documents
Currently valid passport
Health
No vaccination is needed
Average temperatures
27°C winter,
29°C summer

To the south-east of the volcanic island of Upolu, Vavau beach is renowned for the unusual small islet planted in the middle of its lagoon, and for its lush coconut palms leaning over the sand like a soft caress.

Airline Companies
Air New Zealand.
How to get there
From Apia, take the coast road east in the direction of Vavau. Buses quarter the island following more or less flexible schedules... Take care if you hire a car, as petrol is only available in the large towns.
Best seasons
The dry season, from May to October.

Accommodation
Some resorts and small comfortable bungalows nearby, guest-houses and hotels of all categories at Apia.
Local cuisine
Fish, seafood, chicken and pork served with vegetables and fresh fruit…
Shopping
Woven baskets, shell jewelry, carved wood, tropical-style local clothes.

What to see
Lake Lanoto'o with its strange colour, where crowds of goldfish swim; Apia, the capital; the Robert Louis Stevenson Museum, in the writer's old house; the south coast with its superb beaches.
Activities
Sailing, surfing, hiking, canoing, VTT, fishing, kirkiti (a local game inspired by cricket), diving (possibility of diving under the volcanoes, at the foot of enormous cliffs, inside the lava tubes and other underwater caves).
Budget
Rather high.
Contact
http://www.visitsamoa.ws

\+ *The peace and quiet of the place.*

\- *The heat and humidity.*

Index of destinations

Africa

America

Index of destinations

Asia

Europe

Oceania

PHOTOS CREDITS

AFRICA: SOUTH AFRICA, Long Beach (South African Tourism Office); IVORY COAST, Mermaid Bay & Monogaga (Ivory Coast Embassy); EGYPT, Ras Muhammad (Michel Vaugrat); GHANA, Axim Beach (Axim Beach Hotel); KENYA, Kiwayu Island (Vie Sauvage); ILE MAURICE, Deer Island, Belle Mare, Rodrigues (Ile Maurice Tourism Office, One and Only Resorts Le Touessrok) ; MADAGASCAR, Nosy Be (Avalon, Soava Dia), Sainte Marie (Vanillla Café, Soava Dia); MOZAMBIQUE, Barazuto Archipelago (Vie Sauvage) ; SAO TOME & PRINCIPE (Sao Tome & Principe Consulate); SEYCHELLES, Anse Source d'Argent (Alberto Zampieri), Anse Lazio (Jean-Pierre Casadesus); ZANZIBAR, Nungwi (Vie Sauvage).

AMERICA: ANGUILLA, Shoal Bay (Jet Travel); ARUBA, Eagle Beach (Simon Garcia); BAHAMAS, Eleuthera & Exuma Cays (Bahamas Tourism Office); BELIZE, Blue Hole (Belize Tourism Office, Tony Rath), Ambergris Caye (Marty Casado, ambergriscaye.com), BERMUDA, West Whale Bay (Bermuda Tourism Office); BRAZIL, Jericoacoara, Morro Branco, Lencois Maranhenses (Brazilian Tourism Minister); Ponta do Saco (Emsetur); COSTA RICA, Parque Manuel Antonio (Costa Rica Tourism Office), Playa Conchal (Groupe Futuropa); CUBA, Cayo Largo (Cayo Largo Tourism Office); DOMINICA, Batibou Bay (Benoît Gosselet), UNITED STATES, Caladesi Island (Visit Florida); GUADELOUPE, Grande Anse (Guadeloupe Tourism Offiice, Philippe Giraud, Benoît Gosselet); GRENADINES, Tobago Cays (Al Kovsky); HONDURAS, West Bay Beach (Dean Milverton, Leif Elg); CAYMAN ISLANDS, Seven Miles Beach (Cayman Islands Tourism Office); JAMAICA, Negril Beach (Gérald Desaulniers) ; MARTINIQUE, Anse des Salines (Gérald Desaulniers); MEXICO, Tulum (Sophie Laurent), Balandra Bay (Gérard Buhl); NICARAGUA, Montelimar Beach (Intur); PANAMA, San Blas Archipelago (San Blas Sailing, Panoramic Panama, Extreme Panama); PUERTO RICO, Culebra (Angel Perez Pacheco); DOMINICAN REPUBLIC, Isla Saona, Las Galeras (Dominican Republic Tourism Office); SAINT KITTS & NEVIS, Frigate Bay (Gérald Desaulniers); SAINT MARTIN, Oriental Bay (Saint Martin Tourism Office, Francis Penot); TRINIDAD & TOBAGO, Englishman's Bay (John Guye); TURKS & CAICOS, Grace Bay (Mike & Peggy Mellum); VENEZUELA, Los Roques (David Caprese); VIRGIN ISLANDS (US), Trunk Bay (John Hendron).

ASIA: CAMBODIA, Sokha Beach (Don Pirot); INDIA, Palolem Beach (Vinod Nagle); INDONESIA, Kuta Beach (Richard Soberka), Kadidiri (Jean-Claude Mangiapan); MALAYSIA, Langkawi (Langkawi-online.com), Redang (Florence Finsbury); MALDIVES, Bandos, Velavaru, Fun Island (Maison des Maldives); MYANMAR, Mergui Archipelago (Irvine Laidlaw); PHILIPPINES, Boracay, Camiguin, Palawan (Philippines Tourism Office); SRI LANKA, Bentota, Negombo (Sri Lanka Tourism Office); THAILAND, Krabi, Koh Phi Phi, (Thailand Tourism Office); VIETNAM, Mui Ne, Phu Quoc (Vietnam Tourism Office).

EUROPE: CROATIA, Bol (Croatia Tourism Office); SPAIN, Fuerteventura (Miguel Merino, Roman Steinboeck), Cala Turqueta (Clara San Miguel); FRANCE, Calanque d'En Vau (André Bernard, escalade-calanques.com), La Rondinara (Editions Corses), Nonza (Gérard Césari, Eric Orsatelli); GREECE, Elafonissos (Oliver Var), Myrtos (Martin Croele), Navagio (Vasilis Papadimitriou, Elena Konstantinova, Takis); ITALY, Lampedusa (Antonio Meli), Spiaggia di Principe (Leonardo Pirina), Capo Vaticano (Ricardo Matuse); PORTUGAL, Praia Marinha (José Rodrigues).

OCEANIA: AUSTRALIA, Whitsundays & Cable Beach (Australian Tourism Office); FIJI, Yasawa Islands (Stéphanie Bleue), Wakaya (Wakaya Club); HAWAII, Hanauma Bay (Christine Shinavier), Lumahai (Daphné Ferret); COOK ISLANDS, Aitutaki (Didier Gomez); NEW CALEDONIA, Island of Pines, Maré, Lifou, Ouvéa (New Caledonia Tourism Point South); NEW ZEALAND, Abel Tasman Park (New Zealand Tourism Office, Dave Whitney); PALAU, Rock Islands (Palau Tourism Office); FRENCH POLYNESIA, Bora-Bora, Moorea, Rangiroa (Tahiti-Tourisme, Raymond Sahuquet, Lucien Pesquie); SAMOA, Vavau Beach (South Pacific Travel Guide, Green Turtle Tour).

The editor thanks everyone, especially
Claire Cabaret for her expert advice, Céline Acézat,
Astrig Laurent and Colette Rodier for their careful checking
as well as all the tourism professionals and photographers
who have contributed to this document.

Printed in April 2005 on the presses of the
printer ESCOURBIAC - Graulhet - France
Legal Deposit: August 2004 - 3rd edition
ISBN: 2-915648-09-3